MEXICO'S SECURITY FAILURE

Mexico has failed to achieve internal security and poses a serious threat to its neighbors. This volume takes us inside the Mexican state to explain the failure there, but also reaches out to assess the impact of Mexico's security failure beyond its borders. The key innovative idea of the book—security failure—brings these perspectives together on an *intermestic* level of analysis. It is a view that runs counter to the standard emphasis on the external, transnational nature of criminal threats to a largely inert state.

Mexico's Security Failure is both timely, with Mexico much in the news, but also of lasting value. It explains Mexican insecurity in a full-dimensional manner that hasn't been attempted before. Mexico received much scholarly attention a decade ago with the onset of democratization. Since then, the leading topic has become immigration. However, the security environment compelling many Mexicans to leave has been dramatically understudied. This tightly organized volume begins to correct that gap.

Paul Kenny, former lecturer in humanities, King's College, London University, and Visiting Professor, Universidad Nacional Autónoma de México (UNAM).

Mónica Serrano, Executive Director of the Global Centre for the Responsibility to Protect, Professor of International Relations at El Colegio de México, and Senior Research Associate at the Centre for International Studies, Oxford University.

Arturo Sotomayor, Assistant Professor, Naval Postgraduate School.

MEXICO'S SECURITY FAILURE

Collapse into Criminal Violence

Edited by Paul Kenny and Mónica Serrano
With Arturo Sotomayor

 Routledge
Taylor & Francis Group

NEW YORK AND LONDON

First published 2012
by Routledge
711 Third Avenue, New York, NY 10017

Simultaneously published in the UK
by Routledge
2 Park Square, Milton Park, Abingdon, Oxon OX14 4RN

Routledge is an imprint of the Taylor & Francis Group, an informa business

Library of Congress Cataloging in Publication Data
A catalog record has been requested for this book

ISBN: 978-0-415-89327-5 (hbk)
ISBN: 978-0-415-89328-2 (pbk)
ISBN: 978-0-203-80578-7 (ebk)

Typeset in Garamond
by Wearset Ltd, Boldon, Tyne and Wear

Printed and bound in the United States of America on acid-free paper
by Walsworth Publishing Company, Marceline, MO.

SUSTAINABLE
FORESTRY
INITIATIVE

Certified Sourcing
www.sfiprogram.org
SFI-00555

The SFI label applies to the text stock.

CONTENTS

ACKNOWLEDGMENTS

The first thanks go to Cristina Eguizábal who, as program officer at the Ford Foundation office in Mexico City, immediately gave her backing to the idea that lies behind this book. This was to bring together a group from Mexico's dispersed security community, in response to the deterioration of the country's security. That idea led to a joint institutional collaboration between El Colegio de México and the Centro de Investigación y Docencia Economicas (CIDE). After the initial contribution of Arturo Sotomayor, the CIDE side of the project was fortunate to find itself in the hands of Jorge Chabat. Meanwhile Kimberly Krasevac-Szekely had come on board at the Ford Foundation, and generously saw the project through to its next stage.

Throughout, Silvia López Hernández, Jasmín Flores and María de Vecchi at El Colegio de México and Valentín Pereda at CIDE provided much appreciated logistical support. The group's participants were privileged over the course of the years to have a series of off-the record exchanges with leading civilian and military policy makers. It is to be hoped that, in however small a way, their thinking was also influenced by the group's perspectives.

The group also had the invaluable opportunity of holding a colloquium at Nuffield College, Oxford University. Gratitude is due to Laurence Whitehead for making this possible, and to Jane Boulden, Malcolm Deas, Andrew Hurrell, Alan Knight, David Mares, Eduardo Posada-Carbó, Philip Robins and Andrés Rozental, among others, for their insights. Jane Boulden also merits recognition for her altruism in securing translations of the chapters by Ana Laura Magaloni, and Raúl Benítez Manaut and Arturo Sotomayor.

The final transition into this book owes everything to the wisdom and patience of Michael Kerns at Routledge. He endured far more trouble than any editor ought, giving a lesson in ethical intelligence through the grace with which he did so. The manuscript benefited enormously from the comments and proposals of three anonymous reviewers, each of whom helped the ferrying of the book to its destination.

Paul Kenny
Mónica Serrano

ABBREVIATIONS

AFI	Federal Investigation Agency (Agencia Federal de Investigación)
CFAF	Corps of Federal Support Forces (Cuerpo de Fuerzas de Apoyo Federal)
CIDAC	Center of Research for Development
CIDE	Centro de Investigación y Docencia Economicas
CISEN	Center of Investigation and National Security (Centro de Investigación y Seguridad Nacional)
CNDH	National Commission for Human Rights
DEA	Drug Enforcement Administration
DF	Federal District
DFS	Federal Security Directorate (Dirección Federal de Seguridad)
EPR	Popular Revolutionary Army
FARC	Fuerzas Armadas Revolucionarias de Colombia
GAFE	Grupo Aeromóvil de Fuerzas Especiales
HRC	Human Rights Council
ICESI	Citizens' Institute on Insecurity Studies
NAFTA	North American Free Trade Association
PAN	National Action Party (Partido Acción Nacional)
PFP	Federal Preventive Police
PGR	Attorney general's office
PJF	Federal Judicial Police (Policía Judicial Federal)
PND	National Development Plan
PRD	Democratic Revolution Party (Partido de la Revolución Democrática)
PRI	Institutional Revolutionary Party
SEDENA	Defense Ministry (Secretaría de la Defensa Nacional)
SEMAR	Navy Secretariat
SIEDO	Specialized Investigation of Organized Crime
SSP	Secretariat of Public Security

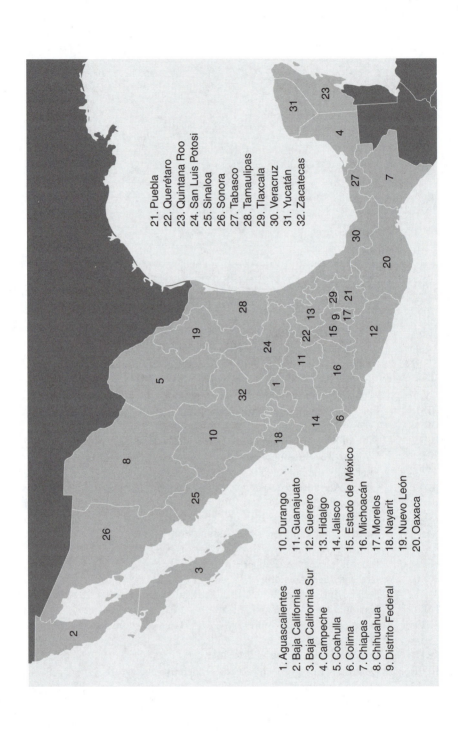

1. Aguascalientes
2. Baja California
3. Baja California Sur
4. Campeche
5. Coahuila
6. Colima
7. Chiapas
8. Chihuahua
9. Distrito Federal
10. Durango
11. Guanajuato
12. Guerrero
13. Hidalgo
14. Jalisco
15. Estado de México
16. Michoacán
17. Morelos
18. Nayarit
19. Nuevo León
20. Oaxaca
21. Puebla
22. Querétaro
23. Quintana Roo
24. San Luis Potosi
25. Sinaloa
26. Sonora
27. Tabasco
28. Tamaulipas
29. Tlaxcala
30. Veracruz
31. Yucatán
32. Zacatecas

INTRODUCTION

Security Failure Versus State Failure

Paul Kenny and Mónica Serrano

The conjunction

The criminal violence that has engulfed Mexico since 2007 has attracted global attention—and scant explanation. Almost overnight, a modern country with a respectable standing in the world had become as violent as Iraq and Afghanistan. What happened?

This book addresses that question, but gives no single-dimension answer. Mexico's insecurity requires different levels of explanation. The disaster has been accumulating on many fronts.

Its most manifest symptom is an uncontrolled spiral of violent deaths. In 2006, 2,221 people were killed in drug-related executions; the following year, 2,673.[1] In 2008: 5,207.

In 2009: 6,587.

In 2010: 12,658.[2]

This rising violence has a context—the administration of President Felipe Calderón. His term of office began in early December 2006. By the time he leaves, in December 2012, on current trends, about 50,000 people will have been executed through his six-year term.

These points are factual; hereafter the conjunction is one of controversy. There are no single—and no neutral—answers to the question of what has happened. In this book we proceed empirically and analytically, but also—inevitably—with its authors' interpretations of the facts. Standard scholarly procedure, we flag it now not because we doubt the truth of those interpretations, but because we know that some will fiercely disagree with them. We believe they are wrong—but we acknowledge their different view. Our responsibility to be objective demands no less.

We have already assumed our stance: the security failure of Mexico is a disaster. For the Calderón government, on the other hand, the fight for security has never been more resolute, and the only disaster would be not to pursue it. We have referred to *people* killed in drug-related executions. The Calderón government for a long time only referred to *them*.

Is Mexico's "reality"—as the government contends—one of relatively *low* violence?[3] Yes, if homicide levels are measured in abstraction. No, if the graphic cruelty of the drug-related executions is a medium of terror. Massacres of dozens of people may be either statistically insignificant, or shockingly symbolic.

For reasons that we shall explain—and with consequences we shall come to—the Calderón government from the start committed itself to minimizing the violence even as first the country, then the world, saw it mushroom. The mismatch of perceptions has been extreme. "Civilian casualties are the least," the president declared—crudely daubing a line between the innocent and the disposable.[4] The criminals' killing of each other was long hailed as an *encouraging sign*—the government's pressure on the drug cartels was working. President Calderón has not wavered from his conviction that the thousands of corpses are the necessary price of a policy for which there is no alternative. This is what we mean by *disaster*—and we mean it as a moral condemnation.

To talk about Mexico today without ethical instincts—revulsion, indignation, pity, fear and anguish—is to sound inhuman. It is right to have an ethical response to Mexico's violence. It can, however, also lead us astray.

Mexico's reality is "beyond horror"—in the words of a former president of Bolivia.[5] Is it? Yes, if the atrocious forms of the criminal killing transfixes attention. No, if an ethical response ought also to be a proportionate response. As distasteful as accountancy on human suffering is, going to non-comparative extremes serves no one's cause. Mexico in 2010 was tragic, but not on the scale of Haiti after an earthquake that killed over 200,000 people. Equally, despite the grotesqueness of the Calderón government's simultaneous argument that the country's violence is both encouraging and low, it *is* a fact that Mexico's homicide rate is considerably below that of its southern neighbors.[6]

So, we talk here of a disaster, not an utter catastrophe; of a collapse into violence, not the collapse of a state. The point is one on which some insistence is due.

Mexico is not a failed state

The title of this book refers to security failure—*not* state failure. The two are not synonymous, although people often assume that they must be. With its levels of insecurity, Mexico—some have been saying—must be a failed state. What else can it be?

A *security* failure.

"Failed state" is a phrase that shuts the lid on understanding, debate and policy—a verdict without appeal. It is used by people who have no need to know more.

We introduce the concept of security failure because we believe there is very much more to be known about what is happening in Mexico. Security failure is a mid-sized concept—bigger than policy failure, smaller than state failure. The criminal violence in the country is not only related to good or deficient political decisions; it is a manifestation of failure in a highly significant sphere of the state—that in which it is expected to provide internal and external security. Mexico has failed in that sphere. Though it is highly significant, it is less than "state failure."

For proponents of "state failure," this is an unacceptable stance. Failure, for them, is an all or nothing condition. Ambiguities and complexities are not welcome. They are promoting an *agenda*.

The state failure agenda is a major obstacle to making sense of a reality like the one currently affecting Mexico. Given how common the assumption is that "state failure" is the paradigm for our case, it is an obstacle we need to remove.

The rise of the failed state idea

Like many ideas that arise with a dramatic claim to "describe reality," the idea of state failure emerged from a history more tangled than it appears; it also emerged carrying baggage.

The globalized discourse of state failure dates from the early to mid-1990s. In the simplistic accounts, the end of the Cold War was the global precondition for disintegrative dynamics within the developing world—for a new international concern with "the 'failed state' part of the world."[7]

In the beginning, this part of the world was overwhelmingly located in sub-Saharan Africa. For a compiler of the "decade's failed states" in the 1990s, only one—Afghanistan—on a list of eight "contemporary classical failed and collapsed states" was not African.[8]

Angola, Somalia, Liberia, the Democratic Republic of Congo, Sierra Leone: these were the textbook cases of state failure. Their uncontrollable disintegrations still inform the most basic understanding of state failure: a loss of central government control over national territory and a breakdown of all state institutions. The failed state was "broadly, a state in anarchy."[9]

No doubt, the catastrophes were proof that state failure was a new phenomenon. But was it global?

The experts in African state failure didn't think so. What was to become a globalized agenda about states failing was at first a discourse specific to Africa.[10] The reason was the unique variable there (and in Afghanistan), colonization—and then decolonization.

The formulations were well-known. Colonial territories had been artificially grafted onto patchworks of competing suzerainties with sprawling areas of statelessness; thus, the colonies were quasi-states built on quasi-states.[11] Then, from 1960, "the symbolic year of Africa's 'independence,'" the last layer of quasi-statehood was added.[12]

"State failure" took hold in Africa because it captured what appeared to be the logical sequencing. From the civil war of the mid-1960s in Nigeria to the collapse of Somalia in 1991, state failure was a death foretold by artificial state formation. In Africa.

Thus, the first question about "state failure" is why should it have been transplanted from Africa? Somalia and Sierra Leone told the story—state failure really amounts to state collapse. The list might have been expanded to include those cases where the UN Charter's Chapter VII was invoked to authorize international intervention: Somalia in 1992–1993, Haiti in 1994–1995, and Albania in 1997. Not a long list. But then, how many other states in the rest of the world were ever likely to replicate their story? "Dozens of states in the current international system are endemically weak, yet only a handful slide into total collapse."[13]

That is common sense. The state failure agenda took off as a departure from it. State failure became less an actual condition than the *risk* of one.

A confluence of actors and trends was behind the snowball effect. State failure meshed with another concept from the 1990s—human security—and so became a concern for humanitarians, NGOs and development agencies.[14] Western media sources were also receptive to dire prophecies of "the coming anarchy."[15] Monitoring agencies like the CIA's State Failure Task Force also emerged, and exemplified the paradox of contemporary global risk management. Controlling for risks often involves maximizing their profile.[16]

Most decisively of all, however, the project of monitoring and controlling state failure coincided with the global appearance of neoliberalism.

The failed state agenda

The combination of events described above yields a fuller explanation of Africa's place in the state failure agenda. It wasn't, of course, true that all African states were headed for inevitable failure in the sense of collapse.[17] To the contrary, post-independent Africa had become home to a particular variant of statehood. It was called the developmental state, a kind of state that neoliberalism was very interested in pronouncing failed.

Africa wasn't alone. Latin America too was host to the developmental state that entered into economic crisis in the 1980s. The original rhetoric of state failure took off from here. The handful of cases would remain no more than that. But state failure became a global monitoring agenda when core international institutions judged that many states in the developing world were heading towards failure.

The conceptual ironies of this turn were many, and are still consequential. In the 1970s neoclassical and political economists talked freely of *government* failure. If neoliberals upscaled this talk into a global verdict of *state* failure, it was thanks to the literature that—in a famous phrase—brought the state back in. It was a literature intimately associated with the promotion of developmentalism.[18]

What this literature wanted to see was national states that were all of the following: interventionist; relatively, but effectively autonomous; socially embedded; socially incorporating and politically mobilizing; legitimate and equitable. The theoretical justifications were explicitly traced back to Max Weber's ideas of a state which ought to be monopolistic of its core functions. An ideal of a state.

As the argument went, neoliberalism did not intervene at all against these states; there was no need to—in the 1980s the developmental state failed by itself. The international environment at the time of the debt crisis may have been markedly unfavorable for developing countries as prices for their commodities plummeted, international credit dried up and interest rates spiked. But these unfavorable trends—ran the neoliberal conclusion—merely "laid bare deficiencies in national development policies"; the "root causes of the crisis" lay with the failures of state policy.[19]

But neoliberalism certainly *did* intervene against those failures of state policy. It did so with a powerful delegitimization. If developmentalists had rested on Weber, neoliberals also took out leaves from his book, drawing on his rich vocabulary of condemnation. The protectionist state was the rentier, corrupt, crony, kleptocratic, prebendal, parasitic, clientistic, populist, illiberal, and above all, neopatrimonial state.[20] The failed state.

State failure in its original sense of state collapse was now left far behind. State failure had become the failure of states to undertake neoliberal reforms. The relevant constituency was now global.[21]

Neoliberalism set state failure off on its global trajectory, but it had also misappropriated the idea of state failure. Considerable conceptual turbulence ensued. At issue was this: how could an ideal of the state have become a pattern of the failed state? The developmental state had gone; but the *aspirations* of that state would remain.

Thus, the most common usage of "state failure" refers to a given state's loss of control over core functions, institutions and the distribution of public goods, and so of essential legitimacy. That is, that the state in question has failed to live up to the mandate for developmentalism's strongly present state. So pervasive, indeed, is that image of the state that one analyst could write that: "when a state has failed or is in the process of failing, the effective education and health systems are privatized."[22]

Such widespread views evidence how, while successful as a critique of statism, neoliberalism was unable to advance a blueprint for a successful new kind of state. Its aim was to whittle down states to their essential "stateness." Yet "the missing dimensions of stateness" remained just that.[23] As theorists juggled the axis of state strength against that of scope (capacities against functions), the outline of an old dilemma was recognizable. Here again was state autonomy *and/or* societal penetration—the developmentalist dilemma. Neoliberalism was an ideology that had killed its opponent's body but couldn't replace its soul. Indeed, for all the sophisticated arguments, the notion stuck that neoliberalism was part of globalization's assault on state sovereignty, and hence that *it* was a cause of state failure.[24]

The paradoxes of "state failure" had become intractable. What was meant? A complete collapse? A neoliberal failure to reform? A developmentalist failure to incorporate goals of social justice and human rights? The discourse had over-expanded, and become incoherent.

The last phase: state failure's securitization

Yet the discourse had also become securitized. By 1997 "state failure" had achieved a position of prominence in the US Defense Department's quadrennial review.[25] When 9/11 occurred, the rhetoric of "state failure" was already set to take its final twist. September 2002's *National Security Strategy of the United States of America* itself avoided the words "state failure," in deference to the primary understanding of this as an extremely rare phenomenon. But the agenda now offered a rich menu of options: "weak, endemically weak, aborted, fragile, ungovernable, shadow, failing, failed, anarchic."[26] The National Security text drew heavily from this wider discourse as it spelled out the risks and threats from weak institutions and corruption—from weak, fragile and rogue states.[27]

The analysts were quick, too quick, to catch the new tone. State failure was to be "not just treated as the local population's Hobbesian nightmare, but also as a potential source of insecurities for the core states of international society."[28] State failure had become symptomatic of "a time of terror."

Literally, "state failure" still referred primarily to state collapse—the handful of cases. But the full connotation of state failure had become the *risk that any number of weak states in the world might become* another Somalia.

Risk perception thus became bound up with risk escalation. How many states really failed? Still the handful.

How many *potential* insecurities were there in the non-core states of international society? An infinite number. Failed states were but a step away from the rogue states in possession of weapons of mass destruction, and from the black holes whence all the other threats to world order were now deemed to emanate—terrorism, transnational organized crime, mass epidemics.

"State failure" denoted fear, and as such could know no bounds.[29] It had been securitized. This book takes a stand against that thrust of the state failure agenda.

The "failed state" precedent: Colombia

As a book about Mexico, this one cannot avoid alluding to Colombia. In the eyes of many, that country was where Mexico is—and, as so often in international politics, precedent rules.

In fact, Colombia was in a far worse place in the mid-1990s. Its conflicts were multidimensional, involving the Medellín cartel's all-out war against the Colombian state; the long but intensifying armed insurgency of the Fuerzas Armadas Revolucionarias de Colombia (FARC); and the ascending power of the ultra-right paramilitaries. In addition, Colombia's long stable political system was then widely being dubbed a "narco-democracy."

Colombia's qualifications for failed statehood were many—the loss of large territory to anti-state insurgents; a humanitarian disaster affecting millions, probably two million refugees; the world's highest homicide figures; mass human rights abuses; ineffective institutions; high corruption. Prima facie, Colombia was a failed state.[30] Certainly more of a candidate than today's Mexico. Yet the story of Colombia reveals how "state failure" does *not* merely describe realities.

Instead, the case of Colombia demonstrated the practical incoherence of the state failure agenda. Its two political halves—the Weberian-developmentalist, the neoliberal—each saw its own state in Colombia.

Looked at one way, here was a state presiding over soaring unemployment (from 7 percent in 1994 to 22 percent in 1999); over increasingly inequitable land distribution; and over a social deficit (67 percent of the population were below the poverty line, in the standard figure). The state had also failed to address the historic wrongs that, in this prism, were behind the civil conflict.

The neoliberal state failure approach to Colombia first saw a state that had avoided the worst of the debt crisis. It noted that in 1991 a new Constitution had decentralized political power. Fiscal decentralization had followed, as had reforms of the country's pensions and social security system. To be sure, corruption and institutional weakness were concerns. Yet the Colombian state had indubitably gone a long way down the road of second generation reforms—becoming "a state in the process of learning how to be a state."[31]

The discrepancy of views was startling. For the developmentalists, the yardstick was that the state makes a "necessary claim to being the guardian of the universal interests of the society over which it has jurisdiction."[32] Able to make no such claim, the Colombian state was not a legitimate state. *Legitimacy* was thus the key variable of success or failure.

For the neoliberals, actions spoke: at the end of the decade Colombia was rewarded with a US$2.7 billion loan by the IMF, conditioned on further reforms. Reform of the state was the key variable.

That these contradictions were deadly serious was soon borne out. The country's leading intellectuals fiercely attacked the claim that the Colombian state—a working democracy—had lost its legitimacy.[33] Those making the claim, it was forcefully put, were in the same camp as the country's revolutionaries.

The Colombian case, then, saw the label of "state failure" being fiercely resisted. It was understood as an attack on sovereignty. In the ensuing battle, the Weberians were routed. The precedent of that was in itself consequential. Humanitarian disasters, soaring poverty and social inequality rates, would *not* count as evidence of failed statehood.

Legitimacy may have been intangible and unquantifiable—yet it had proved to be of transcendental importance. The state could face any number of unprecedented challenges, but its legitimacy could never be put in doubt. The corollary was that not one shred of legitimacy would be conceded to the enemies of the state. President Uribe would consistently deny that Colombia had a civil conflict, much less war. In the 1980s the "guerrilla opposition" of the FARC had routinely been taken as a sign of the state's legitimation deficit.[34] In the 2000s, the FARC had gone from being insurgents with a social cause to no more than criminal terrorists.

Such were the dramatic power politics of re-definition. Such too, however, the price that had to be paid by Colombia for avoiding the "failed state" stigma. For rebranding its enemies was only possible after the state had signed up to the wars on drugs and terror.

Inducement to do so had also been behind the waving of the "failed state" flag at Colombia. So conceptually incoherent as to be of limited use per se, state failure had become politically very useful to the United States.[35] Targeted as a security threat, a weak state like Colombia had no choice but to submit to US-commanded securitization.

This was no light sacrifice. In 1998 the Colombian government had been pursuing a comprehensive peace settlement with the FARC. In 1999 the Pastrana administration presented the first version of Plan Colombia to the United States, a plan with the ambitions of a Colombian Constitution.[36] Peace with the FARC still came high on the wish-list. Further down it, an anti-narcotics strategy was contemplated—a concession to the United States whose grudgingness was signaled by an insistence that the strategy be international. Colombia was in no position to insist. The United States gave US$1.3 billion in 2000–2001: 78 percent of the aid went on military assistance, 7 percent on human rights, 2 percent on judicial reform, 1 percent on peace. By late 2002, more than half of the 2 percent for judicial reform was unspent.[37] In mid-2002, US counter-narcotics had definitively crossed over into counter-terrorism assistance.

The Colombian state had passed the ordeal of "failure." Out had gone the Weberian ideals of a more democratically inclusive, economically steering state; in had come securitization, the "strategic state."[38] Its democratic deficits will occupy us in the Conclusion.

What does the failed state agenda mean for Mexico?

In March 2007 President Felipe Calderón started talking with President George W. Bush about securing assistance for Mexico along the lines of 2000's Plan Colombia. The cases of Colombia and Mexico were not analogous, but analogy prevailed.

Calderón himself had decided on militarization as his response to the country's criminal violence. Still a new president, he had anticipated US pressures. It wasn't enough to prevent an attack from the failed state agenda-bearers.

The attack appeared to have been coordinated. In December 2008 former US drug tsar Barry McCaffrey warned that Mexico was "on the edge of the abyss—it could become a narco-state in the coming decade."[39] In December 2008 a strategic-analysis report from the United States Joint Forces Command labeled Mexico a failed state.[40] And in December 2008 *Forbes* magazine did likewise.[41] Another leading US media source followed suit.[42]

When in 2009 the US Joint Forces Command reiterated that Mexico should be monitored as a "weak and failing" state, a leading Mexican intellectual responded:

> Mexico is a tolerant and secular state, without the religious tensions of Pakistan or Iraq. It is an inclusive society, without the racial hatreds of the Balkans. It has no serious prospects of regional secession or disputed territories, unlike the Middle East. Guerrilla movements have never been a real threat to the state, in stark contrast to Colombia.[43]

The exchange encapsulates much about "state failure" now. The Mexican intellectual was right. Is Mexico a failed state?

Do we find, as in Somalia, a government whose writ extends over only a few blocks of the capital? We do not. Do we see a state with no control over its institutions, from the army to the postal service? Far from it.

Does the state have the authority to instruct the population in how to behave in major crises, such as 2009's swine flu outbreak? It certainly does. Was the country in 2009 the world's tenth largest export and import economy? Indeed it was.[44]

We could go on, but we are of course posing meaningless questions. *"State failure" is a phrase that no longer means what it says.* What the US Joint Forces Command means by "state failure" is a failure by the Mexican state to control security threats. It means, in fact, *security failure*.

The Mexican intellectual was right—but the position he represents is untenable. It takes "state failure" literally, as still being about the handful of cases. Their existence is readily granted. They are all far away from Mexico. State failure has nothing to do with Mexico. As we shall see, this is the official view of the country's political class. It is a view that has also led to disaster, as the chapters in this book establish.

Mexico is not a failed state—but "state failure" stopped gravitating around the handful of cases long ago. Instead, "state failure" is shorthand for a part of the world where emerging risks to international order are perceived to exist. Mexico has sleep-walked into that shadow world.

That world is one of subjunctive grammar and modal logic—a world of what may, might, or could happen or be true. Mexico *could* become a narco-state. Mexico *might* be failing. The statements are somewhere between conjectures, assertions and judgments—provisional yet menacing, retractable but extraordinarily recurrent for the failed state part of the world.

Mexico's president understands this grammar. Early in 2009, in the presidential residence of Los Pinos, Felipe Calderón told the leaders of the party of the PRI (the Institutional Revolutionary Party): "if we don't win that battle [against crime], it could be that the next time you come to Los Pinos you will have to sit down with a drug trafficking president."[45]

In the local as well as global context, then, this is blackmailer's grammar. "State failure" is about the possibility that the most terrible of outcomes could be true—not their probability of being true. It recurs because it cannot be refuted—even when there is no demonstrable risk of the state failing.

The blackmail of "state failure" has a clear agenda: the state under the threat of being judged a failure should opt for military securitization, within the parameters of the twin wars on drugs and terror. This is what the failed state agenda means for Mexico. Reining it in is urgent. But that can only be achieved by admitting to the real charge—security failure.

Security failure

Security failure has two halves. The first refers to the obligation of the holders of state authority to protect the right of citizens to security. The second refers to the regional and international norm that states ought not to threaten the security of their neighbors. On both accounts Mexico has become a security failure.

The core of this book, accordingly, folds along these domestic and international dimensions of security failure. Each of course has its own disciplinary constituency. The greater purpose here, however, is to bind together the two dimensions of security failure. If failing to guarantee internal security makes Mexico an international risk, we need to overcome the old domestic/international divide. What happens inside the state has trans-national reverberations. Some scholars now use the word *intermestic* to catch these dynamics and trends. It means that security issues within a sovereign state can no longer automatically be taken to be a matter for it alone. This in turn cuts the ground from under the feet of a very long Mexican tradition, one exemplified by the Mexican minister quoted by Jorge Chabat: "We cannot accept external meddling in situations which concern only Mexicans." What for decades has been considered an acceptable diplomatic stance now has to be set alongside events ranging from the massacres of Central American migrants within Mexico to the spillover of ferocious Mexican criminal organizations both north and south of the country. The old stance no longer holds.

The external threats presented by Mexico, then, emanate from its internal failures. This situation has not happened overnight. We thus begin this book with a background section where we provide an explanatory-narrative framework. Against the snap judgment of "state failure," we show that long processes of state evolution and external conditioning are behind today's criminal violence.

Security failure at home...

By domestic we understand something that encompasses more than party politics and civil society. Important as these are, we want to bring into focus the institutional scaffolding of the domestic—the state. Our perspective is thus at the outset different from other studies of criminal violence, where the focus is on the nature and capabilities of the state-challenging actors—the gangs and gangsters.[46] Our question is: *what kind of state* is being challenged?

This is the question that the mainstream state failure perspective ought to help us with—and doesn't. That tradition of thinking about the state ended in the unresolved ideological clash surrounding neoliberalism. Out of it, however, came an offshoot sub-branch of the state failure literature that also asks our question. A fruitfully suggestive part of the literature, we shall meet it properly in the Conclusion.

The Mexican state that we find in the chapters by Ana Laura Magaloni, Ernesto López-Portillo and Alejandro Anaya Muñoz is a state in which survive many of the practices and much of the ethos of the authoritarianism that prevailed from 1929–1994. It is a state whose transition to democracy was an incomplete project.

One of the authoritarian hallmarks was a minimizing of domestic security's profile. Security was always "under control"—the array of repressive measures to deal with it was extensive. They remained in place even as the PRI regime mutated towards its end. The technocrats who then assumed power were men who saw little point to government beyond getting the economy on track. Their crowning symbolic achievement, the North American Free Trade Agreement (NAFTA), initiated a major opening of

Mexico to the largest market in the world with next to no thought for the country's security architecture.

In the 2000–2006 administration of President Fox, security also remained off the agenda—until it breached the dykes. Then, in the midst of the spiral of drug-related killings, the Calderón administration would continue to insist that there was little violence in the country—that what violence there was has been blown out of proportion by an unpatriotic media. The threat of organized crime was, in the president's words, that of "a ridiculous minority."[47]

The Calderón administration was in line with the tradition of downplaying security. And yet, as of the president's tenth day in office when he set in motion his full-frontal military strategy against organized crime, security rose to the very pinnacle of the national agenda. The 180-degree turn would never be explained, much less resolved. The country had been sent to war against a ridiculous minority.

President Calderón would say that he had thrown the power of the state into the fight. Time would soon show that the armed branch of the state was insufficient when other critical branches were utterly unprepared. What set out as a war of *us against them* turned into something far murkier— a picture of a state unable to win security for its population largely because of its authoritarian ways and criminal complicities.

Why are there so many powerful criminals in Mexico? A major explanation is offered by Ana Laura Magaloni. Her chapter charts how the country's criminal justice system evolved as a tool of authoritarianism for the control of political opponents and prosecution of minor delinquents, and almost deliberately obstructs the investigation of the powerful. Also compelling is the account provided by Ernesto López-Portillo of police forces that still have every incentive either to protect criminals, or themselves become criminals.

There are, naturally, other factors behind the force of the criminal threat to the Mexican state. But these chapters dent the notion that the threat is extrinsic to the nature of the state in question. Taken together, they do more: their analyses will prompt the reader to ask how could it be that a state in this shape was thrown into a full-frontal war against organized crime?

It is the question raised by the occasion of this book. Our authors are not the first to investigate the issues of Mexican security, criminal justice and police reform. Their predecessors had indeed already sounded some of the alarm bells.[48] Now incredulity appears in order. Criminal violence spun out of control in Mexico precisely when the holders of state power decided to confront it head-on—without first taking the trouble to gauge the quality of state capacity in the sphere of security.

The statistics tend to be sobering in their simplicity. According to government figures, from 2007 into early 2010, 113,000 people were arrested for "crimes against health"—the tag for drug trafficking in Mexico. Over the same period, the prison population increased by *10,384.*[49] The cause of the discrepancy could theoretically have been that 100,000 people, more or less, had been mistakenly arrested. The real reason, however, was that the state simply had no capacity to prosecute them.

Of the 70,000 members of organized criminal groups arrested from 2007 into early 2010, the expert calculation is that 98 percent were released for want of evidence to bring their cases to trial. The calculation was not disputed by President Calderón.[50]

As Magaloni and López-Portillo's devastating enquiries show, the judicial system and the police work harmoniously together in their dysfunctionality. Police investigation and preparation of cases still depend upon the extraction of confessions—a method with a 2 percent success rate, even with the torture that it invites.[51] Thus, the drug-related homicides are also testaments to impunity. The 1,000 executions a month in 2010 would quite possibly yield arrests—but nearly zero convictions. Statistically, the rate may be the reasonable one that the government claims. Yet by any standards, a 98 percent homicide impunity rate is a disaster.

Mexico has a relatively small prison population—of 227,000 in mid-2010.[52] Only 58 percent of that population has been convicted. The prison system is thus over capacity (by 32%). Aside from the 42 percent of its inhabitants in judicial limbo, the overwhelming bulk is composed of small-time offenders. Convicted under the jurisdiction of the country's states, these make up 176,500 of the total. The population of seriously violent criminals, subject to the central state's jurisdiction, has held steady over the last years: 49,217 in 2006; 50,467 in 2010. The country's prisons are thus often more than 100 percent overpopulated with, principally, petty thieves.[53]

As had been the case with the police and the courts, the penitentiary system was also completely unprepared to cope with the corrupting power of the drug lords. The evidence now is overwhelming that the territory lost by the state to organized crime extends from the northern border and cities to its very own penitentiary system.[54]

The president deployed the military when *these* were the front-lines of any war on crime. With virtually no power to investigate, prosecute, convict and properly imprison the criminals, it is hard to avoid the conclusion that the strategy was both to kill them and help them kill each other. By default, it was a strategy to stoke up violence.

A prosecution of security by such extra-legal means will not deliver— but may nonetheless garner societal acceptance. In Alejandro Anaya Muñoz's grimly balanced assessment of the security policy of the Calderón administration in the realm of human rights, this is the core problem. Anaya Muñoz's treatment of it carries a strong echo of Magaloni's. Both are keenly aware of the current of our times that makes human rights tradabl against security fears. Both challenge it, Magaloni with a logical onslaught, Anaya Muñoz from the angle of the manipulability of social fears of insecurity. The disturbing possibility arises that not only has Mexico been sent on an uncontrolled spiral of violence, but that a notion that security must vitiate human rights has set in.

...and abroad

There is an American way of looking at Mexico with which we disagree, but which is understandable. Call it the prohibition prism. In it, no other country sends as many bad things into the United States as Mexico.

Some 90 percent of the cocaine that gets into the United States comes via the Mexican cartels—75 percent of the marijuana and methamphetamines.[55] Mexican cartels now operate, according to the Justice Department's National Drug Intelligence Center, in 195 cities in the United States.[56] With them has come violence and more crime—bloody gang battles in Tucson, 700 kidnappings in Phoenix from 2007–2009.[57] Way beyond the border, Atlanta has become a battleground, its network of freeways going north and east the prize. When, in late 2009, a US police operation swooped down on the cartel of *La Familia*, it took two days to arrest the 303 alleged members in 38 cities, 19 states.[58] The headline: "How US Became Turf for Mexican Drug Feud" speaks for the wider perspective here.[59]

We come to the conundrum that runs through the second core portion of this book. Are neighboring Mexico and the United States enemies or friends? A perennial question, it's one that has rarely been as open as now. The very fact that the question can plausibly be answered either way is the other key conjunctural dimension of Mexico's security failure.

Over the last decade Mexico's interest to the United States has been seen in increasingly negative terms, as an issue of the security threat it poses. The symbol for this is the Wall, inaugurated by September 2006's Secure Fence Act. Against this, 2008's Merida Initiative is the symbol of joint action against the common enemy of organized crime.

Mexico poses threats, real and perceived, to the United States. To talk responsibly about the real threats means drawing a line against the merely perceived. So, readers of this book will find no chapter on illegal immigration to the United States. None of us consider it a security threat. But we acknowledge that many in the United States do—64 percent of all adults, in one poll (and 48 percent of Democrats).[60] That perception of Mexico as a source of spillover insecurity is extremely consequential—that perception of illegal immigrants, tragic. When Arizona is called "the ground zero of illegal immigration," something has gone horribly wrong.[61] As it has when the DEA (Drug Enforcement Administration) claims that every single Mexican undocumented immigrant could be working for a Mexican drug cartel.[62]

The shaping of illegal Mexican immigration into a threat has everything to do with the weight of the drug enforcement precedent. To a significant degree, Mexico is now trapped in the prohibition prism. It cannot exit because prohibition doesn't work.

The most telling example of this is the now buoyant cocaine industry. Coca leaf is not a precious resource—but becomes extremely precious after it has been commercialized as an illicit commodity. If it weren't illicit it would be next-to worthless. What makes it illicit is the policy of prohibition, which is an attempt to stop cocaine and other drugs coming into America by making them illegal. Yet the effect of the policy is to make the drug business fantastically profitable. So the single most important reason for the quantity of drugs entering America is the policy designed to stop them.

Some figures do the talking. They come from the United Nations' 2009 World Report on Drugs.[63] In Colombia—the producing country—a kilo of cocaine was worth US$2,000. In Mexico—the transit country—it had gone up to US$12,500. Once it got inside America that same kilo was worth US$97,000. If the traffickers could get it to Europe, it would be even higher—US$101,000. These are extraordinary profit margins, and incentives.

It wasn't meant to be like this. Prioritizing interdiction—cutting off the supply—seemed logical. If the amount of drugs coming in could be squeezed, wouldn't prices on the street go up? And then wouldn't many users just not be able to afford them? And so it ought to have been, if we were talking about a normal commodity. But cocaine isn't: it's just so dirt-cheap to produce *and replace*. Say the traffickers were smuggling in washing machines; if big consignments got confiscated at customs they'd be looking at a hefty replacement cost. But with cocaine the trafficker is going to be losing US$12,500 if Customs find his kilo. His eventual prize of US$97,000 is so huge that he has already factored in some losses to Customs. As Peter Reuter long ago showed, if the United States had been able to successfully interdict 50 *percent* of all cocaine coming from Colombia, the cheapness of replacement would have meant that less than 3 percent would have been added to its retail price in America.[64] It's all part of the price paradox of illicit drugs. Its practical result is that interdiction ends up *stimulating* production.

As with the drugs, so stricter enforcement against illegal immigration has failed to stem the flow. Even before 9/11, through the NAFTA years, a 75-mile-long metal fence was installed along the border; the number of US border patrol agents increased from 3,965 in 1993 to 11,106 in 2005.[65] California walled itself behind Proposition 187 in 1994. That led the way to Arizona gaining its prominence as a destination. The next step—a fully militarized border—is no more likely to halt those flows into the United States than was the dysfunctional hi-tech virtual fence of President Bush's

2005 Secure Border Initiative.[66] When the land runs out, the seas will remain.

Economic downturn is a more potent deterrent to migration than enforcement—2008's 693,592 detained Mexicans was 17 percent down on 2007's.[67] But tighter enforcement *has* made for a perverse convergence of undocumented migrant and illicit drug flows, stimulating the cartels' involvement in the clandestine immigration business. This in turn does represent a heightening of the threat to the United States—but also to the immigrants, as testified by the 72 Central Americans massacred together in Tamaulipas in August 2010.

Thus, prohibition and its effects are at the bottom of Mexico's security failure. The demands in the United States for illicit drugs and cheap labor are too high—the incentives to meet them too great—to allow the country to succeed in stopping their transit. This *is* a bottom line, and we think it appropriate to fully spell it out. The internal as well as external halves of Mexico's security failure evidently do relate to the ways in which Washington's preferred anti-narcotic policies aggravate the country's problems. To discuss security sector reform in abstraction from the drug prohibition paradigm's *empowerment* of organized crime—as technical studies tend to—appears to us at best ingenuous. So does analyzing United States–Mexico relations without factoring in the dynamic market of nearly 20 million illegal drug consumers in America.[68]

But this bottom line is not the full story. Mexico's internal security failure is also a matter of institutional neglect for which only Mexico is to blame. The country's powerful criminals were cultivated in that context of neglect.

What, then, of its external security failure?

Ending Mexican denial

One of the notable aspects of the Calderón years has been that US-style militarization has gone hand in hand with unprecedented blame of the United States. Former Secretary of Interior Gómez Mont was blunter than us. Mexico's violence, he said, is caused by America's drug market.[69] President Calderón has repeatedly pointed to the flow of weapons from the United States as the cause of the violence in Mexico.[70]

Such blame-shifting positions have many elements of truth in them, are prevalent in Mexico—and are not ours. As with Mexico's internal security failure, there *is* a Mexican responsibility that is not cancelled by the hard truth of the bottom line. This is the argument of the second half of this book. Readers familiar with Mexico will recognize its novelty; for those who aren't, we need to show that statements of the obvious aren't always so in Mexico.

Among the country's political class, it is common sense that Mexico's insecurity isn't Mexico's problem. The stance connects with the deep reluctance to admit that security is a legitimate democratic issue. Here the nub is "interference." Unfortunately for the country, Mexico's political class has long understood security as a subject that allows for US interference. Sovereignty, then, depends upon not breaching the taboo of security. Thus, when Barry McCaffrey's warning became public, he achieved something now rare in Mexican politics—unity. Politicians across the board stood shoulder to shoulder in their condemnation of the *catastrofista*. Likewise, when Ambassador Carlos Pascual was revealed by WikiLeaks to have made some critical statements of fact about Mexican institutional incapacity in combating the cartels, his resignation was demanded and won by President Calderón.[71]

The symbolic meaning in this is hard to overstate—about the only thing Mexico's political class will unite on is its denial of the country's security failure. This denial is without doubt one of the failure's greatest causes. Security is the one great issue over which no one in the political class wants to claim ownership, until they find themselves in executive power. The executive takes momentous decisions on security alone; the political parties out of power are concerned mainly to calibrate the effects of those decisions on themselves. The irresponsibility on both sides is breathtaking; the confusion, woeful. The executive speaks of its security policy as that of the state, while the opposition questions whether the policy was necessary in the first place, and blames its "politicizing" results.

More is at issue in all this than inherited reluctance and nationalist disinclination to rise to the country's security challenge. Some in the political class are corrupt, evidently enough. The infinitely more important matter, however, is that the political class as a whole has shown no willingness to sacrifice any of its members for the cause of a war on crime.[72] This is in startling contrast to the recent trend in Colombia.[73] Behind the militaristic direction the war in Mexico has taken, then, is also the closing of the political class's ranks. Indeed, it has become clearer with time that President Calderón's gambit in December 2006 was, in some part, designed to force the governors of the north to abandon their "passivity"—to speak euphemistically—vis-à-vis organized crime.

What could lift such a political embargo against strong action on the country's insecurity? For its political class to wake up to the crude reality that its posture of rejecting the United States actually translates into subservience to the United States. Because they can't agree on a security framework for the country, the country gets one from the United States. The Merida Initiative wasn't welcomed by the opposition parties, but it wasn't rejected either. When it came down to it, nobody had a better idea. When the Mexican army grows dispirited with its mandate, the Mexican navy is directed to play a more prominent part—by the American ambassador.[74] In reality Mexican nationalism has much to be modest about.

Unjust, onerous, even impossible, Mexico's security situation can be all these and more *and yet it still needs to assume responsibility*. On the one hand,

Mexican organized crime is now a risk, to Europe as well as the United States.[75] On the other, the price for not claiming a stakehold in its security is a loss of effective sovereignty.

That is the implicit premise from which Jorge Chabat sets off in his analysis of cooperation and conflict over drug trafficking between Mexico and the United States. The innovativeness lies in the approach: Chabat isn't rehearsing the history, with its grudges and polemics. The object is, rather, cool dissection: given that drug enforcement cooperation between the two countries is the inescapable reality, what lessons can be learned about the management of conflicts? His finding is that the attainment of tangible goals comes second to the message of Mexican willingness to cooperate. The token of that, Chabat also posits, is now its ability to deal with corruption. If he is right, the corollary is that President Calderón set off to fight his war on completely the wrong front.

Cooperation works on the level of intentions, but generates conflict in practice, because of the dysfunctionality that reigns within security failure. Such is the picture of Mexico's contribution to the war on terror that Athanasios Hristoulas paints. The security map of the world changed for the United States after 9/11: all security threats became interconnected. Drug traffickers, terrorists, human traffickers, arms dealers, computer hackers— all were to be dealt with as parts of a continuous spectrum of "black" networks; security against one was security against all.

Hristoulas' word for Mexico's relation to that vision is "disconnect." The country's different security agencies compete for their slice of the budget without sharing information; compared to Canada's implementation of its border agreement with the United States, Mexico flounders, unable to keep up. Notably, Hristoulas concurs completely with Chabat on the primacy of the problem of corruption for Mexico.

The chapter by Raúl Benítez and Arturo Sotomayor is about what they call Mesoamerica, but one of its strong subtexts has to do with the relation between Mexico and Central America. Taking an idealized view of the region as one largely free of interstate disputes the better to highlight their theoretical model, the authors explore the many ways in which the region has failed to draw together into a security community. The conundrum is why this should be so, given that the states face so many of the same security problems and challenges. The answer is twofold: internal weakness, most notably the lack of civilian control over state security apparatuses, works against cooperation; so too does the divisive influence of the United States, robustly denounced by Benítez and Sotomayor. As for Mexico, the country that ought to be the local regional hegemon instead drags down its Mesoamerican fellows.

The relation between Mexico and Central America has recently become a source of anguish for the latter. In Guatemala, where the murder rate has doubled over the last decade—a level of violence higher than in the civil war—40 percent of the killings are drug-related.[76] The incursion into and takeover of Central American territory by Mexican cartels has put five of its seven countries on the US list of 20 major illicit drug transit or major illicit drug producing countries. Tragically, they contain the region's beacon of tranquility, Costa Rica. Shamefully, its minister of public security has talked of the region "degenerating into another Mexico."[77]

If everybody now understands that as an allusion to a country overrun by criminal violence, in the Conclusion we ask what kind of country—and state—Mexico is evolving into. Building upon the first five chapters, its premise is not especially controversial: a state in which human rights are downgraded may be said to be evolving in an authoritarian direction. In itself, we think this is a bad thing. In a context in which the state does face a criminal challenge, we can go farther: if organized crime in Mexico is in large measure a problem of authoritarian legacies, policies that reinforce those legacies are the next chapter in the story of disaster.

Our overall stance, then, is that the Mexican state is in significant measure responsible for the nature of the criminal threat it faces; and that the external environment for the Mexican state, through prohibition, provides powerful economic incentives to the criminal organizations. An intermestic picture, it's what we see. It's not at all what "state failure" sees.

Its securitizing agenda now harps extensively upon the external, transnational nature of criminal threats to the state. It sees the big continuum, as sketched by Secretary of State Hillary Clinton: "the barbarity that we are seeing from criminals and terrorists in the world today ought to ... require a concerted effort to defeat these violent, terrible actors who disrupt lives from Mexico to Africa and to Afghanistan and beyond."[78] In Mexico it sees drug traffickers becoming terrorists—so that even though there are no terrorists in Mexico, the Merida Initiative was also explicitly a counterterrorist initiative. Most egregiously of all, it sees a drug insurgency.[79]

In other words, it sees a state that ought to maximize its securitization policies.[80] As strenuously as possible, this book contends that those policies are the worst road for a state with security problems like Mexico's to go down. In the short term, they increase violence; in the mid-term, they compromise the integrity of its armed forces; and in the long term, they make the state more authoritarian. The paradox is cruel but undeniable: responding only to the imperatives of the failed state agenda is leaving the Mexican state the worse.

Notes

1 The figure for 2005 was 1,537. *El Universal* 20 August 2009.
2 *Milenio* 2 January 2011.
3 Secretary of the Interior, Francisco Blake Mora. *Reforma* 11 November 2010.
4 *Reforma* 17 April 2010.
5 Carlos Mesa, *Reforma* 20 November 2010.

6   Mexico's annual homicide level is roughly 12 for every 100,000 inhabitants. For 2008, the comparative levels in Guatemala, El Salvador and Honduras were 48, 52, and 58. International Crisis Group, *Guatemala: Squeezed Between Crime And Impunity* (June 2010), 13.

7   Francis Fukuyama, *State Building: Governance and World Order in the Twenty-First Century* (London: Profile Books, 2004), 131.

8   Robert I. Rotberg, "Failed States, Collapsed States, Weak States: Causes and Indicators," in R.I. Rotberg, ed., *State Failure and State Weakness in a Time of Terror* (Washington: Brookings Institution Press, 2003), 10–11.

9   Robert I. Rotberg, "The Failure and Collapse of Nation-States. Breakdown, Prevention, and Repair," in R.I. Rotberg, ed., *When States Fail. Causes and Consequences* (Princeton: Princeton University Press, 2004), 5.

10 Among a mini-deluge of articles on "anarchy" and state failure in Africa, William I. Zartman, ed., *Collapsed States: The Disintegration and Restoration of Legitimate Authority* (Boulder: Lynne Rienner, 1995) is recognized as the landmark volume.

11 The key reference is Robert H. Jackson, *Quasi-States: International Relations, Sovereignty and the Third World* (Cambridge: Cambridge University Press, 1990). See Jennifer A. Widner, "States and Statelessness in Late Twentieth-Century Africa," *Daedalus* (Summer 1995). One may here also recall the claim of world systems theory that, in the past, "weak or nonexistent (colonial) states were needed to allow imperialist exploitation by the core states." Robert R. Alford and Roger Friedland, *Powers of Theory: Capitalism, the State, and Democracy* (Cambridge: Cambridge University Press, 1990), 367—summarizing Immanuel Wallerstein.

12 Alexandros Yannis, "State Collapse and its Implications for Peace-Building and Reconstruction," in Jennifer Milliken, ed., *State Failure, Collapse and Reconstruction* (Oxford: Blackwell, 2003), 64.

13 Jennifer Milliken and Keith Krause, "State Failure, State Collapse, and State Concepts, Lessons and Strategies," in ibid., 13; Sebastian von Einsiedel, "Policy Responses To State Failure," in S. Chesterman, M. Ignatieff, and R. Thakur eds., *Making States Work State Failure and the Crisis of Governance* (Tokyo, New York, Paris: United Nations University Press, 2005), 22.

14 Susan L. Woodward, "The Paradox of 'State Failure': States Matter; Take them Seriously," unpublished paper. The International Network of Migration and Development NGO has accordingly called Mexico "a failed state in terms of guaranteeing security for its population." *Reforma* 6 November, 2010.

15 Robert Kaplan, "The Coming Anarchy: How Scarcity, Crime, Overpopulation, Tribalism, and Disease are Rapidly Destroying the Social Fabric of our Planet," *Atlantic Monthly* 273 (2).

16 Compare Von Eisiendel, 23:

> [The State Failure] task force identified only 12 cases of complete collapse of state authority during the last 40 years, [but] they enlarged the dataset to include almost all revolutionary wars, ethnic wars, genocides and politicides, and adverse or disruptive regime transitions between 1955 and 1994 ... [and came up with] a total of 127 cases.

17 Indeed, experts who took that line ended up in a position—later joined by proponents of "shared sovereignty"—*antithetical* to the state failure project.

For the former, the universal model of statehood might not be appropriate for Africa; for the state failure project, the model has never been in doubt.

18 For influential accounts, see Joel S. Migdal, *Strong Societies And Weak States: State–Society Relations and State Capabilities in the Third World* (Princeton: Princeton University Press, 1988); Peter B. Evans, "The State and Economic Transformation," in P.B. Evans, D. Rueschemeyer and T. Skocpol, eds., *Bringing the State Back In* (Cambridge: Cambridge University Press, 1990); Peter Evans, "The State as Problem and Solution: Predation, Embedded Autonomy, and Structural Change," in S. Haggard and R.R. Kaufman, eds., *The Politics of Economic Adjustment: International Constraints, Distributive Conflicts, and the State* (Princeton: Princeton University Press, 1991). Compare Evelyne Huber, "Assessments of State Strength," in Peter Smith, ed., *Latin America In Comparative Perspective: New Approaches to Methods and Analysis* (Boulder: Westview Press, 1995), 168:

> The prototype of a strong state, then, is a developmental state, that is, a state capable of stimulating industrial transformation as a basis for sustained accumulation in a developing economy, which is at the same time capable of shaping distribution in a less-inegalitarian direction.

19 Merilee S. Grindle, *Challenging the State: Crisis and Innovation in Latin America and Africa* (Cambridge: Cambridge University Press, 1996), 1, 24, 45. For a fully rounded analysis, see Robert H. Bates, *When Things Fell Apart: State Failure in Late-Century Africa* (Cambridge: Cambridge University Press, 2008).

20 Christopher Clapham, 'The Challenge to the State in a Globalized World," in *State Failure, Collapse and Reconstruction*, 32: "the failures of neopatrimonialism ... led to the imposition of 'structural adjustment' programmes."

21 The agenda may be seen in, for example, the foundations of the "single best model" employed by the State Failure Task Force. The model tracks openness to international trade, and "democracy," alongside infant mortality. The scoring for "democracy" rests on such bodies of information as the Polity IV dataset, which doesn't make too many bones about its business-like criteria: three of its five main criteria are "competitiveness of the executive, openness of executive recruitment, and restraints on chief executive." Ross E. Burkhart and Indra de Soysa, "Open Doors, Open Regimes? Testing Causal Direction between Globalization and Democracy, 1997–2000," undated paper, University of Bonn. They also report that: "being dependent on oil reduces the level of democracy by a little over 5 points on the 21-point scale of democracy." Ted R. Gurr, leader of the State Failure Task Force, pioneered the use of the Polity IV Data set.

22 Rotberg, "Failed States," 7. ("Privatized forms" of public goods provision "are possible," he says on p. 3.)

23 Fukuyama, 1–57.

24 David Keen, "Organised Chaos: Not the New World We Ordered," *World Today* (January 1996), 15: "Nor is it enough to point despairingly to 'the collapse of the state' without understanding how international financial institutions have often willfully undermined the state in favor of the 'market economy.'" Compare Fukuyama, 53: "The international community ... is actually complicit in the *destruction* of institutional capacity in many developing countries" (his italic).

25 Juan Gabriel Tokatlian, "La construcción de un 'Estado fallido' en la política mundial: el caso de las relaciones entre Estados Unidos y Colombia," *análisis político* 64 (September–December 2008), 75.

26 von Einsiedel, 16.

27 In her discourse on the National Security Strategy, Condoleezza Rice did make the explicit reference: "We have seen how poor states can become weak or even failed states, vulnerable to hijacking by terrorist networks." Online, available at: www.whitehouse.gov/news/releases/2002/10/print/20021001–6.html

28 Milliken and Krause, "State Failure, State Collapse, and State Reconstruction," 12.

29 See Paul Rogers, *Losing Control: Global Security in the Twenty-first Century* (London: Pluto Press, 2002).

30 Eduardo Pizarro and Ana María Bejarano, "Colombia: A Failing State?" Online, available at: http://drclas.fas.harvard.edu/publications/revista/colombia/pizarro. html accessed 30 May 2003; Philip McLean, "Colombia: Failed, Failing, or Just Weak?," *Washington Quarterly* 25:3 (Summer 2002), 123–134.

31 Former President Belisario Betancur, "Colombia: From the Actual to the Possible," in Eduardo Posada-Carbó, ed., *Colombia: The Politics of Reforming the State* (London: Institute of Latin American Studies, 1995), xviii.

32 Evans, "The State and Economic Transformation," 47.

33 Eduardo Pizarro Leongómez, *Insurgencia Sin Revolución La guerrilla en Colombia en una perspectiva comparada* (Bogotá: Tercer Mundo Editores, 1996), 32. See also 16, 181.

34 Gary Hoskin, "The State and Political Parties In Colombia," in *Colombia: The Politics of Reforming the State*, 58 saw "guerrilla opposition" as having contributed to undermining "the legitimacy of the political system" in the 1980s.

35 So, in a common argument, labeling Afghanistan a failed state was more attractive to the United States than granting the Taliban the legal status of enemy combatants.

36 Jairo Estrada Álvarez "Elementos de economía política," in Jairo Estrada Álvarez, ed., *Plan Colombia Ensayos críticos* (Universidad Nacional De Colombia, 2001), 30–31 lists ten elements, in order: an employment-generating economic strategy; a fiscal and financial strategy of "severe adjustment"; a peace strategy with the insurgents; a national security strategy of armed forces' modernization; a judicial and human rights strategy to guarantee equality before the law; an international anti-narcotics strategy; an environmentally friendly alternative development strategy; a strategy for social participation; a health and education-centered strategy for human development; a strategy for international co-responsibility for an integrated response to the drug problem, including resources for treatment. The budget was US$7.558 million.

37 Ingrid Vaicius and Adam Isacson, "The 'War on Drugs' meets the 'War on Terror,'" *International Policy Report* (Washington, DC: Center for International Policy, February 2003), 6.

38 The concept was coined by Gabriel Marcella in what, in retrospect, was an influential policy brief—*The United States and Colombia: The Journey from Ambiguity to Strategic Clarity* (Miami: The Dante B. Fascell North–South Working Paper Series, March 2003). The brief demonstrates many of the paradoxes of "state

failure" we have been noting. Thus, "it is important to underscore that Colombia is not a failing state" (8) Yet Colombia was also "a nation fighting for its survival" (30). The state should accordingly recreate itself as "a strategic state" (24).

39 Barry R. McCaffrey, "After Action Report." Online, available at: www. mccaffreyassociates.com/pdfs?Mexico_AAR__December_2008.pdf.

40 "Joint Operating Environment 2008," 4 December 2008.

41 Jesse Bogan, Kerry A. Dolan, Christopher Helman and Nathan Vardi, "The Next Disaster," *Forbes* 22 December 2008.

42 Joel Kurtzman, "Mexico's Instability is a Real Problem," *Wall Street Journal* 16 January 2009.

43 Enrique Krauze, "The Mexican Evolution," *New York Times* 24 March 2009.

44 *Reforma* 6 November 2010—reporting the World Organization of Commerce.

45 Quoted in Carlos Monsiváis, "México en 2009," *Nueva Sociedad*, March–April 2009, 43–44.

46 See for examples, Moíses Naím, *Illicit: How Smugglers, Traffickers and Copycats are Hijacking the Global Economy* (New York: Anchor Books, 2006); Juan Carlos Garzón, *Mafia and Co. The Criminal Networks in Mexico, Brazil, and Colombia* (Washington, DC: Woodrow Wilson International Center for Scholars, 2008).

47 *Reforma* 24 March 2010.

48 See Marcos Pablo Moloeznik, "Public Security and Police Reform in Mexico," in John Bailey and Lucía Dammert, eds., *Public Security and Police Reform in the Americas* (Pittsburgh: University of Pittsburgh Press, 2006); Robert A. Donnelly and David A. Shirk, eds., *Police and Public Security in Mexico* (San Diego, CA: University Readers, 2010). Moloeznik (171) records that from 1995 to 2000, for example, the successful sentencing rate in the lower courts was a mere 28 percent. A more recent contribution is Niels Uildriks, *Mexico's Unrule of Law* (New York: Lexington Books, 2010).

49 Miguel Angel Granados Chapa, "Cifras de violencia," *Reforma* 5 November 2011. The fact was first reported by Miguel Carbonell.

50 David Luhnow, "Mexico's 'Eliot Ness' Seeks US Help," *Wall Street Journal* 19 May 2010.

51 Detained suspects with heavy facial bruising are routinely paraded before the Mexican media, attracting no comment.

52 Secretaría de Seguridad Pública, *Sistema Penitenciario Mexicano*, May 2010—for this and the following figures. For a sense of comparison, the prison population of California is 160,000. *New York Times* 6 December 2010.

53 Javier González Garza, "Crisis carcelaria en puerta," *Reforma* 1 May 2010. The reason for overpopulation is that 21.4 percent of the country's prisons are municipal—and hold 1.8 percent of the population. Secretaría de Seguridad Pública, *Sistema Penitenciario Mexicano*.

54 See "Va ex mando de AFI del escritorio al penal," *Reforma* 30 October 2010 for a review of the cases of prison directors arrested for involvement in organized crime. See too Garzón, 159.

55 *Reforma* 9 August, 2009. Mexico's intelligence agency CISEN breaks down the drug flow through Mexico to the United States like this: 40 percent cocaine, 28 percent marijuana, 18 percent heroin, 14 percent methamphetamines. *Reforma* 1 November, 2010.

56 "Atlanta Reeling under Mexican Drug Cartel Violence." Online, available at: www.newsmax.com/Newsfront/atlanta-mexico-drug-gangs/2009/03/10/id/ 328722.
57 "Mexican Drug Cartel Violence Spills Over, Alarming US," *New York Times* 22 March 2009.
58 "US Arrests 100s in Raids on Drug Cartel," *New York Times* 22 October 2009.
59 *New York Times* 9 December 2009.
60 *Wall Street Journal* 27 May 2010.
61 Kris W. Kobach, "Why Arizona Drew a Line," *New York Times* 29 April 2010.
62 Jesús Esquivel, "Allende Las Fronteras," *Proceso* special edition 29 (July 2010), 34.
63 Cited in *Reforma* 27 August 2009. For clarity, figures are rounded down. An estimate for 1998–2000 put the value of a kilo of cocaine leaf at the farm gate in Colombia at US$650, and US$120, 000 at the distribution point in Chicago. See European Commissioner's report, *A Report on Global Illicit Drug Markets 1998–2000*, 75.
64 Peter Reuter, *Can the Borders Be Sealed?* (Santa Monica, CA: A Rand Note, August 1998), 7. Garzón (120–121) records seizures of cocaine within Mexico in 2000–2006 at levels of 12 percent, rising to 13 percent of the 380 metric tons that entered in 2006–2007.
65 Wayne A. Cornelius, "Introduction: Does Border Enforcement Deter Unauthorized Immigration?," in Wayne A. Cornelius and Jessica M. Lewis, eds., *Impacts of Border Enforcement on Mexican Migration. The View from the Sending Communities* (La Jolla, CA: Center for Comparative Immigration Studies, UCSD, 2007), 2.
66 Randal C. Archibald, "US Plans to Cut Budget for Mexico Border Fence," *International Herald Tribune* 18 March 2010.
67 *Reforma* 16 July 2009.
68 *Reforma* 12 May 2010.
69 *Reforma* 5 May 2010.
70 Luhnow, "Mexico's 'Eliot Ness' Seeks US Help."
71 *Financial Times* 21 March 2011.
72 The most prominent recent exception to the rule—Julio César Godoy, reluctantly disowned by the Democratic Revolution Party (Partido de la Revolución Democrática, PRD) late in 2010—effectively confirms it, as we discuss in the Conclusion. Before him the most prominent case was that of the ex-governor of Quintana Roo Mario Villanueva—a fugitive from 2000, apprehended in 2001 and extradited to the United States in 2010.
73 See former President César Gaviria: "We have a much more efficient penal justice system [than Mexico], we send them all to jail: governors, ministers, drug-traffickers, paramilitaries, there are 40 deputies in prison." *Reforma* 15 October 2010. In fact, as one of our authors has pointed out, the case is rather that these high-profile successes gain the Colombian system a reputation that masks deeper problems: in 2008, the Justice Department was able to bring to trial 30 of its 13,000 homicide suspects. Ana Magaloni, "Percepciones de (in) justicia," *Reforma* 23 October 2010.
74 Nick Miroff and William Booth, "DEA Intelligence Aids Mexican Marines in Drug War," *Washington Post* 4 December 2010.

75 "The agencies of public order in Europe are having more and more prob-
    lems with Mexican drug traffickers, particularly in the cocaine business," says
    Carel Edwards, the European Union's drug tsar. *Reforma* 6 November 2009.
    Characteristically of the prohibitionist view, she does not mention the growing
    European demand for cocaine—5.5 million consumers in 2007. Garzón, 131.
76 "Central America: The Tormented Isthmus," *The Economist* 16–22 April 2011.
77 "Drug Wars Are Pushing Deeper Into Central America," *New York Times* 24
    March 2011.
78 *Reforma* 15 October 2010.
79 Secretary of State Hillary Clinton, *Reforma* 17 October 2010.
80 This is both compatible with—and an intensification of—the larger trend by
    which US aid to the developing world has been framed in national security
    terms since the Cold War. The classic study remains Robert A. Packenham,
    *Liberal America and the Third World: Political Development Ideas in Foreign Aid and
    Social Science* (Princeton: Princeton University Press, 1973).

PART I
The Background

1

THE MEXICAN STATE AND ORGANIZED CRIME

An Unending Story

Paul Kenny and Mónica Serrano

What is the relation between the state and organized crime in Mexico? Utter antagonism, as proclaimed by the government? In attempting to present its war against organized crime as a policy of the state, the government has pinned everything on the pure opposition between the state and its enemy, between *us* and *them*. Right from the day that Felipe Calderón finally learned of his triumph in the elections, on 10 September 2006, the grip of that schema was evident. "Today, friends," the president-elect declared, "the future won, a future of hope, of civility opposed to a past of violence." That past, he continued, was one that "despises the law, abhors institutions"; "the Mexico of the future is, precisely, the Mexico of the law, the Mexico of institutions."[1]

That greeting to a new dawn was the origin of a bloodily violent tragedy. Words that were forgivable in the flush of victory became set in stone—the words of a "policy" by which the Mexican state for the first time ever would impose itself on its most powerful criminal enemies. The fantasy would cost dear.

The modern state and organized crime in Mexico have a mutual evolution, a shared history. Some parts of it are better known than others, but our aim here is to see that the parts fit together into a recognizable pattern. As we see the pattern emerge, we also appreciate just how much rash impulses to securitize in response to criminal threats depend upon a deliberate forgetting of history. The fruit of this forgetting is a state that, in taking the fight to the criminals, has also found itself fighting parts of itself. Rather than *us against them*, the reality remains inevitably *a few of us against them and who knows how many of us*. To win the war against organized crime the Mexican state would have to defeat branches *of* the Mexican state. Such is the historical weight of state–crime relations in Mexico.

In this chapter we revisit the beginnings of 100 years ago. Although the panorama could readily reach beyond this the context is still quite long. On the other hand, it could turn out to be *only* 100 years if the illicit drug prohibition regime continues to be as invincible as it has been thus far.

To show how the story is composed, we use narrative explanation along with analysis of the critical moments. Since, by its nature the terrain is often secret and taboo, we also move forwards with some explanatory hypotheses. Our attempt is to introduce the sequence of events not in abstraction, but with agents and actors. The conclusion offers a theoretical reprise.

The young modern Mexican state and the illicit drug market

Some 100 years of US illicit drug prohibition date from the 1914 Harrison Narcotics Law. Before it, opium, heroin and cocaine were licit commodities inside the United States. Mexico's role in supplying them was in the hands of the Chinese entrepreneurs who took refuge in the country after the San Francisco earthquake of 1906. The Harrison Law was specifically targeted against these Chinese entrepreneurs' opium and morphine. They, in turn, made the fortune of the first major Mexican racketeer, Colonel Esteban Cantú.

Cantú had first been sent to Mexicali in 1911, at the outset of the Mexican revolution, with a column to protect the northern region of Baja California from US incursions. In 1914 he declared himself governor, evidently inspired by the sudden profitability of drugs guaranteed by the new law. A career soldier, anti-Yankee patriot who seized the opportunity of prohibition to enrich himself, Cantú was the precursor of many Mexican military men.[2]

Cantú lasted until 1920 when General Abelardo L. Rodríguez, was dispatched to reaffirm the central state's authority over him. Cantú hopped over the border and into obscurity, Rodríguez expelled the Chinese community of Mexicali that Cantú had protected, and installed himself as governor—and monopolist of the opium trade. Rodríguez was also a beneficiary of the "vice" boom on the Mexican side of the border created by the prohibitions of gambling and alcohol. He ruled Baja California until 1929, and in 1932 became Mexico's first millionaire president.

Through the 1920s controls were introduced on the consumption and commercialization of opium and marijuana in Mexico.[3] By the 1930s, as US consuls and Treasury agents amply testified, production of both was booming. The pattern of a century was already set. Increasingly punitive enforcement of prohibition policies had become the sine qua non of the steady growth of Mexico's drug illicit economy.

Something less quantifiable was also happening inside Mexico's corridors of political power. The examples of Cantú and Rodríguez were replicated in other local, vertical systems of political–criminal relations that formed to manage a clandestine economy that stretched across the poppy fields of Baja California, Sinaloa, Sonora, Chihuahua and Durango, and the marijuana lands of Guerrero, Puebla and Tlaxcala. Local authorities protected drug production and trafficking for economic benefits and political subordination.[4] The fact that these were criminal activities counted little: imperatives of economic benefit took priority over legal niceties from a world away. The result was a system of "élite–exploitative" relations in which local political actors maintained the upper hand.[5]

Take a figure like General Rodrigo M. Quevedo.[6] Governor of Chihuahua from 1932 to 1936, his "ownership" of the state lasted far longer. With a brother as mayor of Ciudad Juárez, General Quevedo was in reality the head of a clan that would hold onto power for decades—the power that could control Customs revenues and smuggling to the United States. Competition wasn't welcome. In 1938 the mayor of Chihuahua City, out of Quevedo's circle, was killed by a bomb. When in the same year Senator Angel Posada was gunned down in a hotel in Ciudad Juárez, the General was briefly arrested. The governor of Puebla, and brother of 1940s President Avila Camacho, paid bail. Impunity for the élite was also already part of the package.

Quevedo was a sign of the times. Undoubtedly a strongman, a *cacique*, he was cut from a different cloth than those of the past. Formal rules, like the alternation of power, had to be respected. That meant that local élite alliances had to be struck up, as Quevedo did with Governor Talamantes. The bond with the governor of Puebla was also indicative. The local cacique was also being carried along by the greater impulse towards central unity. The negotiation of the 1928–1929 political pact followed by the creation of the National Revolutionary Party had paved the way for the gradual centralization of political and military power. There would be limits to the autonomy of regional players. That their power often had roots in local drug economies was something of which those at the center were very well aware. In 1931 the penal law was altered to define drug consumption and drug trafficking as federal crimes.[7]

In practice, the law was applied to independent operators like Ciudad Juárez's Ignacia Jasso, by no means the only woman of the time to enjoy a long criminal career.[8] After her second arrest in 1944 Jasso set about paying for the police protection that would finally enable her to hand over the business to her sons in the 1960s. A small player finding her niche, Jasso exemplified the limited, local nature of the whole criminal system. Concentrated in the northern states, the market was in the hands of governors and strongmen.

The gesture towards federal enforcement was one both of control over those powerful figures, and of submission to continued pressures from Washington on the part of successive Mexican administrations. Illicit drug production in Mexico was increasing. By 1943, US authorities estimated that Mexico's opium production had tripled within a decade.[9] Bilateral relations with Washington became strained. Governors in the north of Mexico came under constant suspicion of at least tolerating drug trafficking, while the US vice-consul in Durango reported the participation of Mexican army officers as intermediaries between peasants and opium traders.[10] By the end of the 1940s drugs had become a source of scandal regarding Mexico.

Mexican anti-narcotic agents cooperated with American counterparts, but sometimes only to score a hit against the outfit that they weren't being paid by. Sometimes they kept the drugs they seized.[11] More ominously, as it became clear that drugs were going to represent an industry worth millions of dollars, some new strongmen moved in to organize it. Such was the case of Carlos Villarreal. He was by turns a federal policeman, a smuggler and Ciudad Juárez's mayor between 1947–1949, during which time he set up a secret, élite municipal police force dedicated to drug running.[12] The force lasted until 1952, a local presage of a later national tragedy. Meanwhile, General Quevedo and Co. had become pioneers of cocaine trafficking. Members of other political and military élites were not simply accused of protecting traffickers, but of actively leading trafficking rings.[13] Something had to change.

State-led regulation's rise…

At first, alternative forms of regulation were considered. These ranged from treatment and prevention, increased US aid, comprehensive plans to wean peasants from illicit crops, to initiatives for legal quotas of opium production. Notwithstanding the consideration given to such heterodox approaches, by the early post-war period internal concerns and external pressures converged to produce not just a federalization of drug policies, but a broader institutional overhaul along the lines of Washington priorities.

Both led to the creation in 1947 of the Dirección Federal de Seguridad (Federal Security Directorate, DFS). The new agency saw a transfer of responsibility for the drug issue from the Ministry of Health to the Office of the General Attorney, and it showed a flexing of muscles by Mexican federal authorities. The DFS was a new, US-complementary anti-narcotic bureaucracy, Mexico's FBI. It was also part of the country's broader post-war international realignment. Its mission was to combat insurgents as well as criminals. The days of the local criminal world in Mexico were numbered. In the new, post-war period the state's power and authority were undisputed, and the DFS was but the first of other central agencies.

What happened with the DFS is no secret, but has had only superficial explanation. It is the internal origin of Mexico's security failure. As law enforcement against the drug trade went national, so did the drug trade— *protected* by the DFS. The major institutions designed by the state to fight crime—the attorney general's office and Federal Judicial Police (Policía Judicial Federal, PJF) as well as the DFS—became the country's major criminal mafia, especially in the 1970s. Such was the magnitude of the disaster of making law enforcement a centralized, federal enterprise. Under its founder Colonel Marcelino Inurreta and with Lieutenant Manuel Magoral, the DFS took control of the narcotics business for a couple of decades.[14]

How did it happen? Centralizing law enforcement provided all kinds of bridges for criminals on the margins to come into the center. Indeed, the marginal–center axis is key to understanding this and subsequent phases of organized crime in the country. The marginal, in Mexico, has a name: the municipality. Typically remote and poor, municipalities don't have much, but do have a jealously preserved political and security structure: a mayor, a chief of public security, a police corps. The existence of the municipal bodies underneath the different police bodies of the 32 states of the country explains why to this day Mexico has so many different police forces—1,661 in 2006; 2,022 in 2009.[15] When the DFS was created, centralization was effected, but only the centralization of the top of a pyramid. The inchoate local base was preserved, and with it the social base of organized crime in the country.

The municipality would remain *the* place where Mexican policemen become criminals. Bereft of resources, removed from supervision, hundreds of kilometers away from army camps, municipalities have a formal power structure that is flimsy compared to the weight of ties of kinship and bonds of friendship. Not only do the latter render it easy to co-opt the formal structure; often in the history of Mexican drug trafficking they explain why the whole of a local population has joined in crime. Such was the case of Chihuahua's municipality of Ojinaga, on the US border. Ojinaga became the center of the Juárez cartel's empire, an empire that expanded from the base of the other municipalities on the border.

For many caciques, the local bastion had been good enough for them. They could still exist in the 1970s, men like Pablo Acosta Villarreal who ruled Ojinaga both violently and benevolently—who was, as they say, both feared and respected—and who never left the state of Chihuahua.[16] He imposed order, brought in resources which he distributed to the authorities as well as the inhabitants. Any general looking on with fears of disorder in his mind would have found Pablo Acosta a very reassuring presence.

Yet Acosta was a dying breed. With the DFS drawing local outposts towards the center, empire-building was inevitable. The new criminals would still have a foot in the municipal structure, but would now spin a web of protectors among state police commanders and federal anti-narcotics procurators, and even higher. New players arose like Miguel Angel Félix Gallardo, the first and genuine "boss of bosses." Felix Gallardo moved from the Sinaloan municipality of Mocorito into the state's judicial police, graduated as the bodyguard escort of the governor, thence into leadership of the Pacific cartel in which capacity he became the most wanted criminal in the world.[17] Or there were Rafael Aguilar Guajardo—the DFS commander who founded the modern version of the Juárez cartel—and Amado Carrillo—the ex-policeman—who made it famous.[18] Juárez cartel DFS agent Rafael Chao was another kingpin.[19] Juan José Esparragoza Moreno, one of today's most prominent cartel leaders, was another DFS graduate.[20] Without the DFS, Mexican drug trafficking would have remained concentrated primarily in Sinaloa, the cradle of the majority of the country's most notable traffickers. With the DFS, criminals had a career ladder to higher things.

The DFS was open to criminals because its mandate was not to police, but to "contain." Cold War logics, and the singular importance of keeping Mexico out of the revolutionary currents coursing through Central and Latin America, allowed the DFS to get away with murder. Its use of violence against radical left movements knew no legal bounds. This in turn very quickly gave it an ascendancy over criminals, and not just Mexican criminals. Colombian traffickers who came to Mexico in the 1970s looking for openings were shocked, and deterred, by the methods of the DFS.

The DFS exemplified a lesson for the future, one that would not be heeded. Giving militaristic impunity to state agents was no guarantee of their incorruptibility. Rather, the corruption of the most violent was the easiest; their brutality was a service ready to be hired out. A law unto themselves, the DFS' ascendancy over ordinary criminals was also that of an élite force over social inferiors. Including the PJF, in the 1970s the number of federal agents for the whole country was around 600.[21] Each had a retinue of 15–20 "assistants." Not appearing on the official payroll, these were the agents' bodyguards, enforcers and licensed predators.

The outcome of all this was what is colloquially known as the years of control. More accurately if controversially, it was the state-led model of regulation of the illicit drug market.[22] Leaving to one side for now the question of whether there was an intention to regulate, the operation can be readily visualized. At the top, a handful of commanders took their seats on the criminal organizations' "boards," directing their zones of activity to avoid conflicts. On the ground, drugs were cultivated with permission from military zone commanders who alternated fumigation with fertilizer spraying.[23] And drugs were trafficked through the *plazas*, the strategic transit points through which the drugs had to pass on their way to the United States. The *plazas* weren't controlled by the criminals; they were, instead, checkpoints at which the traffickers were greeted by the police, there to collect their bribes, to monitor the movements of the criminals and to keep tabs on the drug market overall.[24] In return for the "taxes" paid to the police, criminals were provided with protection, and their market activities were effectively regulated. So too was their violence.

For over three decades, state regulation of the illicit drug market in Mexico kept levels of overall violence low, at insignificant levels by today's standards. Faced with an intrinsically violent illicit market, state police agencies successfully reduced violence to a minimum, making the criminal costs of its use prohibitively high. The weapon used was strategic coercion—a compelling mix of threat and sanction.[25] The sanction was the unleashing of brutality, for disciplinary, exemplary ends. In its way it was a fitting expression of the *pax priísta*, of a regime ever able to justify means to sacrifice due process and human rights. And it was the affirmation of the state's monopoly over organized violence.

With the use of force denied them, drug traffickers worked together—even further reducing the need for coercion by denouncing the "tax" defaulters.[26] They shared routes and even protectors. Their emblematic figure from the late 1960s was Miguel Angel Félix Gallardo. A conciliator of rival interests, a tireless negotiator always keen to avoid violence, he could have passed for a professional politician—like his protector, Governor Sánchez Celis. Instead, as he mingled among the élite social circles of Sinaloa later in his career, Félix Gallardo had to be content with passing himself off as a businessman with an unusually diverse portfolio. It was another of the rules. Criminals could be socially welcomed by the regional élites who liked the economic booms their money brought, but political office was to be barred to them. The rule reflected less a sense that something had to be sacred than a desire to show that the politicians were the real bosses.

Likewise, the criminals were forbidden from opening a domestic consumption market inside Mexico. Here there was something sacred. It was one thing for Mexican criminals to become millionaires thanks to the effects of prohibition in making their supply of American demand so lucrative; drug consumption in Mexico, however, would have been a symptom of national laxity for a regime that maintained a ban on the sale of liquor on national holidays.

From a Mexican nationalist point of view, it could appear to have been the win–win of a golden age. Not least for one final reason: the rule of regulation was a time of drug peace with the United States. Although the US Embassy in Mexico very early on reported the links between the DFS and drug traffickers, Washington looked the other way.[27] It would do the same for Central America as a whole in the 1980s. Drug trafficking wasn't a priority compared to real or feared left-wing insurgency.

...and fall

The appeal of the "control" model would remain, and Mexican authorities would continue to rely on many of the old regulatory mechanisms. But the stability won was degenerative for the state, for interconnected reasons.

Regulation presupposed some degree of leverage over criminals, some differentiation of standing. Corruption eventually eroded that. The "tax" the criminals were forced to pay would become their means of overthrowing their regulators, for regulation worked only when the criminal being threatened couldn't be sure of buying his way out. Once he gained that certainty, the threats lost their credibility. Police protection would always be essential, but the status of the police had begun a disastrous slide. They were on the way to becoming the criminals' retainers.

The point of no return came when the Mexican market experienced its big bang. It happened in the early 1980s, it featured a new drug on the market, and it was thanks to the United States. Deployed in a wave of interdiction operations in the Caribbean, US military personnel saw to it that cocaine flows to the United States would be re-routed through Mexican airspace.[28] It was the external origin of Mexico's security failure.

The country went from a production-based type of illicit drug market to a dynamic transit type. Previously, geographically contained zones of cultivation of opium and marijuana created a market amenable to regulation, with low levels of violence. Subsequently, the cocaine transit economy opened up the whole country as a highway to the United States. The business took off, and so did the violence. By the mid-1980s the regulatory system collapsed as the United States' contemporaneous shift to coercive and inflexible enforcement—in its second war on drugs—mortally wounded the credibility of Mexican state-provided protection of drug criminals.

The ignominious end to a whole way of life for Mexican criminals and police occurred on 7 February 1985, the day DEA (Drug Enforcement Administration) agent Enrique Camarena Salazar was kidnapped—then to be tortured and assassinated—in Guadalajara. Camarena was leading an operation to seize six tons of marijuana from the trafficker Rafael Caro Quintero, a producer of the drug on a scale that required 4,000–7,000 peasant laborers on his enormous estate in Chihuahua. In the first version of events, Caro Quintero ordered the assassination. A very wanted man in February 1985, Caro Quintero certainly escaped arrest at Guadalajara airport, by waving his DFS badge. (He was eventually arrested in Costa Rica.) Investigating DEA officers would uncover a trail of official complicity in the murder going up to the attorney general's office.

This first version, however, is incomplete. Caro Quintero, 27 years old in 1985, was in a chain of command.[29] Above him was Ernesto Fonesca Carrillo, who also went to jail for Salazar's killing. Protected and pragmatic, it is inconceivable that they had the DEA man killed without what the second version claims they had—clearance from another US agency. This was the CIA, and the fuller story is about how Mexican state-led regulation also fell apart because of the same factor that had first propelled it—Cold War dynamics.

There are strong grounds for believing that Camarena was betrayed to his killers because he had stumbled upon the joint participation of Caro Quintero's bosses and the CIA in the operation later known as *Contragate*.[30] Circumventing US Congressional pressure from 1982 to ban military assistance to Nicaragua's paramilitaries, the covert operation ferried arms to them via Mexican drug traffickers. In return, the CIA protected the Mexicans' export of drugs to the United States. The arrangement was a significant boost to the power of the Mexican drug lords.

They weren't to know, though, that Mexico had become the battleground for an American inter-agency turf war. While the CIA was calling the shots in Mexico, the DEA had been campaigning in Washington to revive the war on drugs—a war that had yielded such good bureaucratic results for Harry Anslinger's Federal Bureau of Narcotics from 1930 to 1962. The scandal of Camarena's assassination gave the DEA a victory whose fruit was the drug certification process that began in 1986. A global annual review of the efforts of drug-producing countries to curb production required what the DEA had won—an enormous bureaucracy, one that would mushroom to 50 federal agencies, departments and bureaus, and another 50 overviewing Congressional committees and subcommittees.[31] President Carter would be unable to rein it in, neither would President Clinton early on in his first term. The bureaucratization of the war on drugs had come to stay—which is to say, the perpetuation of the "war" by the US agency entrusted with enforcing drug prohibition.

Ostensibly doing no more than register the government's progress in things like drug eradication and confiscation, US certification was the final knell for the Mexican state's regulation of its criminal economy. In 1985 the DFS was dismantled, and Mexico's most reliable police force became the DEA. It would be the DEA that confirmed the deaths of drug lords Amado Carrillo (1997) and Ramón Arellano Félix (2002) ahead of the Mexican authorities; the DEA that taped the conversation in the presidential palace between President Fox's travel coordinator and drug trafficker Héctor Beltrán Leyva; the DEA that investigated President Fox.[32] The freedom that the DEA demanded for its agents in Mexico was a contemptuous message that, at least as far as it was concerned, the drug-challenged country was no longer a sovereign state. The DEA could do this because of its hold over Mexico's political class, through the capacity to conjure scandals out of its drug corruption, both real and hypothetical. With this invigilation, the political sine qua non for "the years of control" had vaporized.

DEA pressure also secured the resignation of the man at the top of the chain of criminal command—the head of the DFS, Zorrilla Pérez. (The PRI tried to assure him immunity by getting him elected deputy, but that didn't wash either. Forced to flee abroad, Zorrilla Pérez was finally arrested in Spain in 1989, quietly released in 2009.)[33] The death of the DFS led to the birth of what eventually became Mexico's Center of Investigation and

National Security (Centro de Investigación y Seguridad Nacional, CISEN). Most of the DFS personnel simply changed uniforms and became the PJF, the entity whose initials became the next emblem of state–crime filiation. Those who were dismissed from the DFS left without even their home addresses being jotted down. Many of these applied for jobs with their former criminal associates; some would become prominent criminals in their own right.

Others became pioneers in a new racket that entered the field now, the private protection industry. As in Colombia and Russia, the emergence of the industry was first and foremost an assertion of the ascendant power of organized crime.[34] Protecting themselves with their own henchmen was in itself a status affirmation, but for criminals to employ former policemen as their bodyguards was appropriately symbolic of the shift of roles in the new era. Between 1970 and 1980 the total number of private security companies increased from 40 to 1,400. Over the same time the correlation between the use of criminal-private security guards and the rise in the kidnapping rate also started to insinuate itself: 32 reported kidnappings in 1970, 120 in 1980.[35]

Another indicator had a bad news story to tell. Through the 1970s homicides remained at around 10–12 per 100,000 inhabitants; by the mid-1980s, this figure had risen to 22.

A last factor, also to become decisive, came into play—the armed forces. Not that they had been entirely out of the picture. In 1948 the first "Great Campaign" to destroy illegal crops had seen Mexican soldiers deployed in Sinaloa. On and off they had taken part in manual eradication campaigns ever since. These campaigns offered a useful rationale for performing other missions far more critical for them like stemming arms smuggling and disarming rural populations in remote zones where the state's authority could do with some assertion.[36] But when first President Miguel de la Madrid and then Carlos Salinas declared drug trafficking to be a national security threat, the military came out of the hinterlands and went to the front line. By the late 1980s, 25,000 soldiers—approximately 25 percent of the armed forces then—were permanently engaged in counter-narcotic operations. The number of federal policemen on permanent anti-narcotics assignment was 580.[37] The army had taken control.

Or so it looked. The very different reality was captured by the great meeting of drug bosses that took place in Acapulco, in 1989.[38] Its purpose was to carve up the north of the country into zones for different operators—both to adjust to the new transit economy, and to take over from where the fall of the central DFS had left matters. The traffickers had control.

The cartels

The 1989 summit was a watershed. Like 1985's critical event, though, it would have different versions. As standardly told, the convener in 1989 was Miguel Angel Félix Gallardo—from the prison cell to which he had been sent earlier that year on the charge of participating in the Camarena murder.[39] Félix Gallardo himself denied responsibility for either event, and identified a top police commander as the distributor of territories to the criminals.[40] Two different scenarios ensue, both overlapping on one point: the rise of a new phenomenon, the cartel.

In the first, 1989 was when the criminals fully came into their own. Félix Gallardo had been the leader of a criminal network based in the city of Guadalajara and operating in Ciudad Juárez. He now attempted to achieve two goals: to make firmer territorial delimitations while drawing the operators together in a brotherly federation. The criminals would regulate themselves, peacefully. Once the territories were allocated the struggle for them would cease. History post-1989 would be about the unraveling of this scheme by a younger generation of criminals.

In the second scenario, despite the blow of 1985, there was still a state-led attempt to rule over the criminals. This could no longer be systematic, however. Instead, it fell to an extraordinarily powerful individual who would rise to the pinnacle of the state's security apparatus—and higher. PJF Commander Guillermo González Calderoni would be widely identified as close to Carlos Salinas de Gortari, president as of December 1988. History post-1989 would be about the penetration of drug trafficking to the pinnacle of the state.

One way or another, 1989 was the birth-year of "the cartel." The name had already stuck in Colombia. In Mexico, it replaced the terms used for criminal drug organizations up to the end of the 1970s—"bands" or "cliques."[41] That usage had clearly signaled that the upper hand lay not with the criminals but with the state's security regulators. "Cartel" reflected the shift in the balance of power. In other ways, however, it was a misnomer.

The ambiguities in the new nomenclature of the criminals were part real, part invented. From 1989 on, it would be the case that criminal organizations showed trends towards amalgamation and integration. The trends weren't strictly those of the classic case of a cartel like Middle Eastern oil countries of the 1980s—a group of producers coordinating to fix levels of production, prices and profits to avoid competition between each other in their market. But a loose analogy could hold, on the occasions when the trends were observable. The trends, however, were to prove unreliable indicators. Time after time, the criminal drug organizations would also exhibit patterns of disintegration so violent as to indicate that no single organization could possibly monopolize the illicit market. At this point, the descriptive use of "cartel" fell away, and its true provenance was revealed. An equivalent to the early twentieth-century trusts in America, "cartel" was popularized by the DEA and other US security agencies as they aggrandized the menace of crime—of, indeed, "organized crime."[42]

Different impulses, then, were behind the rise of the phenomenon of the cartel. From the criminals' side, the weakening of the hold of state regulation could be propitious for their own federation. From a state perspective, after the collapse of the horizontal regulatory model, there could also be a perceived advantage in vertically concentrating control.

The next chapter would be about how both of these assumptions, if truly made, collapsed. *Were* they made? On the whole the criminal calculation seems less clear-cut than the state interest. Félix Gallardo was leader of a loose territorial organization. The same was true of his equivalent on the Gulf side of the country—Juan N. Guerra, uncle of the man who became its longstanding head, Juan García Abrego.[43] Even if he had made the realignment for his own organization, Félix Gallardo was not seeking to encroach into the Gulf. At most, he had laid the foundations for the more territorially firm cartels that soon came, especially the Tijuana and Sinaloa cartels. By Félix Gallardo's own account, he only became a cartel leader upon his arrest.

González Calderoni, on the other hand, had already shown his cards when in 1987 he took the step that cleared the way for a new leader of the Juárez cartel—an operation to arrest Pablo Acosta in which Acosta died.[44] Acosta's subordinate, Amado Carrillo Fuentes, took over. A nephew of Ernesto Fonesca Carrillo, Amado Carrillo would drive the Juárez cartel into a position of pre-eminence, in the process making it the alma mater for many of today's famous traffickers. Here indeed was a super-criminal organization worthy of the name cartel.[45]

Carrillo Fuentes moved out of Ojinaga, and pursued the business plan that would make him renowned as *lord of the skies*. His flotilla of cocaine-transporting airplanes, including a Boeing 727 as well as an assortment of jets, would violate US airspace thousands of times.[46] González Calderoni, meanwhile, had moved on to become the attorney general office's director of aerial interception and operations.[47]

Carrillo Fuentes' security chief was the PJF's head of antinarcotics.[48] By 1988, the Juárez cartel had 30 PJF commanders on its payroll.[49] The operation of Carrillo Fuentes also depended upon the ambiguous mix of incapacity and protection of the governors of Morelos, Campeche, Yucatán, Sonora and Chihuahua. For the first time, with Carrillo Fuentes the sheer power of a cartel could be seen. It had made itself an interlocutor with the state, with González Calderoni—his assets valued by the DEA at US$400 million—its chief associate.[50]

The age of pure corruption

With the ascendance of cocaine, corruption burst all barriers. The profits from supplying seven million-odd cocaine users in the United States were now so immense that increasing the rewards for protection could easily be afforded. The fabulous increase in the value of cocaine over the decade from 1985–1995 also saw Mexican drug traffickers freeing themselves from the role of middlemen for the Colombians, and participating more closely in the whole process from production to supply. This also expanded the need for protection.

Corruption's place in the scheme of relations between state and criminals had now reversed. Then, criminals had been forced to pay to avoid the sanction of violence by state agents. Now, criminals chose to pay, and they could punish non-compliance. The law of *plata o plomo*—silver or lead— was coming into effect. Before, corruption had acted as a form of trust-worthy insurance obviating the need for much violence; now it was becoming another form of violence. The threat of force from the state's representatives hadn't just lost credibility; it had disappeared.

The collapse of the country's police forces was swift and total. As regulators, they had had to keep to their role as police. Now their role was represented by the 40 percent of Sinaloa's police who had warrants out for their arrest from other states.[51] Above all, they worked for the cartels. Police officers would wait for criminals—to escort, not arrest, them. When they did arrest a drug lord, it was to protect him from the DEA and extradition. They would arrive at crime scenes—to dispose of evidence. They accompanied every step in the process of drug transportation. In Quiníana Roo, local, state and federal police waited at airports to unload and re-load the cargoes from Colombia, sending 100 tons of cocaine a month on their way to the United States.[52] Infamously, late in 1991 in the state of Veracruz, PJF agents thus engaged opened fire on an unexpectedly present contingent of soldiers (seven policemen were killed).[53] At the era's end, the all-but whole scale desertion of police into criminal ranks was symbolized by the arrest for money-laundering of Adrian Carrera Fuentes, the director of the PJF during the Salinas years.[54]

Occasionally, police commanders trained their own criminals—converting small-time car robbers like the Arellano Félix brothers, for example, into sophisticated drug consignment thieves.[55] The police might train such criminals, yet they could no longer run them. After the Arellano Félix brothers took hold of the Tijuana cartel, their paying power was too great. Indeed, the extraordinary success of the Tijuana cartel was largely due to the unprecedented corruption drive masterminded by their uncle, Jesús Labra Avilés, who—according to the DEA—started paying out US$1 million a week in bribes.[56] When Benjamín Arellano was put on trial, one of the few watertight charges against him was his million dollar attempt to bribe a general.[57] By the 1990s criminal organizations in Mexico were, in another estimate, spending up to US$500 million a year in bribery—double the budget of the attorney general's office.[58]

The occasional observer of Mexico at the time noted "the burgeoning black economy, including the drug trade."[59] Political analysts remained concerned with the nature of the PRI regime and the party system. Even when noted, the drug trade was seen as a separate, minor issue. Instead, it had become more entwined with the question of the regime than anyone imagined. This was so because of the collapse of the country's police forces into criminality. As the police–criminal boundary was lost, so the political class also lost a buffer between it and tainted money. Corruption became a political force.

"What there was was a growing influence of drug traffickers in the sphere of the [Salinas] government," judged 1982–1986's President Miguel de la Madrid, in a taboo-breaking interview in 2009.[60]

More outspoken was Eduardo Valle, an agent of the attorney general's office of the Salinas years. Entrusted with the hunt after García Abrego, he tired of the tip-offs that always put his prey a step ahead of him. In his 1994 letter of resignation Valle asked:

> When are we going to have the courage and political maturity to tell the Mexican people that we are suffering *a species of narcodemocracy*? Will we have the intellectual capacity and ethical fortitude to affirm that Amado Carrillo, the Arellano Félix brothers and Juan García Abrego, are, in a manner inconceivable and degrading, propellers and even *pillars of our economic growth and social development*? That nobody can outline a political project in which the leaders of drug-trafficking and their financiers are not included because, *if you do, you die*?[61]

The questions raised there were unanswerable, but suggest others about this period in Mexico that have rarely if ever been seriously posed. We shall take them in sequence.

A species of narcodemocracy ... As we shall argue more fully in Chapter 2, it is helpfully corrective to emphasize the democratic hue of the late regime like this. At the time the suggestion would have been heretical, with scholarly attention fixed on the partial, controlled nature of the political opening. While understandable, that narrow focus missed other dimensions of the process underway after 1990's electoral reform law, and after President Salinas' declaration of the demise of the single party. Politicians were going to have to run more costly campaigns. PRI politicians in particular were squeezed. As of the 1970's conflicts between the government and business, the PRI had had to rely on public funding. Now biting fiscal constraints and the programmatic institutionalization of social welfare policy drained its candidates' access to the resources needed for clientelism. At the same time, they faced a vocal demand by opposition parties to regulate their electoral funding.[62] Structurally, then, increased democratic competition laid the condition for drug money to go directly to politicians. This in turn was why, in the electoral reform of 1996, the amounts of public funding for parties would be so exorbitantly high. President Zedillo was not heard properly when he insisted that state security was at stake.[63]

Pillars of economic growth … While the country had followed an inward-oriented model of development, a highly restrictive financial system that limited credit flows had opened a niche for "informal" drug money to find its way into smaller firms. Up until the early 1980s, the economic sphere of criminal influence was regional. Thereafter it went national. The reason lay with another phenomenon that was noticed in all but its criminal dimensions— "the meteoric growth of a new private financial élite" composed of many previously unknown investors.[64] In the wake of the 1982 bank nationalization the De la Madrid administration had desperately wooed capital into an unregulated "parallel" stock market.[65] Its most notorious expression was the private brokerage houses that suddenly emerged in lieu of the banks to handle the financial system's flow of funds. In the 1980s, with liquid asset holders in unchallenged supremacy, in the space of five years the capital assets of those houses grew 600 times. It is reasonable to say that no distinction between clean and dirty money existed. When oil prices collapsed in 1986, cocaine money can only have been perceived as helping dig the country out of a deep hole. The cartel leaders *had* become movers at the highest national level. Ever since, Mexican presidents have had to think carefully about the economic costs of acting against the power of drug money.

If you do, you die … The allusion was to the assassination in March 1994 of the campaigning presidential candidate for the PRI, Luis Donaldo Colosio. Its standard interpretation is that he had refused to accept drug funding.

The slide to violence

Drug trafficking became publicly visible in Mexico in the 1990s. Since then, the common assumption would take root that corruption was an exclusively moral issue. This was misguided.

The fallacy of casting corruption as an issue only of personal morality was expressed in Miguel de la Madrid's 2009 interview when he said he regretted not having known about the immorality of President Salinas and his brothers before he selected him as the party candidate for the 1988 election. A president, that is, made of sterner moral stuff would have kept the door to the cartels shut. On similar lines, much speculation would attach to any public figure able to be associated with the presence of drug criminality. This was particularly so for the governors. Was it a coincidence that the first attorney general in the 1988–1994 Salinas administration had just been governor of Jalisco, the state whose capital Guadalajara was the traffickers' redoubt? And so on.

Actively complicit, or passively compromised? These were the corners into which the question of state–crime relations would henceforth push both administrations and public figures. No doubt, the sowing of such suspicion about the political class was insidious for the late PRI regime. In Raúl Salinas too, there was an apparently plausible case of high corruption. Yet the guessing game would keep on after the regime's end, involving other presidents. In the end, it would prove easier to convict Raúl Salinas of the murder of his former brother-in-law than of money-laundering the US$135 million found in a Swiss bank deposit. Much speculated, little proved. That was the dead-end to which a personalized approach to corruption led.

By the 1990s corruption instead demanded to be understood systemically. Indeed, it demanded a different name. Without a security force to regulate the criminal market, the line between corruption and intimidation vanished. *Coercive corruption* encompassed the justifiable fear as well as pecuniary gain of many bribe-takers.

Following the personalized logic, many would conclude that the Salinas government protected the Gulf cartel—because of a relation between its founder and the Salinas' father so public as to be caught on camera.[66] The origin of the idea that every administration had its favored cartel was another misconception. In the early 1990s, the larger truth was that all of the big cartels were untouched.

The clearest sign of the criminals' new power was the impunity they enjoyed. Carrillo Fuentes missed the mafia summit meeting in 1989 because he was serving time for arms possession; he walked free the next year.[67] The Arellano Félix brothers weren't arrested in 1993 when the Papal Nunciate in Mexico City warned authorities they were going to visit him, as they did (the attorney general adduced that as they were armed arresting them risked violence).[68]

The brothers had killed their way to the top of their cartel, late in 1991.[69] They were following the precedent of 1987's killing of Pablo Acosta—the first time that violence had been used to rearrange power relations within the criminal élite. When in 1993, Carrillo Fuentes' co-founder, the ex-DFS agent Aguilar Guajardo, was assassinated, the new profile of the criminal chief executive officer had emerged.[70] Violence was a requirement.

The next step was conflict between cartels. This had already broken out in 1992. The feud between the Arellano Félix brothers and the organization of Carrillo Fuentes was the first public clash between cartels. It also showed that "cartel" described only half of the picture. In the cocaine era of trafficking lower volumes for higher profits, the cartels assumed more tightly defined geographical identities. Profit maximizers as they were, however, the leaders also retained a quality that had characterized Félix Gallardo and Juan Guerra: they were also clan members. As such, they accumulated vendettas as well as profits.

The Arellano Félix brothers were in the extended familial web of Félix Gallardo. In 1992 five closer members were kidnapped, tortured and assassinated. Carrillo Fuentes had hired PJF officers to send the public "message" to Félix Gallardo.[71] An attempt to assassinate the Arellano Félix brothers in a discotheque then left nine people dead. Then the author of that attempt—Joaquín Guzmán—himself became the object of two assassination attempts. He survived.

But, on 24 May 1993 at Guadalajara airport, Cardinal Juan Jesús Posadas Ocampo didn't. The official version would be that the Cardinal had got caught up in the ambush of Guzmán. That was scarcely likely. The truth of the Cardinal's death appeared to turn instead on his closeness with the Arellano Félix family, and his knowledge of their ties with members of the PRI élite.[72]

1993 was a turning point. A feud between two criminal groups had spun out of control, implicated élite members, and left criminal violence on public display. Prior to this, there was a sign of the sadistically grotesque violence that would later emerge, with the work in Baja California—in the mid-1980s—of the executioner who became known for dissolving his victims in acid. His gang, which worked for the Arellano Félix brothers, disappeared 300 people.[73] Faraway in Baja California, the general mood of peace hadn't been dented. Quantitively, the drug-related violence was still low. Overall homicides, after all, were going down from 1992, as the intensity of conflicts over land in remote rural hinterlands diminished.[74] From 1993, however, the perception changed. Beneath the relative quantitive calm, hitherto sacrosanct social and psychological restraints had been smashed.

Violence had become the trademark of all of the newly ascendant criminal bosses, but it most stood out with Ramón Arellano Félix. He was an utterly new composite figure—the mafioso who killed for business, and the psychopath who could kill a policeman or a wealthy teenager or another *narco* for not showing him respect.[75] That kind of violence wasn't a matter of scale, but of terror. For its message was unmistakably that the perpetrator enjoyed absolute impunity. The source of that, in turn, was corruption. Once the stabilizer of violence, corruption was now its stoker. After 1993, no guarantees existed that the wildly unrestrained new criminality wouldn't strike against the state.

That was the context in which Luis Donaldo Colosio was assassinated in Tijuana. It was followed by the Mexico City assassination of the president of the PRI party (and former brother-in-law of Raúl Salinas), José Francisco Ruiz Massieu. These "criminal events" would be given by a future Treasury secretary as a cause of the devaluation crisis at the end of 1994.[76]

It hadn't come about through either intellectual capacity or ethical fortitude, but 1994 was the year that Mexicans realized that the very top of the official political system was mired in violent criminality. The cartels, for so long protected by the system, were now able to shake it to its foundations. Thus, where some analysts would surmise that organized crime became a problem for Mexico upon its transition to democracy (with its weaker repressive reflexes), this was not the case. Visible above all in the Arellano Félix brothers, the open violence of organized crime instead played a key part in plunging the old regime into its final legitimation crisis. The regime was authoritarian, yet what was its justification if it couldn't repress violence—if indeed it was symbiotic with the expression of violence?

Conclusion

In Mexico, as in many other countries, the presence of an illicit drug economy has long challenged the authority of the state. Now it has seriously disrupted the state's capacity to provide security. In this chapter we have taken the long view. The crisis of today's security failure is pressing, but cannot be tackled without understanding its causes. These are in turn inextricably enmeshed with the evolution of a young modern state.

The state that emerged from the churning process of the Mexican revolution was in many ways as unhappy as its precursor "Porfirian" state—one both centralist and with weak control over its peripheries, particularly the 3,200 km of the border with the United States. To this initial disadvantage was soon added an illicit drug market that would emerge and mutate in Mexico. Three main periods stand out: the appearance of a local illicit drug economy; then the rise of a centrally regulated illicit market; finally the transition to a privatized and increasingly violent drug economy.

This history was intimately linked to the enactment and enforcement of prohibition policies north of the border.[77] Beyond the factors of geographical location and weak central rule, it was also the impact of rising drug control policies in the United States that turned Mexico into an active drug producer.

It was in these circumstances that the question still being heard today first arose: was this illegal market within Mexico a symptom of state failure? The position of the Mexican state was more nuanced. Eradicating all illicit activity by marginal subsistence communities was never an objective. At the same time, however, Mexico's shift towards prohibitionist policies coincided with advances towards the centralization of state power over local and regional strongmen and drug economies. Initially, prohibition was embraced for the sake of assuring that redistribution of power to the federal state.

Thus, even though the market within Mexico was fairly limited to the north, a greater trend was underway. It crystallized in 1947's creation of the *Dirección Federal de Seguridad*, and it represented the prizing away of criminal market regulation from local agents by the first of what would be a cluster of central state agencies. The era of state-led regulation of the illicit economy had arrived.

Regulation: patently, this did not mean enforcement of the law. It meant, instead, coordinating, steering, containing—above all, to reduce conflict.[78] What was going on, in other words, was far more than a mere accommodation of illegal activities by rent-seeking individuals who happened to work for the state. Nor do we argue that goods such as low violence and an absence of an internal drug market were accidental byproducts. Rather, regulation carried with it a systematic intention by the state to control an illicit economy in the ways we have described.

Not every agent in the story acted exactly the same; no doubt, police supremacy over the criminals was sometimes uncertain.[79] Yet the testimony of the actors also shows that the distinction between having the authority to tax the criminals, and merely accepting bribes from them, was meaningful and firm.[80] The money taken went to pay for the uniforms, equipment and offices of the police—to the salaries of the federal agents' escorts. This situation didn't happen by chance; it was designed. Crime was made to pay for the state. The centralized system of corruption built around the PRI rule provided the foundations for a model in which regulation meant coordinated state control of the illicit drug economy.[81]

What was the nature of that economy? Illicit economies have a built-in propensity for violence. This is especially true for illicit drug economies, where the threat of violence is a protection against the risk of fraud. Criminal entrepreneurs operate in a highly uncertain environment, facing problems of trust but also of high labor turnover, short-lived structures, and on-off operations. The criminals' grip on the drug economy is constantly undermined, in turn creating conditions for transactional violence between them. As many have pointed out, criminals in dispute with each other cannot settle their grievances in court. So, along with corruption, the threat of the use of force is an essential feature of illegal market regulation, distinguishing organized crime from "ordinary criminality."[82]

State-led regulation involved dominating this violent structure. Few in the literature have pointed out the possibility of this, yet the Mexican state is not the only case—Alberto Fujimori's Peru is a clear analogy, Alvaro Uribe's Colombia a suggestive one. State-led regulation does not extract the violence intrinsic to the illicit market—it transfers it to the watch-dog.

What kind of state can achieve regulatory control over a set of actors otherwise predisposed to violence? The evident answer is an authoritarian state. In Mexico, local and federal authorities were able to assert their supremacy over the illegal drug economy by monopolizing the means of coercive protection. They were able to do that, in turn, because of the distinctive nature of the *pax priísta*. Isolated from international human rights standards, the PRI regime also enjoyed the permissive international conditions of the Cold War. So the dual mandate of the DFS was also critical: the repression of radical left movements gave it the carte blanche of impunity in its dealings with the criminals too.

The paradox, then, was that the criminals were forced into non-violent behavior while the police were allowed vicious practices that flouted any standard of due process and human rights. For a considerable period of time the threats of force were nasty enough to be credible, and the non-violent elements of the agreement allowed the economy to operate quietly.

Criminals were provided by their regulators with an authoritative mechanism of dispute resolution. Within this framework the criminals' own interactions were distinctly cooperative, such that the quintessential figure of this age—Miguel Angel Félix Gallardo—could perhaps finally think of forming a confederation, a genuine cartel in the economic sense.

Over the course of three decades a number of unspoken rules helped regulate relations between the political class and the criminal markets. Levels of criminal violence were to remain tightly confined. Traffickers were not allowed to emerge as an independent power. And nationalist tenets both reminded traffickers of the benefits of keeping their profits at home and deterred them from developing domestic consumption markets. Regulation also meant containing, not expanding, the size of a market organized around the two main commodities of marijuana and heroin.

If the practical model of state regulation of the criminal market can be said to have had a heart of gold, there it was, in that basket of bargains. The force of its appeal is still apparent in Mexico today when people say that organized crime either can be—or indeed oughtn't to be—"administered."[83]

And in many ways the era of state-led regulation *is* paradise lost. Then, the local and the PJF—not the criminals—controlled the *plazas*, the nuclei of the business. Today the *plazas* are the prize for which rival cartels send their military wings out to do pitched battle, in daylight gunfights in the centers of sophisticated cities. This stunning loss of state territory to the illicit market would have been unthinkable then.

Then, the state fostered trust among criminals, promoted certainty and geared orderly patterns of illicit exchanges. Without the state as referee, the cartels fight to the death. And, even as they fight for supremacy, they also show how much of a misnomer "cartel" is for them—since none of them can monopolize either the violence or the business.

Then there was peace; now there is war. It's easy to see why the assumption that organized crime could be administered again is so popular.

Was regulation viable in the long term, though? Clearly not. Too many factors told against it. To maintain control over the illicit drug market, the complicit state agencies also had to control the deployment of anti-narcotic policies. The United States soon noticed that the Mexican eradication airplane was spraying fertilizer instead of fungicide. When its priorities were elsewhere and its agencies were fighting each other, the United States could not only live with that, but actively fostered the Mexican drug economy. But once the United States rallied behind the pursuit of prohibitionist enforcement, Mexico's security forces would be deemed seriously wanting. Sooner rather than later, Mexico's de facto sovereignty for the United States would be called into doubt by its state–criminal nexus. The invidiousness of Mexico's position couldn't have been greater. Its state was now fatally weakened by its protection of the illicit market; protection of that market now transferred exclusively to the arm of US prohibition, the DEA.

Then too, the other side of the equation with the United States was there—a sudden rise or shift in its drug user population's demand could throw state–crime relations in Mexico out of kilter. In the early 1970s, as the share of Mexican heroin in the US market jumped from 10–15 percent to 80 percent, the ability of federal agencies to wield their authority critically diminished.[84] As new market opportunities arose, the structure of criminal incentives and expected profits altered—and so too did the balance of power on which regulation rested. Coercive power waned before corruption, as criminal actors could afford to pay endlessly for the protection they required. The precedent set in the early 1970s was reinforced by the 1980s with the re-routing of cocaine flows from the Caribbean into Mexico. Regulation fell apart.

By the end of the 1980s Mexico had not only reasserted its position as the main producer of marijuana and heroin for the US market, but had also emerged as a major transit route of over one-third of the cocaine bound to the United States. Estimates of the amount of cocaine flowing across Mexican territory jumped from 30 percent in 1989 to 50 percent in 1998, and upward of 70–80 percent more recently.

Simultaneously, the relative restraint that had long characterized the Mexican cartels was replaced by defiant patterns of behavior by younger criminals. The restraints on violence weren't in fact exclusively broken by the Tijuana cartel, but the brutality of the Arellano Félix brothers was most public. The violence that started in remote Baja California was the death notice of regulation. When the violence left not even the president's family or the official presidential candidate sacred, it was also a sign that regulation had one way or another compromised and made vulnerable people at the highest echelons of state power.

More pervasively, the Mexican method of regulating criminals and their economy had compromised the state. The regime that ran it had engineered a deviant type of order, based on, among other ingredients, corruption and impunity. Its relations with crime were viciously circular: because it was authoritarian, it could control the criminal economy; its means of control deepened its authoritarianism.

The bargains, then, were those of a Faustian pact. In some ways, it has been broken. Then there was authoritarianism; now there is democracy. In other ways, though, the state that authoritarianism inherited to democracy was more damaged than the new actors began to imagine. The enormity of the challenge of reforming that state would mean that, while now there is democracy, then again there might be authoritarianism.

Notes

1   Cited in Anabel Hernández, *Los Señores Del Narco* (Mexico: Grijalbo, 2010), 525.
2   For Cantú, see Francisco Cruz, *El Cártel de Juárez* (Mexico: Planeta, 2008), 33–35.
3   Luis Astorga, *El siglo de las drogas* (Mexico: Plaza Janés, 2005), 19–28.
4   See Luis Astorga, "Mexico: drugs and politics," in Menno Vellinga, ed., *The Political Economy of the Drug Industry. Latin America and the International System* (Gainesville: University Press of Florida, 2004), 8.
5   Peter A. Lupsha and Stanley Pimentel, "Political–Criminal Nexus" (Washington, DC: Institute for Contemporary Studies, National Strategy Information Center, 1997).
6   Cruz, 76–79.
7   Astorga, *El siglo de las drogas*, 43, 50–51.
8   Cruz, 86.
9   William O. Walker III, *Drug Control in the Americas* (Albuquerque: University of New Mexico Press, 1981/1989), 163–166.
10 See "Appendix: Opium Poppy Destruction in Mexico from the American Consulate in Durango to the Secretary of State," in ibid., 225–229.
11 This practice remained in place for decades. In 1937 José Siurob, head of the Ministry of Public Health, reported some of the "problems" encountered with state governors who having confiscated opium, then financed the payroll of security agents with income derived from seized drugs. In confidential interviews an officer of the army reported how eradication operations in Guerrero in the early 1960s were deployed with little or no funding, thus forcing officers to resort to "extreme measures." See Luis Astorga, "Viaje al país de las drogas," *Nexos*, 211, 1 July 1995; Astorga, *El Siglo de las Drogas*, 39. See also the testimonies gathered in Pimentel, "Mexico's legacy of corruption," 182–183; and in Carlos Antonio Flores Pérez, "El Estado en crisis: crimen organizado y política. Desafíos para la Consolidación Democrática," PhD Thesis, Universidad Nacional Autónoma de México, 2005, 111–115.
12 Cruz, 71.
13 See the memoirs of the state's attorney general, Manuel Lazcano, quoted in Astorga, *El siglo de las drogas*, 81, 101. See also Luis Astorga, *Mitología del 'narcotraficante' en México* (Mexico: Plaza y Valdés, 1995), 60–62.
14 Cruz, 219–220.
15 Genaro García Luna ¿*Por qué 1,661 corporaciones de policia no bastan? Pasado, presente y futuro de la policía en México* (México, DF: Secretaría de Seguridad Pública, 2006); Genaro García Luna, *Nuevo Modelo de Policía* (México, DF: Secretaría de Seguridad Pública, 2009).
16 Cruz, 80.
17 Ricardo Ravelo, *Los Capos* (Mexico: Plaza Janés, 2006), 81, 85–86.
18 Ibid., 130.
19 Jesús Blancornelas, *El Cártel. Los Arellano Félix: la mafia más poderosa en la historia de América Latina* (Mexico: Plaza Janés, 2003), 48.
20 Hernández, 385.
21 Ibid., 119.

22 See Mónica Serrano, "Drug trafficking and the state in Mexico," in H. Richard Friman, ed., *Crime and the Global Economy* (Boulder: Lynne Rienner, 2009), 139–157.

23 Hernández, 120.

24 See Peter A. Lupsha, "Drug-lords and narco-corruption: the players change but the game continues," *Law and Social Change* 16:1 (1991), 41–58.

25 Although closely linked to the notion of deterrence, strategic coercion not only seeks to deter other actors from acting when they want to, but also compels them to act when they do not want to do so. Lawrence Freedman, "Introduction," in L. Freedman, ed., *Strategic Coercion* (Oxford: Oxford University Press, 1998), 5.

26 Hernández, 122.

27 Astorga, "Mexico: drugs and politics," 88.

28 See Bruce Bagley, "The Myths of militarization: enlisting the armed forces in the war against drugs," in Peter Smith, ed., *Drug Policy in the Americas* (Boulder Colorado: Westview Press, 1992), 129–150.

29 Hernández, 102.

30 Jorge F. Menéndez, *El Otro Poder* (Mexico: Nuevo Siglo, 2001), 65–66, 103–107 reproduces the testimony of a CIA agent to this effect. Hernández, 88–93, reprises the breaking of the Contragate story in the United States and the five-year-long DEA investigation.

31 Vanessa Peat, *The Andean Cocaine Industry: A Maze With No Way Out? Failures of the US' "War on Drugs"* (Geneva: Institut Universitaire D'Etudes Du Developement, 1998), 60.

32 Ravelo, *Los Capos*, 104, 245, 68. Hernández, 14, 319–320.

33 Miguel Angel Granados Chapa, "Caro Quintero y Zorrilla Pérez," *Reforma* 5 June 2009.

34 See Federico Varese, "Is Sicily the future of Russia? Private protection and the rise of the Russian Mafia," *European Journal of Sociology*, 35: 2 (May 1994), 249.

35 Mónica Serrano, "Latin America: The limits to the state's capacity to enforce law and order," in *Institutional Reforms, Growth and Human Development in Latin America* (New Haven: the Yale Center for International and Area Studies, 2000), 461–482.

36 María Celia Toro, *Mexico's "War" on Drugs; Causes and Consequences* (Boulder: Lynne Rienner, 1995), 13.

37 Ibid., 33.

38 Blancornelas, 47–48; Ravelo, *Los Capos*, 95–96.

39 Ravelo, *Los Capos*, 94.

40 Diego Enrique Osorno, *El Cártel De Sinaloa: Una historia del uso político del narco* (Mexico: Grijalbo, 2010), 252.

41 Hernández, 34, 118. Likewise, there had been a plethora of terms before "drug-trafficker" came into official usage in the early 1960s—from cultivators to racketeers, mafiosi to smugglers. Osorno, 126.

42 Carlos Resa Nestares, "El Comercio De Drogas Ilegales En México: Nueve mitos del narco tráfico en México (de una lista no exhaustiva," unpublished paper (2005), online, available at: www.uam.es/personal_pdi/economices/ cresa//nota0305.pdf

43 Menéndez, 204.

44 Cruz, 294.
45 See Peter Reuter and Franz Trautman, eds., *A Report on the Global Illicit Drug Markets 1998–2007* (Brussels: European Commission, 2009), 88–89.
46 Cruz, 35, 333.
47 Ravelo, *Los Capos*, 147.
48 Hernández, 345.
49 Ravelo, *Los Capos*, 83–84.
50 Jorge Carpizo in Carmen Aristegui and Ricardo Trabulsi, *Transición* (Mexico: Grijalbo, 2009), 65.
51 Former Governor Francisco Labastida, in ibid., 201.
52 Ravelo, *Los Capos*, 154.
53 Hernández, 55.
54 Ravelo, *Osiel*, 79.
55 Ibid., 126.
56 Menéndez, 81–82.
57 *Reforma* 5 December 2002.
58 Peter Smith "Semi organized international crime: drug trafficking in Mexico," in Tom Farer, ed., *Transnational Crime in the Western Hemisphere* (New York and London: Routledge, 1999), 204.
59 Alan Knight, "State power and political stability in Mexico," in Neil Harvey and Mónica Serrano, eds., *Mexico: Dilemmas of Transition* (London and New York: Institute of Latin American Studies, University of London, 1993), 30.
60 Aristegui and Trabulsi, 103.
61 Ricardo Ravelo, *Osiel: Vida Y Tragedia De Un Capo* (Mexico: Grijalbo, 2009), 74 (italics added.)
62 Mónica Serrano, "The legacy of gradual change: rules and institutions under Salinas," in Mónica Serrano, ed., *Rebuilding the State: Mexico after Salinas* (London: Institute of Latin American Studies, 1996), 9, 13, 18.
63 Mony de Swaan, Paola Martorelli and Juan Molinar Horcasitas, "Public financing of political parties and electoral expenditures in Mexico," in Mónica Serrano, ed., *Governing Mexico: Political Parties and Elections* (London: Institute of Latin American Studies, University of London, 1997), 160.
64 Blanca Heredia, "State–business relations in contemporary Mexico," in Serrano, ed., *Rebuilding the State*, 137–138.
65 Neil Harvey, "The difficult transition: neoliberalism and neocorporatism in Mexico," in Harvey and Serrano, eds., *Mexico: Dilemmas of Transition*, 13.
66 Hernández, 191.
67 Ibid., 58.
68 Menéndez, 93.
69 Hernández, 41, 63.
70 Ibid., 35, 41.
71 Ibid., 161–167.
72 Ibid., 77–78.
73 Ibid., 128.
74 *Reforma* 3 October 2009. See Guillermo Zepeda Lecuona, *Crimen sin castigo. Procuración de justicia penal y ministerio público en México* (México: Fondo de Cultura Económica, 2004), 66.
75 Blancornelas, 84, 83, 49.

76 Agustín Carstens and Moisés J. Schwartz, "Mexico's economic programme: achievements and challenges," in Serrano, ed., *Rebuilding the State*, 113.

77 See Mónica Serrano, "Transnational organized crime and international security: business as usual?," in Mats Berdal and Mónica Serrano, eds., *Transnational Organized Crime and International Security: Business as Usual?* (Boulder: Lynne Rienner, 2002), 15–20.

78 See Peter Lange and Marino Regini, "Introduction: interests and institutions: forms of social regulation and public policy making," in P. Lange and M. Regini, eds., *State, Markets and Social Regulation: New Perspectives on Italy* (New York: Cambridge University Press, 1989), 4.

79 In Sinaloa of the early 1970s, for example, a federal police officer was killed for failing to fulfill his duties for traffickers. Osorno, 130.

80 Hernández, 121.

81 As Lupsha put it, organized crime in Mexico operated "with the 'con permiso' and franchise of the state and national institutions, and their representatives." Peter A. Lupsha, "Transnational narco-corruption and narco investment: a focus for Mexico," *Transnational Organized Crime*, 1:1 (1995), 87.

82 J. McC. Heyman and A. Smart, "States and illegal practices: an overview," in J. McC. Heyman, ed., *States and Illegal Practices* (Oxford: Berg, 1999), 5; A. Anderson, "Organised crime, mafia and governments," in G. Fiorentini and S. Petlzman, eds., *The Economics of Organised Crime* (Cambridge: Cambridge University Press, 1997), 46; Tom R. Naylor, "Mafias, myths and markets: on the theory and practice of enterprise crime," *Transnational Organised Crime*, 1: 4, (1997).

83 As urged in Rubén Aguliar V. and Jorge G. Castañeda, *El Narco: La Guerra Fallida* (Mexico: punto de lectura, 2009), 56.

84 The jump followed a successful clampdown on illicit opium cultivation in Turkey. Peter Reuter, "Eternal hope: America's quest for narcotics control," *Public Interest* 79 (Spring 1985), 90; Paul B Stares, *Global Habit: The Drug Problem in a Borderless World* (Washington, DC: The Brookings Institution, 1996), 28; Peter Smith, "Semi organized international crime: drug trafficking in Mexico," in Farer, ed., *Transnational Crime*, 193–217.

2

TRANSITION TO DYSTOPIA

1994–2008

Paul Kenny and Mónica Serrano

In 2008 Mexico's security failure become impossible to hide. By the year's end, as we mentioned in the Introduction, Mexico was suddenly targeted as a failed state. The country's security failure was a matter of state evolution, but the state failure agenda was characteristically uninterested in either that or the further harm that *it* represented for the state. Against this, then, we advance the argument that both drug crime and the war on it in Mexico are politically conditioned. An unobjectionable, even anodyne, argument, it cuts against two common contentions. One is frequent in Mexico: drug crime is merely a matter of law and order. The other is constant for Mexico: there is no alternative to the war on drugs. The aim of this chapter is to show that efforts to de-couple security from politics are unsustainable.

We begin by proposing a new periodization for the last chapter of the country's political history. Against both expert expectations and common hopes, the year 2000 did not mark the country's transition to democracy. Instead, Mexico became a democratic country with the presidential election of 1994.

The independent federal electoral authority gave the following results at the end of August 1994. The Institutional Revolutionary Party's (PRI) candidate, Ernesto Zedillo, won 50.18 percent of the vote. The National Action Party (Partido Acción Nacional, PAN) gained 26.69 percent; the Democratic Revolution Party (Partido de la Revolución Democrática, PRD) 17.08 percent.[1] In 1988's fraudulent election, the abstention rate was 49.7 percent. By contrast, 77 percent of the electorate participated in 1994.

By any standards, this was a compelling result, and yet its crystal-clarity would be misted. Before the result was out, it had already become unacceptable. Analysis of the time had been strong on precedents for

suspicion. Emphasis fell upon the restricted character of political liberalization, the drop-by-drop administering of concessions in an invidious
fashion that divided the opposition parties, rather than upon its cumulative
institutionalizing effects. The assumption that even as it declined the
regime would still keep the levers of control blinded observers to evidence
to the contrary, and to the role of chance. So, while it was true that President Salinas designed political change to maintain the status quo —and
leave room for the transformative economic liberalization of the North
American Free Trade Agreement—his method of rule was increasingly
crisis-prone and destabilizing for the PRI. A government that terminated
with 17 of the country's 32 governorships in suspension was a government
in deep trouble.[2] Then came the uprising in Chiapas. A complete surprise,
the events of 1 January 1994 triggered the democratization achieved with
the opening of the federal electoral authority to citizen control of its governing council. The PRI had lost the means of validating its perpetuation
in power. To remain in power, it would have to do what it did—win a fair
election.

After the result, however, the talk was of the "structural inequities" that
went into Zedillo's victory, talk to which Zedillo himself on one occasion
contributed.[3] From then on, the perception would stick that, while it may
have been legal, Zedillo's win was not legitimate—and thus that democratization remained top of the country's agenda of unfinished business.
Attention was captivated by the survival of the PRI regime, and by the
manner in which it would meet its "true" end. An alternation of the political party in power was all-but universally deemed an essential requirement. Despite the insistence in the specialist literature that uncertainty of
outcome was one of the key features of a transition, leading commentators
were 100 percent certain that the PRI had to lose.

The subsequent story would be one of distortion and disappointment, as
of July 2000 when Vicente Fox won the presidency by a margin of 6.42
percent—a margin given him by voters who transferred from the left PRD
party to support a transition from the PRI.[4] Significant new civil liberties
would be gained in the country, yet the structural discontinuity or rupture
with the past denoted by transition would not occur after 2000. Many
factors contributed to this, but the fundamental reason was that 2000 was
not the breakthrough year: 1994 was, set the path that has been followed
since—democracy without transition.

If this was missed in the specialist literature, it was because of its sche-
matization and fixation with political parties at the expense of state perspectives. If, in turn, the new framework stands out here, it is because the
concern is—to use a new term—security history. The continuity is overwhelming between the two administrations of the supposed post-transition
and the security policy of the supposed last authoritarian (Zedillo) administration. That is, the sequential course of a transition has not held. Indeed,

the Mexican experience runs counter to the logic predicted by transition. Not only has the core condition of civilian control over the military not been met; civilian control has drastically diminished.[5] This has been a continuous process since 1994. With it, the levels of drug-related violence in Mexico have climbed, and eventually skyrocketed. To understand this process is to make sense of the country's security failure.

Crime and politics: the legacy and the precedent

As we saw in Chapter 1, by 1993–1994 the state–criminal nexus came out into the open with publicly violent acts, undermining the PRI regime's legitimacy. Longer-term factors were behind this appearance of violence. When the old regulatory system broke down, it did so in a political context also experiencing significant change. From the mid-1980s, local electoral competition intensified, spreading from the north into the center, and from there towards the south. The consequences for criminals were contradictory. Political alternation and circulation both expanded the set of corruptible actors and disrupted old protection agreements. At the same time, while their corruption power was unprecedented, drug traffickers had to contend with the Drug Enforcement Administration (DEA)—and with the reduced power of Mexican security agencies and politicians to resist its externally driven enforcement. Cocaine seizures went up dramatically from 1987–1989.[6]

The combination of these conditions all made the use of criminal violence more likely. First, the two predominant modern cartels, the Juárez and the Tijuana, squared up against each other. The numbers involved were not great, but very high representatives of the state were swiftly caught up in the violence, indicating that drug trafficking had penetrated farther than anyone knew. At the same time as Colombia was being dubbed a "narcodemocracy," the government insider in Mexico we cited in the previous chapter was taking it as given that his country was no different.

How, then, was the lid put back on the volatile 1994, enabling the PRI to win the election that year? The answer was Chiapas. The armed uprising magnetized the electorate's security fears. It also provided a precedent for 2006's election: the PRD party could be pulverized by a climate of fear. The winning advertizing campaign of 1994 for the PRI featured a child frightened of being kidnapped—and not likely to be reassured by the PRD.

The real causes for fear were to be found in neither Chiapas nor the PRD. In 1994, there were 355 kidnappings in the country; by 1997 there were an estimated 1,047. From 1994 to 2005, this figure probably exceeded 75,000. With scarcely a whisper about it, Mexico was set to become the world's number two country for kidnapping.[7] Here was the most damaging evidence that the country was going through a severe internal security failure breakdown. By 1995, 70 percent of the kidnappings were being committed by police agents. Half of the members of the country's 900 armed gangs in 1995 were police agents. The Department of the Interior put the figure of the 100,000-strong Federal Judicial Police (Policía Judicial Federal, PFJ) captured by drug money at 30–50 percent.[8]

Ernesto Zedillo was both the first president to be elected in a context of security fears, and the first democratically elected incumbent to confront the magnitude of the security crisis. As the campaign manager of Colosio, he was also uniquely positioned to picture the threat of drug trafficking. Zedillo would keep his thoughts on these issues to himself, but it is a reasonable hypothesis that his determination to democratize the PRI out of power was connected with his dismay and alarm at the party's criminal complicities. In March 1995, Raúl Salinas was arrested. In January 1996, Gulf cartel leader García Abrego was arrested and swiftly extradited to the United States. Both were highly symbolic acts, showing a break of the political–criminal nexus.

Both acts had to be highly symbolic. In 1995 the US drug certification process was amended to include the level of drug corruption as an index of a country's commitment to the war on drugs.[9] The index was a matter of US perception. Institutionally too, then, strong moves were made in Mexico. By the end of the Zedillo administration in 2000, some 1,800 agents of the PFJ had been dismissed on corruption or incompetence charges, leaving just 1,200.[10] By 1998, the PFJ was effectively dismantled.

The next step had been prepared. The armed forces were to step in on a firmer basis than that on which presidents in the past had sent out military police into the federation. From 1995–2000 the National Program for the Control of Drugs significantly widened the involvement of the armed forces from eradication to surveillance and the control of air-space.[11] The army as well as air force was granted authority to survey and intercept vehicles— that is, to arrest. The line between anti-narcotic and public order missions was blurred. In a series of rulings the Supreme Court of Justice deemed the support granted by the armed forces to tasks of maintaining public order in times of peace to be fully legal when so requested by the competent civilian authorities.[12]

The security crisis had yielded the political decision to bring the military to the fore. In 1996 *The Accord on the Strengthening of Civil Power and the Function of the Army in a Democratic Society* was signed in Mexico. The army and society were Guatemala's.

The military

The Mexican military stance had become crucial, but also complex. It had different stakes and constraints. The greatest constraint came from outside. The various agencies of the United States manifested varying levels of tolerance for the Mexican cartels, but coalesced around the need to see some action in the war against drugs. The militarization of Mexican anti-narcotic policies was thus galvanized by the need to appease the demands and appetites of the US security agencies. At the same time, it was hard to deny that the country faced a genuine internal security challenge. The rising violence in the north, the crisis of the political system and the disintegration of police credibility all conspired to bring the military institution visibly onto the scene.

Yet it was a development that ran against the grain of decades, and the position of the military élite was uncomfortable. Uppermost on its mind was the uprising in Chiapas of the Zapatista Army of National Liberation. Off-the-record comments confirm what one might in any case expect, namely that the army high command had chafed for an all-out counter-guerrilla offensive—and been hugely frustrated at President Salinas' decision instead to negotiate. The mission to combat drugs was a most vexing distraction, especially when in mid-1996 the Popular Revolutionary Army (EPR) erupted in Guerrero. And to cap it all, the nature of the game with the different US agencies was that no Mexican official—not even Enrique Cervantes Aguirre, secretary of defense—was above suspicion of colluding with the cartels.[13]

What followed was another of those critical episodes whose many versions attest to their many dimensions. On 19 February 1997 the arrest was announced of General Jesús Gutiérrez Rebollo. Head of anti-narcotic policies at the INCD (National Institute to Combat Drugs), he was effectively Mexico's drug tsar. He had, the secretary of defense declared in a press conference, "betrayed" the military institution and "threatened national security" by giving "protection" to one of the nation's main drug lords for several years.[14] The drug lord was Amado Carrillo Fuentes; the scandal was a classic Mexican mystery.

Respected in the army, known outside it, Gutiérrez Rebollo was a secretary of defense-in-waiting. Already difficult to move against, Gutiérrez Rebollo was also arrested at the worst possible moment in February 1997—on the eve of the year's US certification, as Jorge Chabat points out in Chapter 6. Only a very major consideration could have led to the open admission that the military institution itself could be added to the list of the state's crises. For Gutiérrez Rebollo wasn't alone. Three brigadier generals were detained with him. In March, another brigadier general was arrested, this time for links with the Arrellano Félix brothers. By August 1997, 402 military officers were in custody, 15 ranking between lieutenant colonel and general.[15] Like the arrest and subsequent trial of Gutiérrez Rebollo, all of this was brought to light in the most public, and humiliating, manner possible.

The two broad interpretations perhaps converge. The first answers the question of timing: Gutiérrez Rebollo was arrested before the US agency that had found him out went public. This was the DEA. Its service was to itself (the INCD was wound down for a more DEA-like one), but also to the Pentagon, the US mover behind the 1995 National Program for the Control of Drugs. The breaking of Gutiérrez Rebollo and such a significant portion of officers was the breaking of the Mexican military's resistance to its new number one mission.

The other interpretation is more tentative. Before his very brief tenure at the INCD, General Gutiérrez Rebollo had been a very long-serving commander responsible for the whole northwest of the country, its hottest drug area. He was both commander of the Fifth Military Region—covering the states of Jalisco, Zacatecas, Colima, Sinaloa, and Aguascalientes—and chief of the Fifteenth Military Zone, with headquarters in Guadalajara. Moreover, he had been so since 1989, outlasting the rotations of Jalisco's governor, of secretary of defense, and of those required by the military for its commanders. Gutiérrez Rebollo had become a strongman, a *cacique*. As such, he exemplified the new realities of state power vis-à-vis organized crime.

Bald and burly, Gutiérrez Rebollo looked absolutely incorruptible and very tough—no doubt the reasons both the DEA and FBI had liked him, and trusted him with their secrets. Gutiérrez Rebollo was, indeed, the kind of strongman that would have had someone like Carrillo Fuentes quaking with fear—30 years earlier. Now the power was Carrillo Fuentes'.

In this second interpretation, Gutiérrez Rebollo had clearly been a contributor to the rise of Carrillo Fuentes' cartel. That could be justified as reality management. What couldn't was Gutiérrez Rebollo's use of the INCD as a task force directed against the Arellano Félix cartel. Carrillo Fuentes even paid for some of the operations. Gutiérrez Rebollo too was paid, along with his subordinate officers. That is incontrovertible, and sufficed to seal Gutiérrez Rebollo's fate when it was decided to bring him down.[16]

This interpretation, however, still needs to explain why that decision was taken; why, indeed, Gutiérrez Rebollo's case went, in an unprecedented move, to a civilian court, instead of being hushed up. Probably, the US vigilance didn't allow it. Possibly, there was another dimension, the least known. By 1995 it appears that some very senior figures in the army had decided that it was their "patriotic mission"—in the words of one of them, retired General Jorge Maldonado Vega—to form a pact with the cartel of Carrillo Fuentes.[17] Contact was then formalized between Carrillo Fuentes' emissary and Gutiérrez Rebollo; and that was why Gutiérrez Rebollo was promoted, at the end of 1996.

The basis of the negotiation was Carrillo Fuentes' offer that if the Arellano Félix brothers could be eliminated, he would donate half of his riches to the state, before emigrating to attend to his businesses in South America (especially Argentina where he was channeling funds into the presidential election).[18] It was an offer of drug peace for Mexico. Its authenticity would be vouched for in a classified file stolen from the secretary of defense's private secretary. Dated 14 January 1997 it "presented the hypothesis of an understanding between the Mexican government and Carrillo Fuentes."[19]

Gutiérrez Rebollo was in fact arrested on 6 February. While Cervantes Aguirre in the company of half a dozen other top generals had been involved in the negotiation, it was Gutiérrez Rebollo who took the fall when the decision came either from the very top of the state and/or the United States that it was unacceptable. Gutiérrez Rebollo didn't go quietly. He accused President Zedillo's father and uncle of drug trafficking connections. The general produced no proof, but the pursuit of it by others would produce another interpretation of the mystery.[20]

Any of its ramifications suffice to mark the Gutiérrez Rebollo affair as a watershed for the Mexican military. Its position to resist US counter-narcotics priorities was cut away just as its ability to "administer" drug traffickers without being corrupted by them was shown to be chimerical. These were two heavy blows.

Carrillo Fuentes was also cornered. After a hunt for him, he died in July 1997, in what looked like a sophisticated assassination from within his own cartel. The assessment that he was worth US$2.5 billion doesn't have to be spot-on for it to be appreciated that there were strong interests in keeping his cartel in business in Mexico.[21]

The state–security crisis: 1995–2000

The death of Carrillo Fuentes unleashed the first great wave of drug violence the country would see—250 people "disappeared" in Ciudad Juárez, 500 tortured and killed from Tijuana down to Guerrero, across from Jalisco to Veracruz, Sinaloa to Tabasco. The mass graves were still being discovered two years later.[22] The Arellano Félix brothers were making their move, and being repelled. Inhabitants of the cities affected got used to hearing automatic gunfire at night—newspaper readers to learning that the photos of corpses meant that "a settling of accounts" between bands had occurred.

In the mid-1980s the state of Chihuahua had experienced one death every two weeks in connection with drug trafficking.[23] In 1999, in Tijuana and Sinaloa, it was about 500 a year.[24] These were now cartel war zones. Carrillo Fuentes' brother Vicente had become leader of the Juárez cartel. This was now joined by the Sinaloa cartel, led by Ismael Zambada. These were the new faces of Amado Carrillo Fuentes' extensive Pacific organization.

The government said nothing to the public, and publicly reassured the United States. In 1997, through the newly opened diplomatic channel of the High-Level Contact Group between Mexico and the United States, the Mexican side underlined that its drug traffickers had "not been able to reflect their economic power in an equivalent political power." The organizational and cultural shortcomings of the Mexican cartels were eloquently diagnosed. Carrillo Fuentes was identified as "the most powerful Colombian drug trafficker."[25]

Mexico was the direct beneficiary of Colombia's woes when it was humiliated by de-certification in 1996 and 1997 after the revelation of the US$6 million that had gone from the Calí cartel into President Ernesto Samper's campaign. Colombia became the DEA's—and so the world's—first "narco-democracy." Yet Mexico's escape had been close. US pressure wasn't about to go away, and was manifestly a top consideration when the Zedillo administration assembled its policies to deal with the security crisis. Many of those policies "of state" would be adopted by its democratic successors. Their consequences would also be borne by them.

There were two, conjoined policy faces. The High-Level Contact Group was a bid for close bilateral cooperation with the United States, and the Zedillo administration was prepared to unscrupulously use its comparative advantage over Colombia in proximity to the United States to get this. Yet this administration would also exemplify the strategy's brutal limit, after President Zedillo—in Vienna—declared himself in favor of a multilateral approach on the drug issue. His reward was Operation Casablanca, a 1998 US Treasury Department operation against leading Mexican banks accused of laundering US$100 million for the Juárez and Calí cartels. The Mexican government was notified of the operation's success minutes before its announcement.

Cooperation, then, might be sought, but the position of Mexico in the war on drugs was rigidly asymmetrical, that of the suspect junior partner. The perverse dynamic encouraged the Mexican administration to take measures more with an eye to how pleasing they were for the United States than to their costs. This was the other policy face, and it involved inflating the military mission while deflating the police. Here was the seed of ruin.

It dated to 1996–1998, when the PFJ was dismantled. As López-Portillo anatomizes in Chapter 4, behind this was the tabula rasa mentality of Mexican "reform." In response to an institutional crisis of corruption, reinvent from scratch. This was not reform, but institutional disintegration—and renewed crisis of corruption. The pattern was clearer the closer the security agency came to organized crime. The Under-Secretariat for Investigating and Fighting Drug-trafficking; the General Agency for Crimes against Health; the National Institute for the Combat of Drug-trafficking; the Special Attorneyship for Crimes against Health; the Under-Secretariat for International Organized Crime—these new anti-narcotic agencies would all fall like ninepins. The PFJ itself was replaced in 1999 by the Federal Preventive Police (PFP). Its membership was a scanty 27,000.[26]

The ranks of the PGR (attorney general's office), were so decimated by its purging—and the United States so unhappy—that the attorney general of the last years of the Zedillo administration, Madrazo Cuéllar, initiated the policy of appointing colonels and generals to command the worst zones of violence.[27] True enough, corruption in the PGR was so dire that the cartels, it came to light in 2000, were on the brink of paying it to get their candidates appointed to the posts.[28] Yet the replacement of the police by military officers was an astounding admission of the lack of will to undertake the urgently needed police and justice reforms. By the turn of the century, the price was plain—an estimated national impunity rate of 90 percent.[29]

While the police were simply written off, the ending of the period of the armed forces' relative isolation in eradication operations in turn exposed *them* to drug corruption. This wasn't new, but the Gutiérrez Rebollo affair made it a matter of scandal, not slander. The position of the military high command on the war on drugs was along a spectrum that ran from reluctance to fighting to making pacts for peace. Neither proved tenable against US determination. In late 1997 Barry McCaffrey reported with satisfaction that the Pentagon would be training more than 1,500 Mexican soldiers in anti-narcotics procedures, communications, intelligence, special forces methods, aviation maintenance and operation—the full package. There was even talk of the Pentagon training Mexican "rapid response units."[30] From here on the fatal assumption stuck that the war on drugs was to be conducted against a territorially entrenched insurgency. Finally, in exchange for assuming responsibility for the war on drugs and submitting to US dictates, Mexican military prerogatives and authority inside the country now became bolder than any time since the 1930s.

The new position secured by the military brought a bundle of problems. Its undisputed victory over the police carried the high risk of its own corruption. The armed forces remained unconvinced of the advantages of directly confronting the drug enemy, but were more geared up for combat, boding no good for its relation to the civilian population. The army's nationalist pride had been wounded, yet it emerged more powerful in the new democracy than it had ended up being under authoritarianism. Out of this mix something very bad could easily come.

The Zetas

The existence of the Zetas would only become public in 2002; their origin, however, traces back from these years of the 1990s, and raises questions that have never been asked. The Zetas are the most violent of Mexico's cartels.

They were the creation of Osiel Cárdenas Guillén, a former low-level Federal Judicial Police operative who had killed his way to the top of the Gulf cartel—still very much a going concern after the removal of García Abrego, official proclamations notwithstanding. The Zetas were to be his bodyguards, probably to protect him either from the assassins of the rival he was about to kill in mid-1998, or perhaps from the FBI and DEA in late 1999.[31] Cárdenas entrusted the task of assembling his protection force to Arturo Guzmán Decena, a former lieutenant of the army's airmobile division of special forces, the GAFE (Grupo Aeromóvil de Fuerzas Especiales), an élite unit. The Zetas began life with Guzmán Decena's recruiting of more GAFE members.

The formation of some such group had been a matter of time. Back in 1993 Carrillo Fuentes had also been sounding out General Maldonado Vega about training a paramilitary squadron in the use of high-caliber weaponry.[32] Nor was the GAFE the only military corps to work for Osiel Cárdenas: the Twenty-first Regiment of Motorized Cavalry of the state of Nuevo León lent logistical support for the mission of ferrying his drugs over the Rio Grande.[33]

But the formation of the Zetas was qualitatively special. The impact would be akin to that of one of the formidable US paramilitary companies, a Blackwater, one day hiring itself out to a ruthless criminal organization within the United States. The drug-related violence in Mexico was about to assume a new, militaristic dimension. The question is: how accidental was this?

The GAFE had been formed in response to the Zapatista uprising in 1994, and was involved in special operations during the counterinsurgent campaigns in the states of Guerrero and Oaxaca, primarily against the Ejército Popular Revolucionario, the EPR. On some accounts, the GAFE received special training by the US army.[34] With the militarization of PGR posts in the Nuevo León-Tamaulipas corridor, GAFE members also transferred to the front-line of the war on drugs. One of them was Heriberto Lazcano, the Zetas' leader upon the killing of their founder.[35] Other members of the GAFE were assigned to the Special Attorneyship for Crimes against Health, the body that replaced Gutiérrez Rebollo's INCD.[36]

The standard accounts would emphasize that Guzmán Decena and Lazcano were deserters. This appears not to be the case. The groups of GAFE soldiers who went to work for the Gulf cartel also took with them a veritable arsenal of the army's most sophisticated machine guns, rifles, pistols, grenades, bazookas, and telecommunications surveillance equipment.[37] Most eloquently suspicious of all is the name *Zeta* (Z) itself. With 1996's militarization of attorney general posts in the north, the generals were called *Yanquis* (Y), the colonels *Equis* (X), and the rank and file delegates *Los Zetas* (Zs).[38] The state origin of the criminal group is thus flagged.

In mid-1998, while Osiel Cárdenas was planning his élite force, he was—as it happened—being held in detention in Mexico City, having been picked up on the road outside Matamoros at a military checkpoint. Called in for "questioning," he escaped his guards with ease.[39] Also arrested in early 1998, Lazcano was soon released.[40] These were plausibly more than coincidences, indicating instead that the Zetas were a product of the peculiar pressures on, and fractures within the armed forces at the decade's end. With all attention focused on the country's most violent cartel in Tijuana, it is hard not to conclude that its Gulf rival was lent a paramilitary capacity by some within the state's security apparatus.

In 2000, President Zedillo sent out 1,500 troops, backed by 2,000 federal police, first to Baja California and subsequently to Nuevo Laredo and other northern cities.[41] The reason was that the Arellano Félix cartel had been discovered to be in business with the FARC, the revolutionary army of Colombia, and so on the wrong side of the war that mattered most for the United States.

The first significant military deployment in Mexico had also set the stage for its successors: its target was one cartel in particular.

The false start of the Fox administration: 2000–2001

When President Fox came to power in December 2000, both his and his top security advisor's view of the Mexican military was that it had served as one of the key props of the long PRI regime and wasn't to be trusted. They especially didn't like the greater operational powers that the war on drugs had granted it. It was time to withdraw the army from that war.[42] President Fox appointed a civilian, Adolfo Aguilar Zínser, as his National Security Advisor.

At the same time Foreign Secretary Jorge Castañeda took a step on a path that could have led to a redefinition of the country's standing with the United States in general, and its entrapment in the unending and unwinnable war on drugs in particular. Presenting the Bush administration with the cause of Mexican immigrants in the United States as an urgent priority, Castañeda knocked drugs off the top of the bilateral agenda—a feat it had in the past taken major financial crises and a free trade agreement to achieve. The hint, later broadened, was that Mexico would prefer some non-military choices for drug control policies.

These were bold steps. Even before 9/11 derailed the strategy, however, there were also signs that bold steps might lead to back steps in an administration that combined heterodox boldness and conservative timidity. President Fox appointed Aguilar Zínser his ad hoc national security advisor—instead of what he should have been, a civilian secretary of defense. Without any bureaucratic anchorage Zínser was simply ignored by the heads of the country's security apparatus. His post soon vanished.

While the Fox administration was expected to behave like a transition government, then, the more consistent tenor of its acts was continuity, and this was especially visible in the security area. New figures came in at the top, like the former business and TV executive Eduardo Medina Mora, who became head of the CISEN intelligence agency and Alejandro Gertz

Manero, who moved from being in charge of the capital city's public security to the country's. But, from the level of under-secretary down, the personnel remained the same. This would have consequences sooner rather than later.

The need to tackle the country's security infrastructure was partially seen, partially acted on. Concretely, ultimate jurisdiction over the principal federal police forces was transferred away from the Department of the Interior to a new entity, the Secretariat of Public Security (SSP), created at the end of 2000. The move freed up the Department of the Interior from some of its overload, and yet allowed the question of the police to spiral farther away from resolution. The successor to the PJF was to be the Federal Investigation Agency (Agencia Federal de Investigacion, AFI). Yet it had taken time to consolidate. It was created in late 2001 by presidential decree, but would have to wait until in mid-2003 to be judicially incorporated under the attorney general's remit.[43] As for the military, by the end of 2001 it was clear that President Fox, notwithstanding his promises, had no inclination to unsettle it with either a Truth Commission or any other investigation into the country's "dirty war" of the 1960s–1970s.[44]

Avoidance of conflict was in fact the hallmark from the start. The first act of the Fox government was to provide a platform for the Zapatista Army of National Liberation, whose conflict Fox had famously promised to resolve in 15 minutes. After a month's carnivalesque "occupation" of the capital city's main square, the Zapatistas broke off dialogue with the government.[45] Then, when a couple of hundred armed peasants protested at the construction of a new terminal for Mexico City's airport, the administration stepped in—and withdrew the project. If these were the bottom lines, the professionals of violence were not going to be given too much to worry about.

That, however, was a signal that couldn't be sent to Washington. Hence the appointment of attorney general was given to Brigadier General Rafael Macedo de la Concha—a military man for a top civilian post. Macedo de la Concha, who had been the military procurator of justice entrusted with prosecuting Gutiérrez Rebollo and the two other brigadier generals, now replaced a couple of hundred civilian PGR agents with military people.[46] The previous logic of militarizing the most important civil institution of law enforcement was thus ratified, along with the desirability of appeasing the hawkish US agencies.

Possessor of a human rights record that observers considered bad and of a body language that exuded zero tolerance for all criminal behavior, Macedo de la Concha was the perfect messenger for what the Americans wanted to hear—that the Mexican cartels were about to learn what a true strong hand felt like. That was the appearance. In reality the brigadier general was a splendidly misleading totem. He had, after all, reputedly been one of the top military men who had listened to Amado Carrillo Fuentes' peace-bearing emissary.[47]

The real meaning of the appearance of a military figurehead in the government was that it had no desire at all to open a serious conflict with organized crime. That was the context in which a most surprising new chapter opened.

Out of the bag

On 19 January 2001 Joaquín Guzmán, a prisoner since 1993, checked out of the maximum security prison Puente Grande. Famously if erroneously, he did so in a laundry basket. The alarms that went off were not the prison's, but the country's.

Guzmán was the survivor of the Arellano Félix brothers' assassination attempts. A trafficker who had moved tons of cocaine for Carrillo Fuentes, Guzmán had been sent to prison either because his boss was unhappy with his violent profile, or for his own protection. In 2001 Carrillo Fuentes was again the decisive factor in Guzmán's career. Alive, Carrillo Fuentes had organized the first true cartel, amalgamating the Guadalajara, Juárez and Sinaloa groups. Dead, Carrillo Fuentes had left a violent conflict. The true story of Guzmán's escape was that this had been noted and conclusions had been reached by some people very high up in the state security apparatus.

On 19 January 2001, Guzmán's prison was visited by the under secretary of public security, Jorge Tello Peón. In the confusion created by his fleeting dawn visit, Guzmán left the prison in a uniform of the Federal Preventative Police.[48] Guzmán had reputedly been in telephone communication with Alfonso Durazo Montaño, personal secretary of President Fox.[49] Transparently, Guzmán's escape was a matter of state. It had been prepared by the high-ranking group of officials who retained their posts in the intelligence and federal police structures, and executed now by them with the connivance of some in the new president's circle.

On the one hand, Guzmán would do what he indeed proceeded to do at the end of 2001—resurrect Carrillo Fuentes' federation of drug traffickers.[50] Hegemonic criminal control was desirable; Guzmán was the right public face for the cartel to have because he had established himself as a trusted interlocutor with the intelligence–police network. And on the other hand, the Arellano Félix brothers would be eliminated. Hegemony would bring peace.

In March 2001 President Fox went to Tijuana to declare war on the Arellano Félix brothers.[51] At the same time the State Department made public the intention of the United States to arrest the brothers, on either side of the border. In February 2002 Ramón Arellano Félix's solo mission to assassinate Guzmán's key Sinaloan ally, Ismael Zambada, ended in his own killing.[52] Benjamín Arellano Félix was arrested in March 2002, after the DEA had joined the hunt.

It was a clear turning point in the war on drugs—but not the anticipated one. The country's most violent cartel had been defeated. The manner of the victory was a crowning vindication of the so-called kingpin strategy, in vogue after the fall of Pablo Escobar. Once their heads were removed, the cartels would disappear. In time, this would be amended— the cartels would fragment, and be more easily dealt with. The fantasy of a possible happy ending was still the same.

2002 was really a turning point, however, because it brought to light how utterly at cross-purposes the rogue elements of the different security branches of the state had been working. The Gulf cartel had been allowed a concentration of the means of violence with the Zetas; yet the Sinaloa cartel of Zambada and Guzmán had been marked out for special intelligence and police protection. From now on the character of the drug violence would be that of a war between these two arms of the state's security structure.

The terrible secret of the Zetas now came out. Osiel Cárdenas had seen his chance to seize control of Nuevo Laredo, a city always considered the jewel in the crown of drug trafficking to the United States because of the 20,000 vehicles that cross through every day, mostly unscreened, to Interstate 35.[53] Cárdenas sent some Zetas there from Matamoros to oversee cocaine transportation into the United States, but in the first operation they found that the PGR commander they were relying upon had changed allegiance to the Sinaloa cartel and was now intent on killing them. Osiel Cárdenas then sent in all of the Zetas, a couple of hundred. It was February 2003.

The accounts differ, but agree that it was war. In one, it started with the November 2002 assassination of the Zetas' founder.[54] In others, that the Zetas assassinated so many police and local allies of the Sinaloa cartel that Guzmán in turn sent 200 *sicarios*, lodged in 20 safe houses.[55] The Sinaloans' leading enforcer, Arturo Beltrán Leyva, now emerged as a player.

The attempt to monopolize criminal violence had set off something akin to an arms race. The Zetas possessed the exclusive weaponry and deployed the tactical precision that first staggered the FBI.[56] The Sinaloans expanded their bands of contract killers. Hours long shoot-outs ensued, on the streets of large, modern cities across the north from Tamaulipas to Baja California. By the summer of 2003, the official estimate was that 480 people a year were being killed because of their link to drug trafficking in Sinaloa alone.[57] By then the Zetas were considered to be responsible for about 50 percent of assassinations linked to drug trafficking in Mexico.[58]

The Zetas were the violence's prime accelerator. For the first time too, turf war between cartels took the form of a pitched battle for territorial possession. The challenge to the state couldn't be ducked. Briefly, in the summer of 2003, the soldiers did come out of their barracks onto the streets of Nuevo Laredo, the city so rocked by violence that—then unprecedentedly—its airport and border crossings to the United States required securing. Nearly 200 members of the local police were arrested and investi-gated for links to organized crime.[59] It was a belated, and minimal, gesture of authority. It was all there could be.

Collapse

The new defiance of the state was rampant. Again in the summer of 2003, the helicopter of the general of the division in charge of crop eradication in Chihuahua mysteriously crashed into the sierra; in the autumn of that year the helicopter of the attorney general was fired on as it flew over a fumiga-tion operation.[60]

The army was in crisis. In a 2007 Congressional hearing the army itself conceded that during the Fox administration more than *100,000* soldiers had deserted.[61] This was roughly half of the army's total. Low salaries and fear of the cartels' superior firepower were the main reasons. They had also been, inevitably, motives for corruption. In one case, an entire 600-strong infantry battalion had been disbanded on suspicion of being in the pay of the Sinaloan cartel.[62] That was 2002, just before the appearance of an enemy hatched from itself drained the army's will. Not all of the 49 desert-ers a day—18,000 a year—joined the cartels. Not all had to for it to be a disaster.

The police were compromised, at every level. The most telling sign was the increasing assassination, openly acknowledged by state authorities, of both municipal and state police agents.[63] It was in these years that, for example, 80 of the 113 municipal police forces in the state of Michoacán—another of the most violent—became actively criminal.[64] At the federal level, there was disarray, a fall-out from the indecisive sequel to the dis-mantling of the PJF. The AFI replaced it—but, as of early 1999, so had the PFP. The duality reflected the juridical distinction between police with investigatory capacity (the AFI), and that with preventive responsibilities (the PFP). While that distinction held, the competition between them would run for years. The AFI's director was Genaro García Luna. His back-ground was at CISEN, and he was a protégé of Jorge Tello Peón (who resigned after the escape of Joaquín Guzmán). García Luna was also closely associated with a group of former judicial policemen from Mexico City notorious for their extortion, kidnapping and, in one case, criminal record as an accomplice to triple homicide. The group won high posts in the AFI.[65]

In May 2005 the meaning of these realignments became clear. By then, Osiel Cárdenas had been in prison for two years, after imprudently threatening two DEA agents.[66] Heriberto Lazcano became the Gulf car-tel's operational leader. In 2005 he sent some Zetas to assassinate Arturo Beltrán Leyva and his four brothers, along with the Sinaloans' most fear-some hitman—Edgar Valdez Villarreal—and their bodyguards. The battleground was Acapulco, in Guerrero, and the encounter exemplified the contrasting modi operandi of the warring cartels. The Zetas were trained to invade territory by storm; believing in their own invincibility, they would undertake kamikaze missions, sending only four men on this one. Against their surgical violence was an absorbent sponge of intelligence agents and police officers. It wasn't a fair fight. Detained by a mass of the AFI, the Zetas were handed over to Valdez Villarreal. He video-taped his execution of them.[67]

This was the immediate context to the Fox administration's major "Operation Safe Mexico." Launched in June 2005, it concentrated again on Nuevo Laredo. The operation dramatized the government's security dilemma. Nuevo Laredo was both a city besieged, and the heart of the Gulf cartel. Members of the GAFE were sent to pound its streets, but so were 600 federal police.[68] The brief operation was open to being interpreted as another unfair blow to the Gulf cartel.

The Zetas' fury led to their first public accusations of the government's complicity with the Sinaloa cartel. And it triggered a spiral of revenge killings by them. Precisely from this time in 2005 the Zetas initiated the horrific theatrics of violence. Two corpses in Nuevo Laredo appeared alongside the Zetas' written message denouncing the federal support of the Sinaloan cartel. In August 2005 a high-level AFI delegate in Acapulco was also assassinated by them. In April 2006, the heads of two police officers had been placed outside the municipal government offices in the center of Acapulco beneath a sign that warned: "So that you learn to respect."[69] By then the Zetas had enlisted former members of the human rights-violating Guatemalan special forces—the Kaibil.[70] The beheadings were their trade-mark. An army captain and a navy lieutenant in Acapulco were the next victims.[71]

In September 2006 a new criminal organization, La Familia, left its calling card—five severed heads thrown onto the floor of a bar in the city of Uruapán, Michoacán.[72] It was a declaration of war against the Zetas, in the language they alone understood.

The Fox administration security balance

One of the many authoritarian reflexes that were to remain in Mexico was the assumption of presidential omnipotence. From it, President Fox would be widely judged to have been inadequate. In the security realm, this is only partly fair. Illicit market changes also lay behind events.

The drug of the 1990s in the United States, cocaine had become some-what passé for the new generation of drug takers there. To be sure, demand didn't disappear. The US attorney general would accuse the Sinaloa and Juárez cartel leaders of having brought 200 tons of cocaine and heroin into the United States from 1990 to 2008, reaping US$5.8 billion in profits.[73]

But the cartels clearly had to adjust to an important mutation in the illicit market place, as their violence through these years would signal.

They were, to begin with, competing to supply a shrinking market. The ferocity of the mass killings reflected this squeeze: although there was little comfort in it, it appeared true that the intensifying violence between the cartels was a sign of some market disarray. Yet there was market readjustment too, signaled by the clashes between drug organizations that began to proliferate around urban centers and major tourist resorts like Acapulco away from the north. The opening of an internal consumption market was also a crucial element in the general deterioration now occurring.

The total number of the drug-dependent population in Mexico wasn't that large (361,000 in 2008, according to official figures), even if it was growing (203,000 in 2002).[74] The significance of this expansion of the market in Mexico had far less to do with alarmist fears about the population's drug dependency than with the new contingent of actors it brought. These were the amateur consumers-*cum*-dealers. The same had happened back in the 1950s in Italy, when the opening of the local heroin market saw distribution transferred to neophytes.[75] With their participation, the internal market became more decentralized—and the struggle to control it more vicious. In twenty-first-century Mexico these petty dealers of mainly marijuana became the easiest of targets for the professional criminals.

Finally, there was a clear opportunity for criminals who had diversified into drugs like methamphetamines. The leaders in this field had been the Valencia brothers of the Milenio cartel, extending from Guerrero and Oaxaca up through Jalisco to Baja California, having achieved their ascendancy over other cartels thanks to the support of Osiel Cárdenas' Gulf cartel. Back in 2000 a DEA operation had led to the brothers' arrest, but not the dismantling of the cartel. Instead, the remaining operators and assassins concentrated themselves in Michoacán, whence they soon launched a bid for control of the territory of the Gulf cartel in Tamaulipas.[76]

While one market was changing, another was flooding open—that of illegal arms. As has shrewdly been noted, since most of these are unregistered, the amount of them coming in from the United States can only safely be set at 18 percent.[77] Nonetheless, the 2004 lapsing of the ban on the sale of assault weapons in the United States clearly facilitated the rise of violence in Mexico. So did the incapacity of the federal government from 2000–2006 to decommission more than 29,000 illegal small arms, from an estimated total in excess of four million.[78]

As that demonstrates, questions about the seriousness of the Fox administration's commitment to security are also valid. Structural changes may have been underway, but the response to the challenges they created was minimal. The best that could be thought of was a military deployment that merely imitated the one made by President Zedillo. With time President Fox would show himself to be an opponent of such military responses to drug trafficking, so it seems reasonable to infer that the deployment was more for show than for real. Instead, President Fox was strongly identified with a current within and beyond his party that had looked for non-military choices for drug control policies. The president's heart was in his proposal of the early summer of 2006 to decriminalize illicit drug possession; subsequently, he would be an advocate of the legalization of drugs.[79] Overall, the indications are that President Fox did not wish to resort to his military, and only did so under duress. The source of the duress was the same that led to the withdrawal of his 2006 proposal—the Bush administration. The result was that alternatives to military deployment weren't pursued, while the deployment was made only perfunctorily.

Yet this was not the worst of all worlds. The administration had entered power averse to conflict.[80] Managing a solution to the drug violence was to be recommended as a rational strategy. Managing, however, was attempted from a position of weakness and entailed dangerously plain collusion. At the same time, the appearance of the Zetas was a quantum leap in the violence. Dealing with them by favoring their enemy might have seemed the right option; in fact, it exacerbated their violence. *There* was the worst of all worlds.

Early in 2005 President Fox's travel coordinator, Nahúm Acosta Lugo, was detained on suspicion of working as an intermediary for the Sinaloa cartel. Seven weeks of investigation either yielded no proofs or were enough for the scandal to die down.[81] It was accepted as a matter of fact that President Fox "allowed the corruption of people close to him."[82] Other unprovable suspicions would swirl, including the report of the DEA's investigation into the president.[83] Eventually, the relationship between President Fox and his successor would be palpably tainted by something here. When there was every reason for Felipe Calderón to be eternally grateful to President Fox for his irregular role in securing the electoral win of 2006, the new president instead came to speak of him with ascending indignation. "We are paying the consequences of what was not done *yesterday*," President Calderón affirmed—yesterday when, instead of confronting "crime" with determination, it had been either ignored or "administered."[84] That last word looked suspiciously like a euphemism.

The many Michoacáns

La Familia, the Family, announced its claim to the territory of the state of Michoacán with an ineradicably grotesque piece of theatre. No doubt, the challenge was addressed to more than the Zetas. Could such drug violence be tolerated by the next administration? Another critical point, then, had been reached.

The public leader of La Familia was Servando Gómez Martínez. A former school teacher, religious zealot and aficionado of the self-help books of John Eldredge, there was more to him than random violence.[85] Behind the theater, the cartel's rise was the product of a sustained campaign to secure protection at every level of the state, through violent corruption. Municipal mayors were presented with "escorts" of armed criminals; officials were informed that their electoral campaigns were being paid for. Coercion would be used to begin with, but once a critical mass had been reached, the rest of the structure in question would collapse into the hands of the criminals.

Eventually, in May 2009, eight municipal mayors and 22 state bureaucrats were arrested in Michoacán and charged with protecting the cartel.[86] Every police agency in the state, from the federal to the local, was openly accused of the same. Officials arrested included the state's procurator of justice and the former secretary of public security. The whole security and judicial state structure was presumed to be effectively working for the cartel.

This was the challenge. By systematizing their intimidation and bribery, the drug traffickers had achieved a political penetration in which submission and cooperation, the involuntary and the voluntary, had become blurred. Characteristically, when the Zetas moved in on uncharted territories for them, as they did in the state of Durango, they relied more on sheer terror—principally, financial extortion and kidnappings of businessmen.[87] Even so, the Zetas would also be able to enforce the reputed collusion of, for example, 600 informants in all the police and some military forces in the state of Aguascalientes.[88]

The traffickers' insertion was also societal, where the other blurred boundary was between licit and illicit activities. Significant segments of the population had become economically dependent on informal-illicit revenues. In 2010 the State Department estimated that 150,000 people were directly involved in trafficking within Mexico—300,000 involved in the cultivation and processing of marijuana and poppy.[89] By 2009 Mexico's Union of Agricultural Workers in its turn calculated that 600,000 day laborers were working for the traffickers in the fields.[90]

Politically and institutionally embedded, societally accepted—these were the dimensions of the enemy that ought to have given the next administration pause before war was declared. Instead, in Mexico, as elsewhere, troop deployment would be conducted on the assumption that local political orders and society had remained in a state of permanent, irreconcilable confrontation with the drug illicit economy and the drug trade. This was to vastly underestimate the elusive dimensions of both. In the words of a soldier deployed to the north of the country, "this is a war you can't really win ... there are so many more of them than us."[91] The next administration never wanted to hear those words.

The Calderón initiative: 2006

On 1 December 2006, Felipe Calderón took office in a scene of tumultuous parliamentary protest. On 11 December, the new president sent 7,000 troops, marines and federal police to occupy Michoacán. The decision not only showed a narrow understanding of military security; it was forged in the heat of fierce electoral contention.

After his unbelievably close 0.58 percent margin of victory over Andrés Manuel López Obrador, Calderón emerged as a president whose legitimacy was gravely in question. When López Obrador refused to accept the result and called himself the legitimate president, Calderón became the president of the war on drugs.

The decision to deploy military force had many aspects, but the political one was the first. Felipe Calderón had campaigned as the candidate of employment, with no hint that security would be his top priority. He won 35–36 percent of the vote. His deployment of the military was initially approved by 80 percent.[92] In his first 35 days in office, President Calderón made 18 public appearances with the army, navy and public security forces—on one occasion appearing in military uniform, the first time a civilian Mexican president had done so in living memory.[93]

As president-elect, Calderón declared the victory of "the future" over "a past of violence"—a past that "despises the law, abhors institutions."[94] The allusion was to López Obrador's statement during the campaign that, as far as he was concerned, the country's institutions could "go to the devil." López Obrador failed to explain that he meant to say that those institutions were in his view corrupted and biased against him, and the phrase became his albatross, the basis for the campaign of fear by which he represented "a danger for Mexico." President Calderón, in turn, had shown his hand: his defense of institutions was not above vigorously partisan politics.

Extraordinarily, in the early days of 2007 his new secretary of defense, General Galván, delivered a speech at a military commemoration in which he affirmed that "the legality of the supreme commander of the armed forces resides essentially in the verdict of institutions, and these have been overwhelming": the president had achieved "popular approbation." López Obrador was referred to, as was "the serious risk" to the country if the armed forces did not give their total support to the head of the executive.[95] By the standards that had prevailed over the long decade of Mexico's political opening, General Galván had crossed the line of political non-interference with his comments. His predecessors would not have made them. "The armed forces do not function as a political actor or social arbiter," as one of them had said.[96]

The new president started where his two predecessors had left off. Military deployment was to be made, accompanied by more politicization of the military and militarizing of the police—as of December 2006's transfer of 10,000 soldiers and marines to the PFP.[97] The early talks with the United States in 2007 that would yield the Merida Initiative also echoed the special form of bilateral cooperation initially sought by the Zedillo administration. And like his predecessors, President Calderón laid down no exit strategy. But where they had been in it only for the short haul, President Calderón informed the country's citizens that "the Mexican State, your government, are firmly resolved to wage that battle." It would last until the country's streets and cities were recovered; it would take a lot of time and resources; and it would cost human lives.[98] The president didn't say that there would be police investigations, mass arrests and prosecutions according to the rule of law. He would use force, he insisted, "despite the costs of human lives."[99]

The same old story...

So flamboyant was the fanning out of troops into the cities of Tijuana and Monterrey and the states of Guerrero and Tabasco that attention was drawn from the president's choice of top civilian personnel in the security sector. Medina Mora became attorney general; García Luna was promoted to secretary of public security. These appointments showed that the new president was entirely happy to endorse the policy of reality management under President Fox, the later accusations notwithstanding. In 2008 President Calderón brought back Jorge Tello Peón to be his security advisor.

Greater militarization, that is, disguised overall continuities. Just as with the early Fox administration, so now one cartel in particular was targeted. The signal that public enemy number one was the Gulf cartel was sent with the January 2007 extradition to the United States of Osiel Cárdenas, and the deployment of thousands of soldiers in Tamaulipas, where his brother had taken over the running of the cartel.[100] Meanwhile Joaquín Guzmán was left in peace in his mountain hideaway in Durango, where he publicly married a beauty queen in July 2007.[101]

More than official Mexican collusion was at work here. The Gulf cartel's Zetas had caught the attention—and imagination—of strategic analysts in the US army. There was evidence that the Zetas were incurring deeper and deeper into Texas, both setting up money-laundering businesses and subcontracting criminal gangs in Dallas.[102] The Zetas were also presumed responsible for the kidnapping of US citizens on both sides of the border.[103] The US securitizing machinery went into action, and the Zetas morphed into an insurgency seeking to capture the Mexican state.[104] Through 2007 into 2008 the founding commanders of the Zetas were hunted down by the Mexican army, from Tamaulipas to Campeche.[105]

Internal and external considerations, then, had produced a policy continuation: the cartel most responsible for the violence would be the most hunted. It was rational. The problem was that it required the opponents to be rational too. Criminal logics, however, defied official prediction. What ensued was the breakdown of any hope of containing the violence.

...until 2008

One unexpected thing appears to have happened, and one unexpected thing definitely did. In mid-2007, a truce was brokered between the Zetas and the Sinaloan federation.[106] The violence was hurting both, and causing unease with their Colombian suppliers. Once again in the history of Mexican drug trafficking, the leading criminal organizations were prompted to carve up national territory and cooperate after a fashion. Once again, that is, the criminal organizations showed an impulse towards monopolistic unification.

And, in what we know for sure, yet again the counter-impulse was stronger. The war resumed. This time, however, the renewal of fragmentation was different. The greater federation also split asunder. That it had held together for so long was remarkable—it had survived the 2004 assassination of Rodolfo Carrillo Fuentes and his wife, presumably on the order of the Sinaloans.[107] The betrayals now, though, were more intimate. Joaquín Guzmán hailed from the same Sinaloan village as the Beltrán Leyva brothers and had familial ties with them; many concur that they had protected him both inside and outside of prison; and one of Guzmán's sons had married one of Arturo Beltrán Leyva's daughters.[108] The bonds of clan couldn't have been tighter. Yet Arturo Beltrán Leyva had emerged as the holder of the cartel's power of violence, as indeed its equivalent of the Zetas. His next move was anticipated. In January 2008, Arturo's brother Alfredo was arrested by PFP officers, on the order of Guzmán and Zambada.[109] War broke out.

Beltrán Leyva went over to the Zetas. Vicente Carrillo Fuentes also left the Sinaloans. These re-alignments would have been bad news had they concerned only the trafficking organizations. They didn't. The cataclysmic meaning of the new war was that the state security institutions that one way or another had been protecting the Sinaloans for years were suddenly forced to choose between Guzmán and Zambada, or Beltrán Leyva and the Zetas—and face the consequences of their choice. The conjuncture was as unanticipated as appalling.

Out of it came a national situation in which the country's third highest-ranking police officer, Edgar Millán, was assassinated, in May 2008. A situation, some have added, in which the country's drug-tsar head of SIEDO (Specialized Investigation of Organized Crime), José Luis Santiago Vasconcelos, and the secretary of the interior, Juan Camilo Mouriño, were killed when their airplane exploded and crashed over Mexico City, in November 2008.

Conclusion

2008 was when the security situation suddenly spiraled out of control. The year before the *overall* homicide total had even experienced a significant dip—8, 868. This contrasted with the 15,625 of a decade earlier.[110] Within the 2007 figure, though, specifically drug-related killings were showing a steady increase: 1,537 in 2005; 2,221 in 2006; 2,673 in 2007.[111] That was the trend that had to be reversed.

Instead, within a year, drug killing increased dramatically, by 146 percent—5,630 executions in 2008.[112]

In 2007 drug violence was killing 7.32 people a day; in 2008, 15.42.[113]

In this chapter we have argued that the dominant trend leading to this outcome was political. The argument has two principal strands.

First, we have attempted to offer an alternative to the country's political narrative for the last decade. That narrative became blocked when the supposedly transition government of Vicente Fox failed to behave as expected. 2000–2001 saw, precisely, a government that had secured the first president to come from the opposition but that was frightened of being transitional. The real turning point, then, had come out of an entirely different process, one in which the old regime fell into democracy. The process began with electoral reforms whose integrity and effect were underestimated. It became definitive with an election in 1994 that was far more equitable than 2006's. And it was consolidated when the PRI lost control of the lower chamber in 1997.

Once we adjust the transition myth, other corrections can be proposed. We can dispel the idea that the country's collapse into criminal violence is fundamentally associated with the change from an authoritarian to a democratic regime—an idea commonly linked to the view that transition to democracy disrupted arrangements between the criminals and state authorities. No such overnight change occurred in 2000; to the contrary. Nor, as we saw in Chapter 1, is the claim that each PRI administration favored one cartel over others tenable. Whether authoritarian or democratic, authorities faced the same reality: that as of the mid-1980s the state's capacity to regulate the cartels was in irreversible decline. That growing incapacity eventually became a factor in the PRI regime's fall.

Once false discontinuities are set aside, true continuities stand out. Here we find the second strand of our overall argument. From 1994 on, successive administrations all confronted an unprecedented challenge from the criminal organizations active in the illicit drug market. All responded in the same way. Newly elected democratic administrations resorted to militarization. Certainly, there were some important differences. But structurally, all built the same—privileging the military with an enhanced presence in the civilian sphere. There was an anomaly here, and it merits emphasis.

Faced with the threat of the Zapatista uprising, and with a military high command chafing to repress it, the last president of the old regime opted (after a week) for peaceful negotiation. Faced with the disturbance of public order by criminal violence, the new democratic administrations resorted to militarization. The contrast can be made more starkly. The old regime was shaken by a handful of highly symbolic acts of violence; the democratic administrations would either show no reaction to the killings of thousands of people in drug-related violence, or would rejoice in them.

What was happening? Part of the answer was the pressure exerted on the Mexican political system from outside just at the very moment when it lurched into democracy. 1995's drug certification process was a terrifying challenge for the initial 16 selected countries. Failing to pass it meant loss of US aid, of US financial incentives to companies to trade with the country, of US guarantees to investors in the country.[114] For Mexico, in the throes of a major currency devaluation crisis, decertification would have destroyed its financial credit, its political credibility. So unthinkable was decertification that the Mexican military had to buckle to the securitizing of drug trafficking. The moment of crisis was reached in early 1997, on the eve of the third certification. In an unprecedented move, General Gutiérrez Rebollo was handed over to a civilian court—to humiliate the army, not to show that civilians controlled it. Thereafter, the use of the military in the war on drugs has been unquestioned.

There was another part of the answer. The solution forced onto the three administrations wasn't entirely to their disliking. More clearly with Presidents Zedillo and Calderón, the assumption was that Mexican soldiers were more determined and less corrupt—more moral—than the Mexican police. The moment of crisis here had been the crumbling of the PJF, the equivalent of the disbanding of the FBI in disgrace. The disaster left paralysis in its wake. Notably, it was the least military-inclined president, Vicente Fox, who initiated the move to replace the PJF. But it was a provisional step, revealing the larger absence of will to exercise control over the country's federal police.

Both reasons meant that, while the more genuine transitions to democracy in Latin America saw militaries return to their barracks, in Mexico the opposite was the case. At root, there was a problem of imagination. The civilian administrations all confronted security challenges; reluctantly or enthusiastically, all were unable to consider alternatives to the use of the military institution. Insensitivity to values in the way of that use, like the sanctity of civilian life, increased.

While the military were deployed the problems of oversight and intra-bureaucratic competition also intensified. Command of the country's federal police was captured by a small group on the basis of its claim of indispensable intelligence prowess. Through a series of treacherous bureaucratic battles, the secretary of public security emerged as more powerful than the attorney general. Only supervision from the secretary of the interior might have stopped this, but that had gone. It meant that de facto autonomy was granted to the federal police agency to craft the strategy for the cartels. The lack of coordination between the different agencies fighting drug crime would be frequently noted.

Yet that problem went far deeper. Taken together, the formation of the Zetas and the release of Joaquín Guzmán showed that different state actors were far more than merely uncoordinated. The two criminal organizations attached to both of these names would dominate the next decade; both were empowered by those different actors, and by larger laws of consequence. The Zetas were the paramilitary outgrowth of the logic of militarizing the state's presence in the northeast of the country. Guzmán's Sinaloa cartel was the inheritor of the practice of marking out one cartel for especial protective favor—a practice that began with Guzmán's model, Carrillo Fuentes.

At cross-purposes, the different state segments shared the same aim. It was, indeed, the constant aim that makes it possible to talk of a state policy vis-à-vis the illicit drug market in Mexico. This was to reduce its violence. It had been done successfully in the decades of regulation; it was a priority in the democracy that came out of the shocks of the years 1993–1994. The policy, then, was to target the most violent cartel. A domestic priority, it was often compatible with US wishes. It was rational—and it was the root of the tangles.

Confronting the most violent was rational given the impossibility of opening a many-front war against all of the cartels. This was impossible because the institutional crisis effectuated by corruption—understood as the ability of the illicit actors to enforce the supply of official protection—had left the state prostrate. So targeting the most violent cartel fitted with the reality of the state's position ever since, with the ascendancy of Carrillo Fuentes' Pacific group, the illicit market became so powerful that drug organizations claimed a right to interlocution with the state.

The interlocution held out the promise of what the democratic administrations most wanted: peace. Self-evidently, for them this was the only winnable goal of the war on drugs. The perverse effects of prohibition denied any other, and condemned the greater part of the war on drugs to be a simulation (one reason why "war on drugs" often appears in inverted commas). At the same time, it was indisputable that there were political, economic and military considerations that worked against an all-out war on all of the Mexican cartels, and layers of societal support for them. Combining the impossibility of the "war" with the strength of its enemy (giving the cartels a combatant status is another reason), it was a fair conclusion that: "Mexico is a failed State only if one accepts the idea that the goal is to attack the drug-traffickers."[115]

But *some* drug traffickers would be attacked. By the time of Carrillo Fuentes, the rules of selection were established. All the criminal organizations were violent, but those that achieved most interlocution with state authorities would be deemed least violent. This meant that the competition between the criminal organizations was also competition for that most favored status vis-à-vis the state. The Arellano Félix brothers were hunted after the assassination of Cardinal Juan José Posadas Ocampo advertized their loss of that status; the Zetas became more violent as it became clearer that they would not attain it.

Once a cartel was singled out as an enemy of the state, the attack on it would have very little to do with military force. Instead, the process began with wearing down its protective resistance. The state *was* strong enough to mobilize its forces on this selective basis, and no cartel could withstand the resulting political-security embargo. Once the walls of complicity were breached, intelligence work quickly and easily did the rest, and—with the arrest or death of the cartel's leader—a "victory in the war against drugs had been won."

Necessarily, while one cartel was so openly targeted, there was an investment in the stability of the quieter others. An amorphous gray zone expanded between the state and these other cartels, in which collusion might be active or neglect benign. As they monitored the situation, though, the relevant state authorities kept uppermost on their mind the issue of how to manage the constant threat of violence. Essentially, state policy could gravitate towards either of two options.

One was to do what General McCaffrey reported in 2008: "the strategy articulated by Attorney General Eduardo Medina Mora is to break up the four major drug cartels into 50 smaller entities and take away their firepower and huge financial resources."[116] Medina Mora clearly drew his inspiration from the Colombian experience with the Medellín and Calí cartels.[117]

The second option was to help build up one cartel to a position of such dominance in the illicit market that it would effectively put the competition out of business.

In fact, the second option was the only one. The full Colombian experience was that a duopoly had again emerged, now divided between the FARC and the Colombian paramilitaries. The instinct to fuse, the ambition to secure supremacy and achieve monopoly, was wired into the illicit drug corporations. If fragmentation fell within that greater logic, then encouraging a predominant criminal entity in order to take a controlling advantage of it could become the favored policy option—and could be why Medina Mora, not García Luna, lost his post. Indeed, a mirror process was underway within the state apparatus, as the different police and intelligence agencies engaged in a struggle for supremacy. An omnipotent agency dealing with an omnipotent cartel would have been an outcome consistent with the precedent laid down by González Calderoni and Carrillo Fuentes. The disaster of the decade was instead that different branches of the security apparatus had the same idea at the same time, and backed different horses.

The Zetas were assembled and Joaquín Guzmán was promoted in the context in which the Arellano Félix cartel was identified as public enemy number one. The Tijuana cartel was no doubt weakened by the appearance of two enemies. But those enemies had in the process been strengthened, and soon represented a greater threat than the Tijuana cartel.

The subsequent targeting of the Zetas then exposed the other great problem with the state's chosen strategy. Rationally coherent, it couldn't cope with the inconsistency of the criminals. No one could have anticipated that, after grotesquely executing each others' men, the Zetas and Beltrán Leyvas would find common cause. Suddenly, a quite different criminal reality came into view, wrong-footing the options that the state might think it had with the cartels.

The cartels were composite creatures. On the one hand, they were both vastly wealthy and ruthlessly efficient modern corporations. Osiel Cárdenas always talked with pride of "my company"; famously, in 2009–2010, Joaquín Guzmán joined the *Forbes* magazine club of the world's super-rich (he came in with US$1 billion).[118] As the sub-secretary within the Ministry of Agriculture responsible for the promotion of agricultural business said, there was much to learn from both the technological know-how and market strategies of Mexican drug-trafficking. (He was fired for his statement of the obvious.)[119]

On the other hand, though, the strongest cartels were clan-like. They structured themselves around as many personal bonds as possible, to preserve trust and unity. This intensified their external conflicts as vendettas arose. Nonetheless, this composite character of the cartel was compatible with state designs—until 2008.

Then, the split within the Sinaloan federation showed that even when a major cartel had conglomerated, objective factors would drive even the most closely bonded criminals away from cooperation into violent competition. In part, this reflected the "internal paranoia" that could grip organizations whose leaders who had risen to the top through violence.[120] And in part, it followed the ebb and flow of the greater market logic that ruled the criminals. Essentially, there were incentives for them to aim for monopolistic control—and incentives for them to wrest it away from those who attained it. Monopolization was thus an inherently unstable, self-defeating process. The big cartels accordingly operated by unpredictable logics of alignment, conflict, and re-alignment for which the state could have no managerial policy.

There was one final corollary. While the war between the cartels appeared to be one of natural selection, in which only the strongest would survive, in fact, due to the chaotic fluidity of the battleground, the weaker cartels tended to survive. They could adapt by entering into alliances with former enemies who might now, with a new common enemy, be their friends.

For the state, there really only was one solution. But it was also the only thing not possible—to fight them all.

Notes

1 Mónica Serrano, "The End Of Hegemonic Rule?," in Mónica Serrano, ed., *Party Politics in "An Uncommon Democracy": Political Parties and Elections in Mexico* (London: Institute of Latin American Studies, 1994), 13. The figure excludes annulled votes.

2 Mónica Serrano, "The Legacy of Gradual Change: Rules And Institutions under Salinas," in Mónica Serrano, ed., *Rebuilding the State: Mexico After Salinas* (London: Institute of Latin American Studies, 1996), 17.

3 His victory, he said, was legal but "inequitable." Cited in Sergio Aguayo Quezada, *Vuelta En U: Guía Para Entender Y Reactivar La Democracia Estancada* (Mexico: Taurus, 2010), 129.

4 Ibid., 137.

5 See, for example, Adam Przeworski, "The Games of Transition," in Scott Mainwaring, Guillermo O'Donnell and S.J. Valenzuela, eds., *Issues in Democratic Consolidation* (Notre Dame, IN: University of Notre Dame Press, 1992), 105.

6 María Celia Toro, *Mexico's "War" on Drugs; Causes and Consequences* (Boulder: Lynne Rienner, 1995), 35–36.

7 IKV PAX Christi, *El secuestro es un negocio explosivo* (Utrecht, July 2008), 20–21; Fred Burton and Scott Stewart, "Mexico: The Third War," *Stratfor*, 18 February 2009.

8 Cited by Peter Andreas, "The Political Economy of Narco Corruption in Mexico," *Current History*, April 1998.

9 Juan Gabriel Tokatlian, "La construcción de un 'Estado fallido' en la política mundial: el caso de las relaciones entre Estados Unidos y Colombia," *análisis político* no. 64 (September–December 2008), 85.

10 *Proceso* 31 December 2000.

11 *Reforma* 9 October 1995; *Oxford Analytica, Latin America Daily Brief*, 1 June 1995.

12 Santiago Corcuera Cabezut, "Propuesta de una iniciativa para retirar a las fuerzas armadas de las funciones de seguridad pública," in Jorge Luis Sierra Guzmán, ed., *El Ejército y la Constitución Mexicana* (Mexico: Plaza y Valdés, 1999).

13 Ricardo Ravelo, *Los Capos* (Mexico: Plaza Janés, 2006), 171.

14 Cited in Carlos Fazio, "Mexico: The Narco General Case," online, available at: www.tni.org/article/mexico-narco-general-case, December 1997.

15 Ibid.

16 Agustín Ambriz, "Informe militar sobre el general Gutiérrez Rebollo: otros oficiales del Ejército, agentes y comandantes del INCD y de la PGR, cómplices de Amado Carrillo," *Proceso* no. 1060 (February 1997).

17 Ravelo, *Los Capos*, 171–181. The account rests upon a copy of the testimony of General Maldonado Vega to the PGR.

18 Jorge F. Menéndez, *El Otro Poder* (Mexico: Nuevo Siglo, 2001), 116.

19 Fazio, "Mexico: The Narco General Case."

20 José Reveles, *El Cártel Incómodo: El Fin De Los Beltrán Leyva Y La Hegemonía Del Chapo Guzmán* (Mexico: Grijalbo, 2009), 87; Anabel Hernández, *Los Señores Del Narco* (Mexico: Grijalbo, 2010), 214, 225.

21 Francisco Cruz, *El Cártel de Juárez* (Mexico: Planeta, 2008), 124. Hernández, 220 makes a case for Carrillo Fuentes' death by plastic surgery as fake.

22 Cruz, 124–125, 127.
23 Menéndez, 108.
24 Jesús Blancornelas, *El Cártel. Los Arellano Félix: la mafia más poderosa en la historia de América Latina* (Mexico: Plaza Janés, 2003), 115.
25 Tokatlian, 88.
26 Raúl Benítez Manaut, "La encrucijada de la 'guerra' y la inseguridad," *Reforma* 11 April 2010.
27 Ravelo, *Los Capos*, 30, 45, 56–57.
28 Ibid., 58.
29 The impunity rate can be estimated in different ways. The national rate considers the average probability of arrest for a perpetrated crime, whether reported or not. An alternative formula considers the average number of arrests in relation to reported crimes. According to the latter the impunity rate in Mexico in 2000 was 11.4 percent per 100 reported crimes. The key variable, then, is the average of those reported crimes. According to some sources, only one out of every five crimes was being reported—and in only 5 percent of these was the alleged perpetrator brought before a court. Guillermo Zepeda Lecuona, *Crimen sin castigo. Procuración de Justicia y Ministerio Público en México* (Mexico: CIDAC-FCE, 2004), 84, 218–220. See also Instituto Ciudadano de Estudios sobre la Inseguridad, "Quinta encuesta nacional sobre inseguridad," online, available at: www.icesi.org.mx/documentos/encuestas/encuestasNacionales/ ENSI-5.
30 Fazio, "Mexico: The Narco General Case."
31 Ricardo Ravelo, *Osiel: Vida Y Tragedia De Un Capo* (Mexico: Grijalbo, 2009), 136, 144, 166, 175; Juan Carlos, *Mafia and Co.: The Criminal Networks In Mexico, Brazil, And Colombia* (Washington, DC: Woodrow Wilson International Center for Scholars, 2008), 86.
32 Ravelo, *Los Capos*, 164.
33 Ravelo, *Osiel*, 236.
34 Hernández, 401.
35 Ibid., 399–402.
36 Ravelo, *Osiel*, 174, 168.
37 Ibid., 176.
38 Garzón, 87–88.
39 Ravelo, *Osiel*, 130–132.
40 Hernández, 401.
41 Online, available at: http://fmso.leavenworth.army.mil/documents/mexico_ evolve/.html.
42 Menéndez, 22–23.
43 Miguel Angel Granados Chapa, "Desorganización policiaca," *Reforma* 3 November 2010.
44 Aguayo Quezada, 150–153.
45 Andrés Aguayo Mazzucato, *La tragicomedia del Foxismo* (Mexico: temas' de hoy, 2010), 150.
46 Menéndez, 25–26; Ravelo, *Los Capos*, 46, 56.
47 Ravelo, *Los Capos*, 184.
48 Hernández, 293, 321.
49 Ravelo, *Los Capos*, 69–70.

50 Hernández, 361.

51 Menéndez, 31.

52 Ravelo, *Los Capos*, 104.

53 Sam Logan, "Mexico's Uppermost Threat is Organized Crime," 1 May 2006, International Relations and Security Network, online, available at: www. mexidata.info/id869.html.

54 Hernández, 407.

55 Francisco Gómez, "Cárteles en guerra al norte del país," *El Universal* 26 June 2005.

56 Hernández, 404.

57 *El Universal* 18 and 29 October 2003; *Reforma* 6 June 2003, 18 October 2003.

58 *El Universal*, 6 June 2003; *Reforma* 30 August 2003.

59 *Milenio* 17 August 2003; *Reforma* 2 August 2003; *El Universal* 30 August 2003.

60 *El Universal*, 6 June 2003, 29 October 2003.

61 Testimony of Secretary of Defense Guillermo Galván, online, available at: www.cdn.com.mx/?c=118&a=2908. See too *La Jornada* 7 August 2005; Jorge Carrasco Araizaga, "Al amparo castrense," in Rafael Rodríguez Castañeda, *Los Generales: La militarización del país en el sexenio de Felipe Calderón* (Mexico: temas' de hoy, 2010), 24, 48.

62 Diego Enrique Osorno, *El Cártel De Sinaloa: Una historia del uso político del narco* (Mexico: Grijalbo, 2010), 112.

63 *El Universal* 18 and 29 October 2003; *Reforma* 6 June 2003 and 18 October 2003.

64 Sergio Aguayo Quezada, "Sopa de cifras," *Reforma* 12 May 2010. The figure came from the office of the attorney general in 2008.

65 Hernández, 433–436.

66 Ravelo, *Los Capos*, 196.

67 Hernández, 418, 428. Subsequently, 103 members of the AFI in Acapulco were detained and investigated; their monthly fee was said to be US$50,000. David Aponte, *Los Infiltrados: el narco dentro de los gobiernos* (Mexico: Grijalbo, 2010), 39–40.

68 Hernández, 426.

69 Manuel Roig-Franzia, "Drug Violence Soars throughout Mexico," *Washington Post* 1 May 2006.

70 "The Spread of Mexico's Drug Wars," *Stratfor Today* 27 June 2006, online, available at: www.stratfor.com/spread_mexicos_drug_wars.

71 "Drug-related Violence Moves Into Acapulco," *Boston Globe* 30 July 2006.

72 "Human Heads Dumped in Mexico Bar," *BBC News*, 7 September 2006, online, available at: http://news.bbc.co.uk/2/hi/americas/5322160.stm.

73 *Reforma* 21 August 2009.

74 *Reforma* 20 July 2009.

75 See Vicenzo Ruggiero, *Crime and Markets* (Oxford: Oxford University Press, 2000), 17–25.

76 *Reforma* 27 July 2009.

77 Rubén Aguilar V. and Jorge G. Castañeda, *El Narco: La Guerra Fallida* (Mexico: punto de lectura, 2009), 68.

78 Aguayo Quezada, *Vuelta En U*, 263.
79 *Reforma* 13 November 2009.
80 "He was afraid," recorded Jorge Castañeda of President Fox in answer to the question of why no reform of the state was undertaken. Carmen Aristegui and Ricardo Trabulsi, *Transición* (Mexico: Grijalbo, 2009), 78.
81 Hernández, 425–426.
82 Former Attorney General Jorge Carpizo, in Aristegui and Trabulsi, 71.
83 Hernández, 14, 319–320.
84 *Milenio* 20 December 2008. Italic added.
85 *Reforma* 21 July 2009.
86 *Reforma* 14 July 2009.
87 *Proceso* no. 29 (July 2010), 11.
88 *Reforma* 17 October 2009.
89 Cited in Jamie Sánchez Susarrey, "P19," *Reforma* 16 October 2010.
90 *Reforma* 30 October 2009.
91 Marc Lacey, "In Drug War, Mexico Fights Cartel and Itself," *New York Times* 30 March 2009.
92 *Milenio* 26 February 2007.
93 Daniel Lizárraga and Francisco Castellanos, "El presidente militarizado," in Rodríguez Castañeda, *Los Generales*, 19, 17.
94 Cited in Hernández, 525.
95 Lizárraga and Castellanos, 27.
96 Secretary Cervantes Aguirre in February 1997, cited in Fazio," Mexico: The Narco General Case."
97 Lizárraga and Castellanos, 20.
98 Presidency of the Republic, 27 April 2007. Cited in Hernández, 476.
99 Lizárraga and Castellanos, 21.
100 Ravelo, *Osiel*, 238.
101 *Reforma* 22 August 2009.
102 *Reforma* 15 December 2009.
103 Hernández, 464.
104 Max G. Manwaring, "A 'New' Dynamic in the Western Hemisphere Security Environment: The Mexican Zetas and Other Private Armies," September 2009, online, available at: www.StrategicStudiesInstitute.army.mil/.
105 George W. Grayson, "Los Zetas: the Ruthless Army Spawned by a Mexican Drug Cartel," Foreign Policy Research Institute, May 2008, online, available at: www.fri.org/enotes/200805.grayson.loszetas.html.
106 Hernández, 486–491.
107 Ibid., 390.
108 Ibid., 495.
109 Ravelo, *Osiel*, 112.
110 *Reforma* 27 August 2009, 3 October 2009.
111 *El Universal* 20 August 2009.
112 "Mexico: asesinatos del narcotráfico han crecido un 146%", Infolatam, online, available at: www.infolatam.com/entrada/mexico_asesinatos_del_narcotrafico_han_c-12566.html.
113 *El Universal* 20 August 2009.
114 Tokatlian, 85.

115 George Friedman, "Mexico and the Failed State Revisited," *Stratfor Global Intelligence*, 6 April 2010.
116 Barry R. McCaffrey, "After Action Report," online, available at: www.mccaffreyassociates.com/pdfs?Mexico_AAR__December_2008.pdf.
117 Interview with Mónica Serrano, London, October 2010.
118 Hernández, 322; Aguayo Quezada, *Vuelta En U*, 256.
119 *Reforma* 30 October 2009.
120 Garzón, 164.

PART II

Security Failure at Home…

3

ARBITRARINESS AND INEFFICIENCY IN THE MEXICAN CRIMINAL JUSTICE SYSTEM

Ana Laura Magaloni

In recent decades, violent robbery, various kinds of kidnapping, murder, and street violence have become distressingly familiar in many parts of Mexico. A palpable sense, or perception, of insecurity is now an integral part of many people's everyday life. As in other similar cases, the public clamors for something to be done. And the politicians? The politicians get tough on crime, in sound bites but also in policies. And yet the crime rates either don't go down, or when they do the generalized sense of insecurity doesn't.

Understandable as they are, both the public clamor and the political discourse distract from the true problem: why has the criminal justice system in Mexico so spectacularly failed to tackle serious crime? To be even more emphatic: why can the current justice system in Mexico do nothing but fail? That is the question this chapter seeks to answer. In so doing, it also hopes to contribute, in however small a way, to a refocusing of the energies behind the public's indignation. To be succinct, there is little point in placing demands on a dysfunctional system, and every point in working for a new one. Yet, as we shall see, this may well demand a shift in citizen attitudes too. Specifically, for all of its instant appeal, the get-tough approach is the wrong one in Mexico.

I use *arbitrariness* as the word to flag that approach here. The tough strategy for crime rests on the all but explicit premise that a measure of arbitrariness by the police and the public prosecutor's office is a "necessary evil" in the new crusade against crime. Whether it be someone's constitutional rights getting trampled on, or the wrong suspects going to jail, or a little rough treatment in the police station's interrogation room—such things are prices well worth paying if crime can be fought more efficiently. Arbitrariness, in other words, means the freedom of agencies and agents entrusted with upholding the law to violate it. And out there in public space, it means that ordinary people accept that public security and justice are negatively correlated. That is, enhanced public security is seen as a good that ought to override the rights of the accused who, if innocent, are like bystanders caught up in an accident—victims of the rules of arbitrariness.

Rather than take my stance on anything like the fundamental nature of certain rights, my aim is to cut through this entire debate by exposing the absolute falsity of its foundation. Using statistical analysis I shall contend that the evidence shows that the more arbitrary the criminal justice system is, the more inefficient it is too. Inefficiency and arbitrariness are, in the case of Mexico, positively correlated.

Statistics, it's hardly controversial to say, cannot win a case by themselves. So I also draw allusively upon some of the now-familiar ideas of Douglas North and the new institutionalism, using them to buttress the evidence with a plausible explanation for it. While that may sound dispiritingly deterministic, we shall also find ourselves in some still new territory as we reach this conclusion: Mexico's well-nigh perfectly inefficient justice system tells us that the story we thought had happily ended with the transition to democracy is in fact far from over. In this respect, crime in Mexico *is* a political topic—but in a manner that goes deeper than slogans and headlines. The dysfunctional justice system in the country, source of such anguish and torment to so many citizens, is the system of a part of the country that remained authoritarian. And *that*, in turn, is where the answer to the conundrum about crime rates is to be had: democratic Mexico has a criminal justice system that is only equipped to work for authoritarian Mexico.

To begin substantiating this assertion, I first turn to the most salient context, which can be no other than the explosion of crime within the country.

Crime rates (Mexico City)

Mexico City—the Federal District—is not quite symptomatic of the whole country, but it is significant. The data on criminal activity there over the last six or so decades is also complete and reliable enough to warrant special attention. Figure 3.1 charts the reports of that activity from 1940.

As can be readily seen, there have been three trends: a decrease, from 1940 to 1960; stability, from 1961 to 1979; and a surge from 1980 to date, with a small dip right at the end. Thus, it is from 1980 onwards that crime became a serious problem in Mexico City. From then on crime rates rocketed at such a rate that in one single year, 1995, crime per capita could increase by 35 percent over the year before. How was it that this acceleration happened just after a long period of stability?

The most obvious answers are to be found in the economic and political changes of the time. From the mid-1980s the country's economic

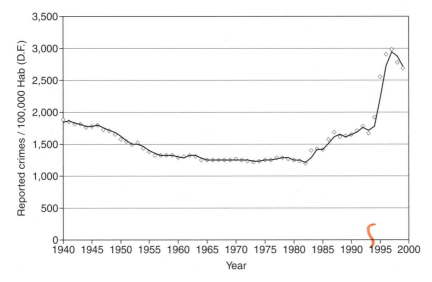

FIGURE 3.1 The number of reported crimes in the Federal District has accelerated since 1980 (source: Rafael Ruiz Harrell).

development model was in recession; in parallel, the political system began to crumble. On the one hand, the collapse of the Gross Domestic Product (GDP) in 1983, 1986 and 1995 brought the woes of unemployment, shrinking credit, inflation, currency devaluation. On the other, these conditions created the climate for the mobilization and articulation of social forces demanding democratization. Difficult as it is to measure or quantify the correlation between recession and political change, we can surely discern the dynamics of both variables in the past couple of decades in Mexico, differentiating them from previous decades.

The following chart shows the evolution of both annual GDP growth and crime rates during the studied period. Again, what stands out is the stability of both indicators until the early 1980s, and the contrast with the large subsequent variations, especially in 1983, 1995 and 1996, the years of severe economic recession.

Taking a step further, it is also useful to locate the existing correlation between the two variables. One doesn't need to claim that GDP growth is the only variable explaining the change in crime rates to still note the coefficients that the analysis shows of a simple linear regression between both variables. Thus, according to our estimates, an increase of one percentage point in GDP corresponds with a fall of 0.90 percent in crime rates (significant with a 99 percent reliability). That may well seem a common-sense result. Yet, if we look a little more attentively at the chart that relates the two variables, one fact jumps out: the negative tendency of the relationship

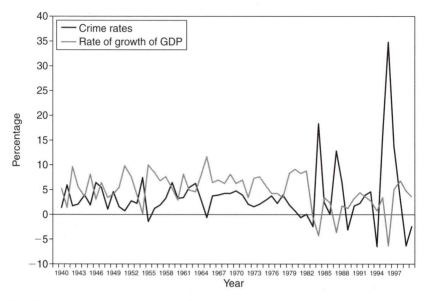

FIGURE 3.2 GDP vs crime rates (source: INEGI, Instituto Nacional de Estadística y Geografía, and Rafael Ruiz Harrell).

between two variables is mainly due to rare events of major economic downturns, that is, the points where the rate of GDP growth is strongly negative.

So what happens in our calculation if we eliminate the points where the GDP growth rate is negative? Despite leaving a large number of observations for analysis, the relation between the two rates actually stops being strong (an increase of 1 percent of GDP would result in only a 0.23 percent drop in crime rates) while also ceasing to be statistically significant (only a 76 percent reliability).

It is, then, important to emphasize the idea that, contrary to what common sense would dictate, crime rates in general have a rather low correlation with economic growth rates, and it is only when a situation becomes critical that crime rates escalate. In other words, crime rates overall do not follow a linear pattern in relation to economic growth. We can only assume that when the threshold of an economic recession is crossed, a strong reaction mechanism is triggered. Equally, we can posit that once an accelerated increase in crime rates occurs, it is very difficult to reverse, since the variables impacting this increase may very well not have the power to reduce it.

Economic crises are social phenomena. They cause potentials for tension, conflict or unrest, and crime rates are accordingly very sensitive to them. By the same logic, political crises also exert a decisive influence, making it possible to explain why in the Mexico of 1994, even as the economy was growing by 3 percent, crime rates would rise in almost the same proportion as during the crisis of 1983. For 1994 was the year of the armed uprising of the Zapatista Army of National Liberation in Chiapas, and of the assassinations of the ruling party's candidate in the presidential election and of its secretary general. These events generated an extraordinarily tense and uncertain climate, signaling as they did that the hegemony of the Institutional Revolutionary Party (PRI) was approaching its end. It was a time when the informal rules that had governed the country for 70 years really began to break.

In sum, the rapid rise of crime rates that we can chart in Mexico City, and that is now the stuff of daily headlines about the country's other urban centers, is a product of the social scarring left by the deep economic and political crises of the 1980s–1990s. Such is the background, one that few would quarrel with.[1] What comes next—the capacity of the state's institutions to respond effectively to this significant and unprecedented threat—is where the tricky part begins.

The formal and the informal in the Mexican judicial system

The legislative design of the institutions responsible for the detection and punishment of criminal behavior in Mexico has the basic features of a federal political system. There are 32 systems of local attorney generals and courts, and one with a national character. The distribution of judicial power between the federal and local governments is determined primarily by the type of crime at issue. Federal authorities prosecute and punish crimes that fall under the umbrella of "national security"—drug trafficking, organized crime, the carrying of firearms. Local state authorities deal with so-called ordinary crime—homicide, robbery, rape, assault, and so on.

This is the first level of description, and one can immediately see the first ambiguity—the blurred, contested jurisdictional responsibility for certain crimes. Crucially, organized crime in practice fits in both local and national categories. On the whole, though, the majority of reported crimes across the country are classified as local crimes, an average of 85 percent in the last decade or so according to data from the government report of 2007.[2]

The institutional design of the apparatus of public safety and criminal justice is formally similar in all states. On the one hand, the work of monitoring and immediate assistance in the streets and neighborhoods falls to the PFP, the preventive police force, assigned to the secretary of public security. Publicly visible, this police force is stringently restricted in its role: it *only* has preventive police functions, *no* criminal investigative functions. Instead, once a crime is committed, the processes of both investigation and the indictment of a suspect before a judge are the responsibility of the attorney general, either state or federal, depending on the case.

The figure on whom the system really depends, however, is the public prosecutor. Both the investigation and the road to indictment are conducted under his aegis. At his command, he has: the Policía Judicial Federal (PJF), the judicial police force, tasked with preliminary investigative work; the expert teams (ballistics, forensics, DNA); and a cohort of lawyers to aid him in presenting a case before a judge. The realities behind such an impressive-sounding job are not hard to guess. The public prosecutor is a lawyer, not a detective; responsible for criminal investigation, he is not competent for it; little to no *professional* criminal investigation is carried out. I emphasize as I do because of course a deal of information is accumulated—the size of bullet holes religiously recorded, and so on. And indeed, anything that the preliminary investigators pick up can and does become evidence for the prosecution, without the defendant's lawyer knowing. But of rigorous investigative follow-through, there is next to nothing. The institutional design provides no incentive for it. This is the great accident in the design.[3]

Its cause lies in tradition, in the perverse precedent set by the decades of overall stability from 1940 to 1980. With such low crime rates, gearing up a justice system to solve crime was far from a priority. Many would argue that the PRI served as the deterrer of anti-social criminal behavior, and it seems reasonable to hypothesize that the role of the attorney generals was more one of social containment, focusing on threats from subversive groups, than the control of crime.

It's hard to say, because the opacity of the justice system during that time means that today it is very difficult to reconstruct its history. We do not have solid evidence to prove what we all suspect happened in the cells of the attorney generals' offices, nor do we have data about how the police and public prosecutors responded to reports of crime, and much less do we have evidence about the incentive system by which the attorney generals rewarded or punished the performance of the police and public prosecutors.

What we can say, however, is that the system of criminal justice operated under two basic informal rules. First, attorney generals operated behind "closed doors," with high levels of arbitrariness and without any legal or political consequences, so long as they stayed within the bounds of the PRI party code. Complementing this, other courts would be weak and submissive, structurally disinclined to challenge the political power embodied in the executive figure of the attorney general.

Constitutional precedents of those years confirm the existence of these rules. The Supreme Court and the circuit courts steered clear of any kind of control of arbitrary police work and of the technical quality of criminal investigations. Their formal rulings underwrote the informal workings of the system. Prosecutors would be free to proceed to trial based on evidence that they had gathered.

Thus, the Supreme Court held on many different cases that arbitrary and prolonged detention by the police was not sufficient to nullify the confession of the accused. For example, the court ruled that evidence of physical abuse of the accused during the arrest did not invalidate a confession if it was "corroborated by other evidence in the files."[4] Prolonged detention by the police or the prosecutor was not itself a material cause for judicial review, on the ground that federal courts could not restore constitutional rights once violated.[5] And great stock was placed upon the pivotal function of the confession in the preliminary criminal "investigation." The defendant might even be able to prove that he had been subject to prolonged detention by agents of the public prosecutor or the police, but his confession would still be valid, on the grounds that he had been "in complete freedom to express all of the circumstances relating to the development of the facts"—in the absence of proof to the contrary.[6] The confession, the defendant's first statement delivered in the office of the public prosecutor, was the declaration with most probative value, because of its spontaneity.[7] And lack of defense counsel in the preliminary investigation did not imply any defenselessness of the accused, since it wasn't the fault of the office of the public prosecutor if the defendant didn't exercise his right to appoint a lawyer.[8] So the Kafkian list went on.[9]

These constitutional precedents were binding for all courts, for all judges assessing the cases presented by the public prosecutor. As could be expected, the confession of the accused in the cells of the attorney general became the "cornerstone proof of the criminal trial." The criminal investigation, if it can be called that, was primarily based on coercion, intimidation and physical abuse of a detainee by the judicial police and the public prosecutor, with the purpose of extracting confessions. Criminal judges, for their part, adhered to the precedents of the Supreme Court and gave full probative value to the confession, finding it sufficient to convict the accused.

The negative effect that these informal rules had on attorney generals in the country has become quite evident in recent decades. Patently, the absence of political and legal controls was fertile ground for corruption. Furthermore, without a judiciary that would ensure the minimum technical quality of accusatorial evidence as well as most basic requirements of due legal process, police and prosecutors had no need to professionalize or raise the quality of their criminal investigations. The Mexican criminal justice system became a system dependent on testimony and confessions. Collecting evidence (even collecting fingerprints), conducting a professional investigation, were considered unnecessary. The confession as "cornerstone proof" was sufficient to close the case and convict any suspect.

Come the 1980s–1990s, and crime didn't just shoot up; it also became a much more complex, dynamic and violent phenomenon. Facing it was a system of arbitrary and corrupt criminal justice, one all but bereft of investigative capacity. Needless to say, it was no contest. Indeed, the impotence of the judicial system would become another significant incentive for criminals.

Clear as that now is, the deeper puzzle is also worth stating. It's easy to see how the criminal justice system was drastically challenged—less so to explain why it was so unable to adapt. This inability of the prosecutors and judges to adapt to the new criminal environment of the country has been without a doubt one of the most unusual factors of these institutions in the last decades. For, almost three decades on, and the old authoritarian practices have not been banished completely. Although the levels of extreme duress and torture of detainees no longer exist in the systematic manner of the years of authoritarian rule, the attorney generals did not abandon the practice of relying on the statements of the accused and witnesses in order to bring cases before trial. That is, the very condition for brutality remained in place—and torture does still occur. Defendants continue to suffer from isolation, the absence of a lawyer and intimidation during the investigation. Also, as we shall see, judges continue to support the poor quality of work by the attorney generals and close their eyes to the arbitrariness of police and public prosecutors.

This has generated a vicious circle. On the one hand, the attorney generals continue to win, on national average, 85 percent of criminal trials using the old authoritarian tactics.[10] In this sense, the criminal court judges have no incentive to compel the prosecutors to improve the quality of their investigations. On the other hand, the authoritarian tactics are not effective in detecting and apprehending major criminals and professional organizations. The result is an enormous inefficiency in the criminal justice system in the country.

The magnitude of the inefficiency of the criminal justice system

Their 85 percent success rate notwithstanding, one of the most emblematic characteristics of the attorney generals is their ineffectiveness. According to estimates by Guillermo Zepeda in 2004, only 10 percent of reported crimes end with a formal charge by the public prosecutor before a judge. Moreover, of this 10 percent, in 44 percent of the cases the trial never commenced because the police failed to issue an arrest warrant. Thus, only six out of every 100 reported crimes are tried in a court of law. In 85 percent of this 6 percent the attorney generals are the victors.[11]

This level of inefficiency can be explained by several factors, of which two seem to me preponderant—corruption, and the lack of a system of professional criminal investigation. I concentrate on the second, for reasons that include the difficulty of empirical corroboration, but also because the obvious has been overlooked, namely that it is exceedingly hard to envisage any judicial system doing its job of apprehending and sentencing criminals without police intelligence.

Police intelligence can mean different things. It can be profiling patterns of individual criminal behavior. It can involve testing fibers and DNA. But whatever it is, it begins where the coerced self-incrimination of the suspect is understood not to be an option. Police intelligence is the most fundamental element of any criminal investigation: to build a coherent story based in proofs that allow the judge and society to know what happened and who is the most likely person responsible.

That all this has yet to be established in Mexico may be gauged by a glance at the statistics in Table 3.1.[12] They show the percentage of inmates sentenced by type of crime in 2005. (The reason for report "all" and "recent" is that we are seeking to solve a statistical problem: given that the survey population in detention is a snapshot at a given time, and that minor offenses are given short sentences, the picture tends to overestimate more serious crimes. Therefore, we also take a second snapshot, with people who have been in custody two years or less, and in this way we try to solve these statistical biases.)

As one sees, in both columns, almost 70 percent of the prison population in our two specimen places are serving time for some kind of robbery. Looking more closely, in Mexico City almost 47 percent of inmates in 2005 are in prison for a minor theft, without violence. In the State of Mexico the percentage is 25 percent. This is a clear indicator of a distortion that a

TABLE 3.1 Types of criminal sentencing (2005)

	All (%)		Recent (%)	
	Mexico City (DF)	State of Mexico	Mexico City (DF)	State of Mexico
Theft	40.6	18.8	46.9	25.1
Armed robbery	20.1	36.7	27.2	42.3
Assaults	2.3	1.3	3.7	2.9
Murder	8.9	11.2	4.1	6.3
Involuntary manslaughter	5.1	7.2	2.9	4.0
Kidnapping	4.9	4.6	2.5	0.6
Sexual crimes	5.5	9.2	2.1	8.0
Carrying an illegal firearm	1.7	1.5	1.2	0.6
Crimes against public health	7.5	6.9	6.2	9.1
Other	3.4	2.6	3.2	1.1
Total	100.00 (657)	100.00 (607)	100.00 (243)	100.00 (175)

Source: Survey of Prison Population, CIDE, 2005

policy decision has brought about in the capital, namely the rewarding of police officers and the public prosecutor for the number of arrests made and cases brought to trial. The policy was designed to prove to the public that tough actions are being taken against crime; its consequence is that the criminal justice system is largely dedicated to catching the weakest links in the criminal chain.

It shouldn't go without comment either that the percentage of 25 percent for the State of Mexico is not an acceptable figure either. To have one-quarter of the prisons assigned for petty thieves is scarcely an achievement to be lauded. Indeed, we have data on the value of the goods stolen. As may be seen in Figure 3.3, they tell their own story.[13]

In other words, the trend of the criminal justice system in Mexico City and the State of Mexico is to increasingly punish thefts of small amounts (US$1–US$38) and punish fewer instances of thefts of more than US$3,006. The fundamental difference between 2002 and 2005 can be seen in this light. While in 2002, 25 percent of those sentenced for theft were charged for stealing amounts in excess of US$3,006, in 2005 this was 5 percent. And similarly, while in 2002 25 percent of those sentenced for theft stole amounts less than US$38, in 2005 this was 45 percent.

Both risible and tragic, these figures open a window onto the way things really work on the ground in the country. The resources and energies of the police and criminal justice system are concentrated on apprehending and sentencing the pickpocket in the subway because he can be caught in the act and because his confession will be plausible evidence.

Indeed, the survey also tells us about this. In the Federal District (Mexico City), 92.5 percent of the inmates stated that they were presented

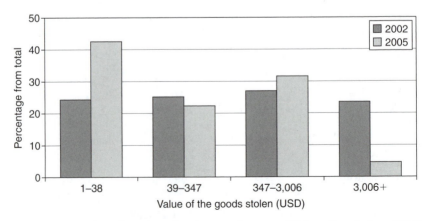

FIGURE 3.3 Value of goods stolen (source: Surveys of Prison Population, CIDE, 2002 and 2005).

with no warrant when they were arrested; 93 percent of inmates also said that when they were arrested, they were taken to the public prosecutor's office or to a judicial police unit. These data are evidently consistent with each other. What they mean is that 93 percent of Mexico City's prison population was caught in the act, or in equivalent flagrancy. And what that means is that 93 percent of arrests made were not the product of any criminal investigation. In only 7 percent of cases did the public prosecutor go to a judge with a request for an arrest warrant, demonstrating that he had conducted an investigation and concluded he had sufficient evidence of the guilt of his suspect to bring him to trial.

The exact percentages may of course be slightly off, but for the sake of argument it can be put like this: in Mexico City, nine out of ten criminal trials are not the product of a police investigation.

The all-round corollaries are devastating. On one side, the system—from police up to the attorney general—is geared *not* to go after professional criminals. Definitions will differ, but most would agree that professional criminals are people for whom the sums we are talking about here are peanuts, and that they are exceptionally unlucky if they caught in the act. Their activity is complex, uses all manner of modern technologies, and can *only* become evidence upon investigation. In their predatory and violent guises, these are also the actors that most concern the general public. Yet, from the attorney generals down, the system has all but stated that it has next to no structural capacity to cope with them. Impunity for the professional criminals is part of the package.

On the other side, more and more effort goes into the minor offenses, the cases ideally where the evidence can be collected after the arrest has been made. Here too things are bleak, as the survey again reveals. Take the inmates imprisoned for crimes against public health. A lot are small time drug pushers (prostitutes are the other main group). The average market value of the drugs they were selling was US$110. In only 10 percent of the cases did the value exceed US$3,900.

Or take kidnappings. One-third of those in prison for kidnapping reported operating either alone or with one partner. In half of the kidnappings US$3,000 or less was obtained.

Drug dealing and kidnapping are of course both abhorrent. Yet that doesn't need to blind us to salient reality: those who get caught and sentenced are overwhelmingly the small fry, not the professionals.

In short, then, we have a criminal justice system in Mexico City that is highly inefficient in two major ways. It is only able to resolve 10 percent of the crimes that are reported. And 93 percent of cases that go to trial get there without preliminary police investigation. The city's attorney general office, as in the rest of the country, has not been able to transform itself into anything remotely resembling a credible institution for professional criminal investigation. Why?

Institutional inertia

When it comes to crime, the country faces new generations of ruthless criminal operators—and a set of dysfunctional institutions whose leading characteristic is resistance to change. What there is, in other words, is a textbook case of institutional inertia, with path dependence largely explaining the story.[14]

My central argument is the following: the Mexican criminal justice system was designed to function in an authoritarian political context and in a country with a low crime rate. Despite the disappearance of those two conditions that made it work, the operators of the system modified neither their routines nor work methods. That is, the role of the police, the prosecutor and the judge remain very similar to that during the old regime. The system worked in three phases during the years of authoritarianism. First, the police obtained information to build the case, intimidating and harassing witnesses and accused. Next the prosecutor tried to make it seem that the police brutality hadn't existed, and so built a file with a lot of paperwork and many formalities. Finally, the judge ratified what the police and prosecutor had done, exercising no control over either their arbitrariness or the quality of the evidence.[15]

Today neither the political conditions nor the criminal context exist that allowed the criminal justice system to work as it did. However, the available data allows us to conclude that in public prosecutor's offices and criminal courts those work routines and practices that took shape in the years of authoritarianism have persisted. In particular, two key factors have not changed over the years. First, the central source of information for building an indictment still lies with the detained and the witnesses, thus allowing for arbitrariness and intimidation during police arrest. Second, criminal judges in the majority of cases continue to support poor cases and sentence in favor of the prosecutor. Both factors are clear remnants of the authoritarian regime.

Already evident, then, path dependence has set in. Even as the evidence of incapacity mounts up, the old ways reproduce themselves indefinitely. The attorney generals are trapped in their own bureaucracies, institutional histories, old patterns of behavior. Developing the skills needed to tackle crime today has not registered as a priority. It can't. Not, at least, while the two key foundations of the system remain set.

The first foundation is this: *the central source of information on which indictments are based remains the testimony of the accused themselves, and hence the arbitrariness of the public prosecutors prevails.*

The fact that 93 percent of the inmate population in Mexico City have been arrested in flagrante delicto is the clearest indicator of the exorbitant reliance of the prosecutor on defendants' statements or information. The strong implication is that when the system cannot arrest a suspect in this manner, the case practically cannot be solved. That is, the prosecutors have not learned how to assemble the puzzle by collecting and analyzing information and scientific evidence relating to the crime. As in the years of authoritarianism, the probability of entering a preliminary investigation depends, essentially, on whether they already have a suspect "in their power."

Obtaining the information needed by defendants continues to require a great deal of arbitrariness similar to the years of authoritarian rule, something that criminal judges prefer to ignore. Prolonged isolation, absence of counsel and failure to inform defendants of their basic constitutional rights are also part of the recurrent practices in the agencies of the public prosecutor's office. Below are some data from the 2005 CIDE survey that show this, highlighting the basic information that the public prosecutor ought by law to provide the detainee.

Regarding the right to have counsel, just 30 percent of respondents reported having a lawyer in the police office and 70 percent rendered their statements without any legal advice.

It is important to state that, in Mexico City, torture in prisons has declined significantly. That aside though, the facts that so many detainees still report being held incommunicado during the police arrest and that they do so not knowing their constitutional rights and without legal advice point to the persistence of authoritarian practices in the agencies of the public prosecutor and the police. And of course, also as in the years of authoritarianism, a very high percentage of the public prosecutors' trials end with a conviction. That is, the judges as well continue repeating the old pattern of behavior as they clearly set the bar of reasonable doubt very low for the public prosecutors.

Which brings us to the second foundation: *the criminal court judges tend to support rather than object to poor prosecutorial investigations.*

In Mexico, on national average, 85 percent of the judges' sentences are in favor of the public prosecutor. This data could, it is true, be interpreted in at least three different ways: (*a*) that the charges brought by the public

TABLE 3.2 Information not provided to defendant by the Public Prosecutor

Information not given to defendant	Percentage
Defendant did not have the the difference between the police investigation phase and the criminal trial phase explained to him/her.	91
Defendant was not informed of the right to remain silent.	80
Defendant was not informed of the right to make a telephone call.	72

Source: Survey of Prison Population, CIDE, 2005

prosecutor have a high professional quality; (*b*) that the public prosecutor only presents cases to the judge in which there is compelling evidence; or (*c*) that judges' sentencing is based on a pre-set punitive approach, one adopted for reasons quite outside of the law. A qualitative study of criminal sentences conducted by Luis Pásara, who analyzed 100 trials in Mexico City and interviewed several judges about their sentencing, confirms one's inclination to believe that Mexican justice mostly fall within the third interpretation.[16]

Of the 100 cases he examined Pásara found that in only one of them had there been an acquittal. This, despite the many cases in which it appeared that evidence was not robust enough to convict. Clearly, various criteria of judicial interpretation have to be at work for the prosecutor to be so unjustifiably favored. For example, Pásara notes that judges routinely take the view of the facts proposed by the prosecutor. And, in order to reject certain elements that appear to contradict the version of the prosecutor, specialized judicial criteria are used. One such is the "divisible qualified admission," that is, the granting of probative value to everything that coincides between the defendant's statement and what the prosecutor argues, and the denial of any probative value to contradictory factors. In other words, judges are predisposed to look for and value only what fits with the prosecutor's case. Then there is the criterion by which the defendant's denial of the "facts" presented to him is to be discarded, on the grounds that the denial is "defensive"—he is only trying to avoid being convicted. Finally, the constitutional jurisprudence that continues to be enforced is that the first statement of the accused, acquired during the preliminary investigation in conditions of solitary confinement, has the most probative value because it is the "most spontaneous."

In sum, judges cannot act as arbitrators in a real legal battle; the old pattern of tilting the field in favor of the public prosecutor continues to prevail.

The constitutional judges, including the Supreme Court and the federal circuit courts, have also not been able to fully modify the judicial behavior patterns typical of the authoritarian era. The uncontested constitutional precedents that have been issued since the constitutional reform of 1994 have not differed substantially from those of previous years. In a study that I conducted with Ana Maria Ibarra into the defendant's constitutional right to have an adequate defense during the investigation and trial (article 20, sections IX and X of the Constitution), this is clearly demonstrated.[17] The constitutional interpretations remain formalistic, impotent to end the authoritarian practices and without tangible impact on the effectiveness of the constitutional rights of the accused. Without the guarantee of a real and effective legal defense, it is difficult to imagine that the accused is entitled to a fair trial.

Indeed, one might gather up all of the strands here with an assertion that I trust will seem logical as well as controversial. It is this: *both for justice to be done on any meaningful scale and for the Mexican criminal justice system to start working, far many more defendants on relatively minor charges need to be found innocent.* This of course is counter-intuitive for public opinion, anxious to see arrests and convictions. But, as things now go, the genuine fears of the public are all too easily turned into the alibi for a system that fails the public every day.

The only possible path towards beginning to resolve the enormous weakness of the Mexican criminal justice system is to uproot and break the authoritarian practices that characterize it. That is, the issue is that the operators of the system—the police, prosecutors and judges—must learn to work without violating either law or the Constitution. This, however, is extraordinarily complicated in a country that is going through a deep crisis of security, as Mexico is.

Conclusion

The central idea that this chapter has argued for is that, contrary to what has often been said in public debate in Mexico, arbitrariness and inefficiency are the twin partners of the country's criminal justice system—two positively correlated phenomena. "Getting tough on crime" sounds right, but is the wrong approach.

In certain contexts, being tough on crime *can* be effective. It can even be conceded that authoritarian practices can sometimes also be effective in providing public security. But our context is Mexico. Getting tough on crime would merely reinforce the worst aspect of a system that has evolved for very specific reasons, and would further inhibit the development of the capacities required for a system able to confront a type of crime that is growing in its complexity and in its violence.

What data we have show that Mexico's criminal justice system has been trapped by the inertia of old authoritarian patterns of behavior. The authoritarian political initial conditions coincided with—if not they didn't create—very low crime rates. This was the setting into which stepped the figure of the public prosecutor. Everything conspired to give him a free, as well as tough hand. Extracted in the cells of his office, the confession of the intimidated, coerced defendant became the "proof" on which criminal proceedings were based. The Supreme Court came up with the legitimating jurisprudence, setting absolute probative value on that confession.

From the 1980s onward, as a result of economic and political crises in the country, crime increased exponentially, mutating too into hugely lucrative, and violent, industries. The deficiencies of the country's criminal justice system were brutally exposed. It lacked a professional criminal investigation apparatus because one wasn't required in the years of authoritarianism. The system was geared to punishing criminals who either confessed or whose apprehension in the act confessed for them. The new generations of criminals couldn't be investigated, much less prosecuted.

Typically where a situation of high impunity criminal rates prevails as it does in Mexico, people say that the justice system has broken down. The true problem is that it hasn't. It has, instead, remained intact, locked in its insufficiencies. This incapacity to adapt, over so many decades now, is genuinely surprising. Explaining it properly is not easy.

Institutional inertia is clearly a large factor, but as an explanation needs to be unpacked with care. People learn ways of doing things, follow work routines, respond to incentives, believe they are being productive. This institutional history is one that is played out every day in the work of regular staff at all levels working in the criminal justice system of Mexico. If, in turn, we do not understand the belief system of such institutional actors, their ideas and prejudices, it will be impossible to reform those institutions. More still, understanding the depth of the inertia with which bureaucracies function makes it imperative that any project of reform pay special attention to the quality of the human resources. It may be that a successful reform of the Mexican justice system requires a significant process of weeding out and forming of new cadres.

Once we focus fully on institutional inertia—address it upfront as an urgent problem—the reform paths can become clearer. To begin with, there are the things not to expect. Evidence of incapacity such as soaring crime rates, dramatic changes in context such as from the 1980s to now—none of such things will trigger changes in institutional practices. Nor will isolated regulatory changes. Nor will increased budgetary resources, even if they come with US strings attached. Institutional history is stronger than all of these. And, let it be added, it is far more powerfully path-setting than the voices of the citizenry.

So what can be projected? First, a drastic change to the working methods within the agencies of the public prosecutors' offices, by which I mean a shift away from the confession to investigation, and within the judiciary, which should impose far higher burdens of proof on the prosecutors. New methods of management in themselves are of value if they succeed in blocking the repetition of learned behavior patterns. A realistic expectation might well begin by aiming little higher than that.

Second, while they are never sufficient, incentives for system operators to change are also important. The reward of good performance cannot be discounted. But good performance has to mean something new, if not traumatic to the operator accustomed to viewing an 85 percent successful conviction rate as a tremendous success. Incentives have to be disentangled from the incentive to repeat learned behavior.

That this is a knotty area may be demonstrated by returning to the research of Luis Pásara. As we saw, the judiciary operates with several criteria of judicial interpretation that provide an incentive to unjustifiably favor the prosecutor. Amending those criteria suggests itself as a good reform, as indeed it would be. But what if judges are in fact acting on other incentives?

Pásara found just this to be so from the judges who told him that convictions result in fewer problems for them than acquittals. Such is the mistrust of the judiciary (based on the egregious behavior of some its members), such the level of suspicion that judges can be bought, that blanket conviction recommends itself as a proof of incorruptibility. One judge even noted that acquittals cannot be issued without consultation with the public prosecutor to determine that there really is no crime to prosecute, while the judicial council of Mexico City also starts an administrative procedure to verify that no corruption has occurred. Weakness and fear, that is, are also motives that need to be identified and understood as well as incentives.

Finally, it is perhaps no accident that we end by touching on the latent variable of corruption. The extent to which the deficiencies of the current justice system are being actively maintained in order to protect professional criminals from investigation can only be a matter for surmise. But it is fair to conclude that the satisfaction of those criminals with justice in Mexico must run very high.

Notes

1 See Gaviria J. Londoño and Guerrero, eds., *Asalto al desarrollo. Violencia en América Latina*, (Washington, DC: Inter-American Development Bank, 2000).

2 Poder Ejecutivo Federal, *Primer Informe de Gobierno 2007*, (Mexico City: Anexo Estadístico, 2007).

3 Ana Laura Magaloni, "El detective: eslabón perdido del sistema de investigación criminal en México," in Gerardo Laveaga, ed., *65 propuestas para modernizar el sistema penal en México*, (Mexico: INACIPE, 2006).

4 Tesis 139–144, Segunda Parte, Séptima Época, Primera Sala, Seminario Judicial de la Federación (November 1980), 36.

5 Tesis 64, Segunda Parte, Primera Sala, Semanario Judicial de la Federación (April 1974), 22.

6 Tesis 41, Segunda Parte, Primera Sala, Semanario Judicial de la Federación (May 1972), 15.

7 Tesis XLIII, Segunda Parte, Sexta Época, Primera Sala, Semanario Judicial de la Federación (January 1961), 37.

8 Tesis 63, Segunda Parte, Séptima Época, Primera Sala, Semanario Judicial de la Federación (March 1974), 23.

9 See for example: Tesis 193–198 Sexta Parte, Séptima Época, Tribunales Colegiados de Circuito, Semanario Judicial de la Federación (April 1985), 342; Tesis I, Segunda Parte-1, Octava Época, Tribunales Colegiados de Circuito, Semanario Judicial de la Federación (January–June 1988), 199.

10 Guillermo Zepeda, *Crimen sin Castigo: Procuración de Justicia y Ministerio Público en México* (Mexico: Fondo de Cultura Económica, 2004), 267.

11 Ibid., 212–221.

12 Marcelo Bergman, ed., *Delincuencia, marginalidad y desempeño institucional. Resultados de la segunda encuenta a población en reclusión en el Distrito Federal y el Estado de México* (Mexico City: División de Estudios Jurídicos, CIDE, 2005).

13 Marcelo Bergman, ed., *Delincuencia, marginalidad y desempeño institucional. Resultados de la encuentra a población en reclusión en tres entidades de la República Mexicana: Distrito Federal, Morelos y Estado de México* (Mexico City: División de Estudios Jurídicos, CIDE, 2002).

14 S. Page, "Path Dependence," *Quarterly Journal of Political Science*, 1 (2006), 187–215. See also V. Fon and F. Parisi, "Litigation, Judicial Path Dependence and Legal Change," *European Journal of Law and Economics*, 20: 1 (2005), 43–56.

15 Ana Laura Magaloni, "El Ministerio Público desde adentro: rutinas y métodos de trabajo en las agencias del MP," Documento de Trabajo, División de Estudios Jurídicos, CIDE, 2009.

16 Luis Pásara, "¿Cómo sentencian los jueces en el DF en materia penal?," Documento de Trabajo 6, División de Estudios Jurídicos, CIDE, 2002.

17 Ana Laura Magaloni and Ana María Ibarra, "La configuración jurisprudencial de los derechos fundamentales. El caso del derecho constitucional a una "defensa adecuada," Documento de Trabajo, División de Estudios Jurídicos, CIDE, 2007.

4

ACCOUNTING FOR THE UNACCOUNTABLE

The Police in Mexico

Ernesto López-Portillo

While a substantial international literature on police accountability has formed over the last years, it was not until the last decade of the twentieth century that systematic study of the Mexican police began. This situation creates anomalies. On the one hand, we can have a good idea of what ought to be the norms of police behavior; on the other, our empirical knowledge of what actually happens inside the Mexican police is only beginning to take shape. Experts are few, serious independent studies are scarce, and official reports by the police themselves are still notable for their lack of sufficient up-to-date information. Not that there isn't quantitative data available. The numbers of officers, the duration and contents of training courses, types of equipment and weapons—the researcher can discover about everything from these to the voluminous legal mandates and organic structures of the various police forces in the country. But from a qualitative analytical perspective, the information needed to assess the overall police force condition remains extremely scarce.

In many ways, this is as it has to be. For the first reality about the police in Mexico is their high degree of fragmentation. There are approximately 1,600 municipal, state and national, or federal, agencies in the country. Neither are agencies at the same level by any means comparable. Mexico City's federal district is policed by about 85,000 officers; the state of Campeche by about 2,000. The municipal police of Chihuahua in the north was the first agency in Latin America to be accredited by the Commission on Accreditation for Law Enforcement Agencies, Inc. In Guerrero, in the south, there are municipal law enforcement agencies that do not even have sufficient funds to build their own offices.

The information deficit regarding the Mexican police has become a pressing concern for government and public alike, in the context of the surge of violence related to organized crime. Some 9,000 people were killed by criminal organizations during the six years of the Vicente Fox administration, 2000–2006; 11,483 from 2007 to June 2009 alone.[1]

The stark figures since then are known. Less so, however, is that they are only matched by the figures for the funding of public security agencies. In January 2008, President Calderón announced that "the 2008 local public safety funds from the federal budget will be increased by more than 90 percent with respect to 2007."[2] As for the budget allocation for the federal agencies of the attorney general's office and the Ministries of Public Security and National Defense, from 2008 to 2009 their share increased by 29 percent.

The paradox could not be plainer: violence has spiraled out of control in tandem with very significant increases in public security spending. The strange symmetry, indeed, goes back to the early 1990s, when criminal violence began to make itself felt—and when funds for public security reforms began to flow, under President Ernesto Zedillo. In 1994, 276 million pesos were spent on public safety. By 2005, that figure would be 13,451 billion pesos—50 times greater than 11 years earlier.[3] And finally, between 2004 and 2008, the budget for the Federal Ministries of National Defense, the Navy and Public Security, plus the Contributions' Fund for Public Security, rose from 49 billion pesos to 83 billion pesos.[4]

Such a trend is not easily reversible, even as more than around eight out of ten Mexicans say they have little or no confidence in law enforcement around the country.[5] A current reform drive, to be implemented by the Secretariat of Public Security (SSP), aims to improve professionalization, technology and control systems, focusing especially on state-of-the-art information systems. Maybe it will work, but one doesn't have to be a doomsayer to doubt it. Increased spending will not likely correlate with greater success in fighting organized crime. The perverse dynamics between law enforcement and crime in Mexico are too deeply entrenched for any quick solution or any quick technological fix. Police reform *is* an urgent necessity, but the path to it has to be taken patiently. This chapter is a sketch of what that path might be, starting out from real existing conditions.

The official take on law enforcement

Article 21 of the Mexican Constitution states that public security is entrusted to the federal government; to the 31 states and the Federal District (DF); and to the 2,439 municipalities. This is in accord with the constitutional precept that all levels of government work in coordination, in this case to establish a national public security system. Thus, public security is a joint responsibility of the three levels of government.

In total, there are 2,088 police institutions in Mexico. The great bulk is made up of the 2,022 municipalities that have police.[6] The states and DF have two police bodies apiece, *la Policía Preventiva* and *Investigadora*, which also represent the two national-federal forces. The preventive police are the overwhelming majority and are recognizable from their uniform; the crime investigation police wear plainclothes. The federal government, the states and DF have both types of police; municipalities have only uniformed police. Over 91 percent of the total forces are municipal and state police. Table 4.1 shows the distribution in 2009.[7]

In 1995 a general law on public security was issued, announcing the first meaningful attempt to reform the country's police forces. There were to be public safety policies whose implementation and results would be subject to evaluation. Ground rules for joint operations were established. The organization, performance and training of forces were to be improved. Criteria for the allocation of federal financial resources were agreed. Rules were set in place for hiring and promoting officers, along with both disciplinary and reward systems. Technological upgrading was to allow for the systematizing and exchanging of all types of police information—for a national police information system.

To make all this happen, coordination agreements were signed between the federal government and the states. And at the apex of this structure was set the National Security Council, comprised of the secretary of the interior; the attorney general; the secretaries of national defense, the navy, federal public security, and communications and transportation; the governors of the states and DF; and one executive secretary of the national system for public security.

A raft of new legislation has come alongside the resolutions emitted by that body. In 2009 alone came: a federal police law; the new organic law of the attorney general's office; a general law of the national system of public security; a law of confiscation of criminal properties. Extant laws, from the penal to those to do with general health, have also been modified as part of the effort to deal with drug dealing. In the process, new faculties have been granted to the country's police bodies.

And finally, according to a new government plan, the president will give an annual progress report on the police.[8]

TABLE 4.1 Distribution of police forces

Police	Force	Percentage
Preventive municipal	159,734	39.00
Preventive state	186,862	45.63
Judicial state police	26,329	6.43
Federal police	32,264	7.8
Ministerial federal police	4,347	1.06
Total	409,536	100

The unofficial take on law enforcement

Diagnoses of what is wrong with the Mexican police differ, yet the consensus that something *is* badly wrong is universal. The police themselves share it.[9] And it is an attorney general who states that "some municipal police forces ... do more to support organized crime than for public security."[10] The dreadful standing of the image of the police has now to be added to the list of obstacles to the institution's ability to renew itself.

The list is long. Functional problems range from poor coordination between the three levels of government to an unreliable national telecommunications network. Structural problems go from the aversion to investigative work amply discussed by Ana Magaloni in Chapter 3, to the failure to consolidate a national register of the police service. There is also the social problem about the police: the career is largely for those close to the bottom of the social ladder.

> In May 2006, out of 292,124 state and municipal preventive police officers in the country, 68.3 percent had some primary school education; 25.2 percent completed middle higher education; and only 4.5 percent completed higher education. The remaining 2.5 percent had not completed any type of education.[11]

Reinforcement of this negative profile comes from the medical survey conducted by the Mexican Institute for Social Security between 1997 and 2004 of 193,762 public security, justice department and prison officers, 88 percent of them male. With an overall average age of 34, 61.52 percent had a medical condition such as obesity, high cholesterol, high-blood pressure, dental cavities and vision problems; 10,042 officers were deemed unfit for service.[12]

In 2004 and 2005, the National Evaluation Center (Ceneval) conducted a psychological evaluation of 15,708 police officers, assessing emotional stability, motivation, social judgment, respect for rules and authority figures, and interpersonal skills. Only 33 percent were judged to have the skills needed for the job. There were reservations about 10 percent, while 22 percent were recommended for preventive counseling—to deal with traits like low self-esteem, poor impulse control, and a passive attitude to the job. The remaining 35 percent were either recommended for ongoing counseling or an in-depth psychological evaluation.[13]

Such glimpses into the realities of police life allow one to make a connection with a more commonly known facet: low salaries. In August 2009, the Federal Public Security Ministry published data on the income of police officers in most of the country's states.[14] I reproduce it in Table 4.2.

No doubt, the attempt there to tabulate the risk of police exposure to corruption errs towards crudeness. On the other hand, methodological scruples ought not to blind one to correlations as compelling as that between the wide-spread desertion of police forces in Michoacán over to the cause of drug traffickers and miserable salaries. Indeed, the general picture is irrefutably clear: in 26 out of the 32 states, police officers take home 3,000–6,000 pesos a month, consistently lower than the regional minimum wage.

The depth of the problem is obvious. It is, in a word, poverty. There is every incentive for the poorly paid local officer to work for the criminals. As stated by the secretary for public security, "every police officer on the [drug trafficking] payroll receives an average of 4,100 pesos [a month], in other words, even the price of corruption is low for organized crime."[15] Low for criminals—not so for police.

The official discourses on law enforcement—that what is needed are hi-tech information systems, that a National Security Council is overseeing cooperation at every level of government—disguise or distract from such unpalatable truths. Without a grasp on them, however, there is little hope of understanding the character of the criminal opponents which the state has now committed such resources to fighting. Organized crime, it may be ventured, has taken such a strong hold in Mexico because, amongst other key factors, it was able to recruit local police forces to their side.

In the municipalities above all, criminals became active economic actors where the larger state was felt to have withdrawn, no longer funding this or that program, not providing infrastructure or sending resources, just not there. To become a municipal police officer became far less a decision to represent authority than a survival strategy for young, under-educated and unhealthy males whose career alternatives were seasonal labor, crossing to the United States, or crime. In other words, poverty created an initial structure of affinities between the police and the criminal—one that was waiting for the hundreds of police who were fired during the reforms of the 1990s. And if the criminal could double the salary of a police officer, he gained a whole web of social solidarity for his corruption. Naturally, intimidation and violence were part of the package. But the embeddedness of organized crime in Mexico is inexplicable without the societal complicity that came with winning over people like the municipal police officers from Tijuana who worked for members of the Arellano Félix cartel.[16] For many—not all—but for many local police, it became irrational to fight crime.

Police supervision

Advanced theories on policing stress that one of the main challenges for any law enforcement agency is to keep control over what its police officers do.[17] This challenge has historically manifested itself in serious deficiencies in supervision.[18] It is very likely that most of the stories of police-related scandals worldwide revolve around the issue. Supervision matters. Without it, accountability is a non-starter.

TABLE 4.2 Salary deficit of the police forces

State	Number of officers	Average income per month Mexican pesos*	Average income per month US$****ª	Minimum wage Mexican pesos**	Minimum wage US$****	Monthly wage deficit per officer Mexican pesos	Monthly wage deficit per officer US$****ª	Deficit %	Monthly susceptibility to corruption, Mexican pesos	Monthly susceptibility to corruption US$****ª
Aguascalientes	2,895	5,823.70	447.63	7,878.43	605.57	2,054.73	157.93	35.28	5,948,443.35	457,220.86
Baja California	7,897	11,112.20	854.13	9,044.58	695.20	–	–	–	–	–
Baja California Sur	2,298	6,987.50	537.09	8,415.92	646.88	1,428.42	109.79	20.44	3,282,509.16	252,306.62
Campeche	2,129	5,866.50	450.92	9,868.97	758.57	4,002.47	307.65	68.23	8,521,258.63	654,977.60
Coahuila	5,294	5,481.50	421.33	8,138.87	625.59	2,657.37	204.26	48.48	14,068,116.78	1,081,331.04
Colima	2,319	4,932.10	379.10	7,558.08	580.94	2,625.98	201.84	53.24	6,089,647.62	468,074.38
Chiapas	12,380	5,287.50	406.42	6,413.13	492.94	1,125.63	86.52	21.29	13,935,299.40	1,071,122.17
Chihuahua	6,770	5,676.50	436.32	8,036.44	617.71	2,359.94	181.39	41.57	15,976,793.80	1,228,039.49
Distrito Federal	84,659	8,034.60	617.57	12,027.83	924.51	3,993.23	306.94	49.70	338,062,858.57	25,984,846.93
Durango	3,681	6,000.00	461.18	6,434.07	494.55	434.07	33.36	7.23	1,597,811.67	122,814.12
Guanajuato	10,652	5,164.00	396.93	7,396.93	568.56	2,232.93	171.63	43.24	23,785,170.36	1,828,222.16
Guerrero	10,126	3,961.40	304.49	7,238.74	556.40	3,277.34	251.91	82.73	33,186,344.84	2,550,833.58
Hidalgo	6,540	5,407.50	415.64	7,444.65	572.23	2,037.15	156.58	37.67	13,322,961.00	1,024,055.42
Jalisco	19,896	7,100.70	545.79	8,211.59	631.18	1,110.89	85.39	15.64	22,102,267.44	1,698,867.60
México	59,622	7,167.70	550.94	9,025.73	693.75	1,858.03	142.82	25.92	110,779,464.66	8,514,947.32
Michoacán	9,510	4,598.80	353.48	7,456.34	573.12	2,857.54	219.64	62.14	27,175,205.40	2,088,793.65
Morelos	5,625	5,932.50	456.00	8,576.86	659.25	2,644.36	203.26	44.57	14,874,525.00	1,143,314.76
Nayarit	2,809	6,179.00	474.94	6,735.70	517.73	556.70	42.79	9.01	1,563,770.30	120,197.56

State									
Nuevo León	11,333	6,421.50	493.58	10,105.43	776.74	3,683.93	283.16	57.37	41,749,978.69	3,209,068.31
Oaxaca	11,807	6,099.10	468.80	7,099.40	545.69	1,000.30	76.89	16.40	11,810,542.10	907,804.93
Puebla	14,261	5,632.90	432.97	8,215.71	631.49	2,582.81	198.52	45.85	36,833,453.41	2,831,164.75
Querétaro	3,516	7,324.00	562.95	10,062.81	773.47	2,738.81	210.52	37.40	9,629,655.96	740,173.40
Quinta Roo	4,659	6,287.70	483.30	7,269.56	558.77	981.86	75.47	15.62	4,574,485.74	351,613.05
San Luís Potosí	7,931	6,918.50	531.78	7,824.70	601.44	906.20	69.65	13.10	7,187,072.20	552,426.76
Sinaloa	8,054	6,948.50	534.09	6,328.89	486.46	–	–	–	–	–
Sonora	6,377	5,924.70	455.40	7,297.69	560.93	1,372.99	105.53	23.17	8,755,557.23	672,986.72
Tabasco	9,880	5,108.50	392.66	7,805.93	599.99	2,697.43	207.34	52.80	26,650,608.40	2,048,471.05
Tamaulipas	7,975	11,946.50	918.26	8,279.04	636.36	–	–	–	–	–
Tlaxcala	3,606	6,545.90	503.14	7,450.43	572.67	904.53	69.53	13.82	3,261,735.18	250,709.85
Veracruz	18,522	3,154.30	242.45	7,509.13	577.18	4,354.83	334.73	138.06	80,660,161.26	6,199,858.67
Yucatán	6,927	3,975.50	305.57	6,508.82	500.29	2,533.32	194.72	63.72	17,548,307.64	1,348,832.26
Zacatecas	2,975	6,327.40	486.35	6,908.70	531.03	581.30	44.68	9.19	1,729,367.50	132,926.02

Notes

   * The average mean for all basic security personnel, from cadets to third officers, guards to agents and patrol car drivers.

   ** The figures reflect the GDP per capita adjusted by the regional average salary, not the cost of living in each state.

   *** Calculation by Genaro García Luna.

   a Dollar exchange rate taken from the Bank of Mexico, 23 November 2009.

I do not know of one single specialized study on police supervision in Mexico, even though dozens of senior and middle-level police officers have confirmed to me that supervision is their greatest challenge. For low-level police officers supervision is primarily a means of control and abuse.

Police accountability evaluation projects have found that supervision comprises formal and informal processes. From what we know of the practices of police supervision in Mexico their formal function is to provide a symbolic routine that gives the appearance of institutional control over police officers. The most notable example is the "roll call" at the beginning and end of each shift, an archaic practice that has nothing to do with modern, dynamic and effective supervision of the officers during their shifts, out on the streets. But in its innocuousness, the formal function gains by comparison with the informal.

The informal side to the practice of supervision is a ritual in the exercise of power and abuse. The codes can be extremely harsh. The first informal sanction that I heard about involved the banning of a police officer from any operational work for at least two years. The officer's crime was to have contacted colleagues in other countries without authorization from his superiors. At the most violent extreme of the spectrum, officers describe sanctions which include physical violence against them if they do anything that is not approved by their superiors.[19]

As may readily be seen, upon entering the "police world" one immediately runs up against rules and practices that have next to nothing to do with ensuring what most citizens would understand as police accountability. Instead, the principles of this world are there to ensure the discipline necessary for the superior officer to prevail. Across the board, Mexican law enforcement agencies have in common a vertical structure connecting hierarchical levels through chains of submission. Behind the headlines of cases of police brutality lies this shadow world in which the victimizers are also the victims.

A historical take on law enforcement

On many counts, the image of the police in Mexico could scarcely be worse. So it may appear quixotic to say that one of the top priorities for any serious reform ought to be the protection of the human rights *of the police*. But that is my claim.

Behind it is a distinctive historical experience. Out of the long complex process of the Mexican revolution, in which the military was so potent as actor and threat, the institutional basis of the police was negligible. A separate police ethos—one, for example, making them the friend of the citizen in distress—conspicuously failed to develop. Instead, institutionally the police in Mexico may best be described as a sort of residual outer limb of the armed forces. Today, as for a century, the state finds the primary use of the police to lie in control and, when required—as it was in the case of Atenco, in the State of Mexico, in May 2006—repression of the population. In other words, the country remains stuck with the police force of the authoritarian regime, one utterly incompatible with practices of democratic law enforcement and a non-oppressive relation to the citizenry. Hence the schizophrenic situation dramatized by an event like Atenco: a human rights culture has been developing in many areas of Mexico, but for the police who committed 209 serious violations of human rights over two days, that culture has nothing to do with them.[20]

It could hardly be otherwise. The Constitution may say what the police are supposed to do, but one searches constitutional law in vain for a system of rights for the police. The administrative abuse of officers occurs in a legal vacuum.[21] Neither does one find any documented experience of broad, sufficient and stable protection of police officers in Mexico, either during or after their professional careers. The most in-depth studies we have show instead that Mexican police officers live in a state of institutional abandonment and social isolation.[22] If human rights are not a meaningful referent in their own experience, their failure to recognize others as possessors of rights can come as no surprise.

The concrete outcome of the Mexican state's lack of interest in the institutional culture of its police is, no doubt, an extremely brutalized world unto itself. Not for nothing are there virtually no norms and protocols for the use of firearms by the police.[23] The almost unchecked power to use force at will has certainly been conducive to violent police practices. One could even speculate that for many police the power that comes from their gun serves as a significant, if compensatory, symbolic assertion of their identity. But what we also know is that the Mexican police have a marked tendency, when abusing their power, to pick on the helpless, the case in point today being the many Central American illegal migrants who are kidnapped and ransomed by the police in some of the Mexican states through which they must pass.

To say that protecting the human rights of Mexican police is an urgent task implies no softness of judgment. Indeed, the case for the prosecution isn't finished.

Police corruption

The generic term "police corruption" is a superficial shorthand for a deep, complex reality, one in which the rules and practices by which superiors enforce their power are matched by other values and attitudes. Submission, that is, is only one side of the story in the police world: the other is loyalty.

If the hierarchy is secure, formal and informal privileges flow more freely. New and young officers are initiated into the benefits of submission, at once becoming parts of the pyramids through which funds flow to the veteran and senior officers.[24] The privilege of the superior is both of prevailing without resistance from his subordinates, and of securing the lion's share of bribes. Around the superior, typically, is an inner circle, one whose membership will usually be reflected in the formal structure. Lower ranking officers have to spend a lot of their time cultivating relations with this group. Even before starting on the job, the rookie learns the informal practice by which alignment with the group will be rewarded.[25] If successful, he can hope to one day attain the same position, with its closer access to the privileges that the superior distributes.

From the outside, all of this is plain wrong. On the inside, the system of privilege distribution that goes by the name of "corruption" is an entirely justifiable, necessary compensation for the insufficiency of the wage packet. You do indeed get what you pay for. The neglect, that is, of police rights has long been accompanied by a budgetary neglect that has left the police in Mexico little alternative but to create their own self-financing rules.

And at some level, this is understood in wider society. A 2007 study revealed that 22 percent of Mexicans believe that if somebody's salary is insufficient to support them, it is indeed allowable to accept "something slipped under the table." Some 21 percent admitted to having slipped something under the table to the police in the last year. Of that 21 percent, 83 percent had bribed the traffic police (who receive bribes either in their caps or copies of the traffic regulations). Overall, 38 percent believe that bribes are necessary in dealing with government authorities in Mexico. And, over the years 2001 to 2007, 80 percent rated the police as being corrupt.[26]

Police unaccountability

Empirical observation, data, studies, the direct opinion of the police themselves—all concur on the chronic inconsistency of Mexican policing standards and practices. At this minimum level, the problem is one of a pervasive unwillingness to reliably record information on pretty much anything—from the individual performance and behavior of police officers to the effective use of resources; from crime rates to calls from the public. There is no evidence that the police use evaluation instruments on public satisfaction with their service—from their treatment of suspects and victims. Only as an exception, usually in cases or situations that have attracted media attention, are either victims or external surveys consulted. Fundamentally, the Mexican police fail to meet professional standards for the provision of public information because they do not like accounting for themselves.

Hence they are not accountable to independent specialized agencies that could have legal powers to receive complaints against the police, or could publish reports on their performance. Indeed, they are barely accountable to

Congress, to the criminal justice system and to human rights commissions. They have no policies or mechanisms to ensure the transparency of their budgetary management. In general, they do not tolerate scrutiny by specialized institutions and individuals from civil society and academia. And, unsurprisingly, they have not developed mechanisms for dialogue and cooperation with communities to secure their trust and assistance—an omission that has led to the lynching of undercover officers in the recent past. In general, the Mexican police have no capacity to establish lasting partnerships with other institutions or with civil society in crime prevention.

The material effects of all of this can be deadly, both for citizens and the police themselves. In the majority of cases, police forces keep no track on the use of firearms. The officer who discharges his weapon while on duty can cause injury and even death without an investigation being automatic. Accordingly, force is often used beyond reasonable limits. At the same time, as bungled operations with police fatalities repeatedly demonstrate, the police tend to depend on their weapons to make up for inadequacies in basic training.

Even when things go badly wrong like this, the unaccountability paradigm ensures that there are no consequences for the police as institution. In effect, the institution stands in the same position as the individual officer whose acts are unbounded by accountability. Do the police comply with their mandate? Are they effective in the combat of crime and violence? The evidence says no and that they are not. Yet these fundamental criteria have become irrelevant to the police institution.

The question that then arises is whether this situation has come about by the accidents of ineffectiveness or the design of malice. In a context like the Mexican case, where the institutional and social dimensions of law enforcement on the whole have a weak relationship with the legal mandate per se, the answer cannot break down the precise impact of either, but rather has to point to their mutual synergy. Some of the incapacity, that is, may just be due to ineptitude. But the bigger picture is one in which the rules of the game for the police are geared towards the incentives of their own opportunity, not towards defending society's rule of law. Ineptitude isn't entirely innocent.

Presumably, this is also the conclusion that has been reached by recent administrations. The police receive no government, legal, budgetary or fiscal support consistent with an accountability police model in a democracy. There is clearly no expectation in the political class that the police define their mission as a public service for the protection of human rights, and no sign of any effort to change that. To the contrary, President Calderón's decision to put the army at the front of the war against drugs was an explicit confession that the Mexican police were hopelessly compromised by their ties to organized crime.[27] Once again, the police were to participate only as juniors in a mission whose logic was military.

Conclusion

Police reform is extraordinarily complex, and the world is full of failed stories of police reform.[28] The Mexican case shows that, even where there is an urgent need to implement reform—even where some funding will go to this aim—politicians can still be of two minds. Not only is it especially hard to begin processes of change in settings of chronic institutional weakness; but change itself is risky. Imposing new rules in an effort to formalize and so change current practices instills uncertainty into an order that, however dysfunctional, is still an order—one held together by the principle of vertical control and by mechanisms of distribution of privileges. All of the incentives point towards the reproduction of the current informal rules.

That is why comparative international theory about police reform emphasizes both that it ought to be a process, and that success depends substantially on police officers' perception of a benefit.

Police reform is not synonymous with mere top-down structural changes. No other mistake is as fundamental as assuming this. The list of police agency makeovers recorded in Chapters 1 and 2 of this book ought to be eloquent testimony to the futility of the tabula rasa approach which has so often been taken in Mexico. The appeal of the approach, of course, is explained by corruption: where it is so pervasive, why not just purge the bad agency and start all over again with a clean one? Intuitively right, this has been going wrong now in Mexico since 1994. Changes in standards and institutional structures—as well as greater resources—do not by themselves produce different police behavior. The lesson is very clear: if police mandates and formal structures lack a new rationale to organize them, then formal changes will have no impact on daily policing.

Central to any new rationale has to be the replacement of informal incentives with new formal incentives.[29] That certainly means dealing with the scandal of the salaries, but can also mean toughening internal control mechanisms, in a tradeoff between higher rewards and sanctions. Current government proposals including a greater role for polygraph examining of police officers—a dismal but also salutary admission of realities—may be appropriate. A large-scale professionalization policy based on a merit system and training to help dignify the work of the police (and prison officers) sounds more promising; for the best incentive of all is to earn a decent wage doing a job, in reasonable conditions, that enhances self-respect. Yet as things stand, the police lack the basic incentive to perform and feel rewarded by an honest job well done.

A commitment to the rights as well as the responsibilities of the police, through public education campaigns, must, then, be part of any reform. This is the essential quid pro quo that needs to be struck if the Mexican police institutions are to attain a professional performance that is respectful of citizens' human rights. At present, those institutions lack the minimum controls required—and that, in turn, tells us that Mexico has still a long way to go in its consolidation of democratic rule of law.

In a democratic nation where the rule of law prevails, there is a higher-level mandate for every public role. No government act may jeopardize or violate the fundamental rights of citizens, under any circumstances. This is constitutionally guaranteed, and if say the police were unhappy about an aspect of citizen protection they would have to lobby to get the Constitution changed. In a democracy, the police must comply with their given mandate to enforce the law and protect citizens. This may appear as a constraint, yet it lends both legitimacy and effectiveness to policing.

The ineffectiveness of the police in Mexico, as in other such cases, is directly connected to their lack of restraints. For all the disdain of them, there is a conventional view of the police—shared by other government agents, by the public and naturally the police themselves—by which they are solely responsible for determining how they will comply with their mandate. After 15 years of legal and institutional public security reforms, despite democratic transition, that is, the police still reflect the authoritarianism of their origins.[30] Conceived as an instrument of political control rather than of citizen protection, the police also still steer far more by the stars of informal than of formal rules. This is what makes their accountability such a remote prospect without a reform process specifically designed to bring accountability to bear on them.

In an ideal world, there are different dimensions of police accountability.[31] Within the police themselves, internal accountability would keep all kinds of tabs on officers, from reporting work to filing complaints. Were the Mexican police to be fully politically accountable to the state, they would be so to the three branches of government—to the policy and conduct guidelines of the executive, the legal standards of the judiciary (including things as basic as the prohibition of torture), and the overview (particularly the budgetary overview) of the legislature. Should the police in Mexico become accountable to the public, they will open themselves to scrutiny by the media, NGOs, and the communities they serve. And were independent external accountability mechanisms to be used, they would handle complaints against the police and investigate and monitor police actions, with the cooperation of the police. In a very ideal world, every police officer would carry with them a copy of the UN Code of Conduct for police.

An ideal world is far off, yet none of these dimensions of accountability ought to be beyond reach. What is required, as international comparative studies tend to agree, is political decision and leadership. For the real issues are far clearer than the technicalities of police reform typically allow people to see. Is it time to counterbalance an unrestrained police with the democratic values of accountability? Why should democratization not touch the police? No doubt, police reform is a complex process, but in Mexico the conditions for initiating it ought not to continue sliding away.

Notes

1 *Milenio* 12 January 2008; *El Universal* 18 June 2009. See also the August 2008 report, online, available at: www.sipaz.org/informes/volf13no3s.htm#i.

2 XXII Sesión del Consejo Nacional de Seguridad Pública, 9 January 2008, online, available at: www.presidencia.gob.mx/prensa/?contenido=33230.

3 Ernesto López-Portillo, "Mexico," *World Police Encyclopedia* (New York: Routledge, 2006).

4 Roberto Zamarripa, "Tolvanera/La Amenaza," *Reforma* 14 January 2008.

5 Instituto Ciudadano de Estudios Sobre la Inseguridad (ICESI), 2009 National Poll on Insecurity, online, available at: www.icesi.org.mx.

6 Genaro García Luna, *Nuevo Modelo de Policía* (México, DF: Secretaría de Seguridad Pública, 2009).

7 Ibid.

8 Programa Sectorial de Seguridad Pública 2008.

9 See Elena Azaola, *Imagen y autoimagen de la Policía de la Ciudad de México* (México, DF: Ediciones Coyoacán, 2006).

10 "Reconoce Medina Mora apoyo policiaco al Narco," *Reforma* 4 January 2008.

11 García Luna, *Nuevo Modelo de Policía*.

12 Efrén Arellano Trejo, *Contenido y Perspectivas de la Reforma Penal y de Seguridad Pública* (México, DF: Centro de Estudios Sociales y de Opinión Pública, de la Cámara de Diputados, 2010).

13 Mercedes Peláez, *Profesionalización de los cuerpos de seguridad del estado* (México, DF: Instituto de Investigaciones Jurídicas de UNAM, 2006).

14 García Luna, *Nuevo Modelo de Policía*.

15 Silvia Otero, "Cuesta a Narco $4 mil al mes "comprar" a un policía: SSP," *El Universal* 25 June 2007.

16 Roberto Zamarripa, "Al servicio de los Arellanos," *Reforma* 31 July 2007.

17 See David H. Bayley, *Changing the Guard. Developing Democratic Police Abroad* (New York: Oxford University Press, 2006).

18 See Samuel Walker, *The New World of Police Accountability* (Washington, DC: US Library of Congress Cataloging in Publication Data, 2005).

19 This paragraph is based upon research conducted by the NGO Instituto para la Seguridad y la Democracia (Insyde). Sources are protected by anonymity, but their testimonies are processed in working papers, online, available at: http://insyde.org.mx/images/cuaderno_trabajo.

20 Insyde and Centro de Derechos Humanos "Miguel Agustín Pro Juárez," *De Atenco a la Reforma Policial Democrática. Una mirada propositiva en clave de Reforma Policial Democrática y Derechos Humanos* (México: Estado de México, 2006).

21 See R. Arturo Yañez, *Policía Mexicana cultura política, (In)seguridad y orden público en el Gobierno del Distrito Federal* (México, DF: UAM-X-Plaza y Váldes, 2000).

22 María Eugenia Suárez De Garay, *Policías: Una Averiguación Antropológica* (Guadalajara, Jalisco: Oficina de Difusión de la Producción Académica del ITESO, 2006).

23 Ernesto Mendieta Jiménez, Samuel González Ruíz, Edgardo Buscaglia, Fernando Ventura, and Gleb Zingerman, *La fuerza de la razón y la razón de la fuerza. El uso legítimo de la violencia* (México, DF: Instituto Nacional de Ciencias Penales, 2009).

24 Author interviews with police.

25 See Ernesto López-Portillo, "Seguridad Pública," *Nexos* 249, September 1998.

26 Alejandro Moreno, "Encuesta/Concentran mordidas agentes de tránsito," *Reforma* 12 October 2007.

27 "President Felipe Calderón admitted that there is corruption in all levels of the police and that's why he ordered the use of the army in the fight against drug traffic," Notimex, *Milenio* 27 November 2009. Compare Secretary of Public Security García Luna: "Police who have been arrested for criminal activities but who win immunity from prosecution and remain active, some of them now within the federal police are tied to crime." Cited by Daniel Blancas, "Con amparos policías federales ligados al crimen siguen activos," *La Crónica* 14 November 2009.

28 Commonwealth Human Rights Initiative, *Police Accountability: Too Important to Neglect, Too Urgent to Delay* (India, New Delhi: 2005).

29 See David H. Bayley, *The Police Abroad: What To Do and How To Do It* (Washington, DC: National Institute of Justice, 2001).

30 See Comisión de Derechos Humanos del Distrito Federal, *Informe Especial sobre los derechos humanos de las y los agentes de las corporaciones de policía de la Secretaría de Seguridad Pública del Distrito Federal* (Mexico: Corporación Mexicana de Impresión, 2009).

31 For a full treatment, see Aneke Osse, *Understanding Policing: A Resource for Human Rights Activists* (Amsterdam: Amnesty International, 2006). Compare Rachel Neild and David Bruce, *The Police that we Want: Handbook for Oversight of the Police in South Africa* (Johannesburg, South Africa: Centre for the study of violence and reconciliation with the Open Society Foundation for South Africa and the Open Society Justice Initiative, 2005, online, available at: www.justiceinitiative.org/publications.

5

SECURITY VERSUS HUMAN RIGHTS

The Case of Contemporary Mexico

Alejandro Anaya Muñoz

During 2005 and 2006—the final two years of the presidency of Vicente
Fox, the levels of violence associated with drug-trafficking in Mexico escalated in an alarming way. Public opinion was routinely shocked by news
reports of brutal killings, dismemberment of bodies, beheadings and an
impressive use of heavy weaponry in a turf war between drug cartels. Initially, violence appeared to be limited to the border region in the north of
the country, particularly to the city of Nuevo Laredo, in Tamaulipas—a
key point of introduction of illegal drugs into the United States. But eventually, shoot-outs started to take place and dead bodies to appear in other
states like Guerrero, Tabasco, Quintana Roo and Michoacán. The reaction
of the Fox government to the situation in Nuevo Laredo and elsewhere was
Operation Safe Mexico (*Operativo México Seguro*), based on the massive
deployment of members of the Federal Preventive Police (PFP) and the
military. The objective was to circumvent corruption within the local
security apparatus (municipal and state police were seen as part of the problem), and ultimately to deter violence—basically through a "show of
force."[1] But as the Fox period approached its end, the number of executions
continued to grow. Apparently, this situation was welcomed by some government officials who perceived that it was the outcome of a successful
strategy leading to the detention of major drug lords. They argued that
violence did not affect the rest of society.[2]

In this context, Felipe Calderón was elected president of Mexico in mid-
2006, taking office on 1 December. In the very first minutes after he formally became president of Mexico—and even before his inauguration
ceremony—Calderón named his security cabinet, made up of the attorney
general and the Secretaries of Interior, Defense, Navy and Public Security.
Hours later, in a speech given to his supporters at the National Auditorium

in Mexico City, Calderón clearly underlined the importance of security issues within his government's agenda.

> Today, delinquency aims to frighten and paralyze society and the government; public insecurity threatens everybody and has turned into the main problem of states, cities and entire regions. One of the three priorities that [my government will pursue] is, precisely, the fight to recover public security and legality.[3]

Comparative experience shows that when a government faces real or perceived challenges to national or public security and thus underlines the importance of the security agenda, respect for human rights (particularly rights related to due process and physical integrity) is put under severe strain.[4] Has this been the case of Mexico? Have human rights been affected by the current Mexican government's emphasis on security? This chapter explores these questions, looking at the design and the implementation of Calderón's security strategy, during the first three years of his administration—2007 to 2009. The chapter traces the government's preferences in the design of its security approach, reviewing the National Development Plan (PND); the constitutional reform bill proposed by Calderón to renovate Mexico's penal justice system; and his decision to further militarize the struggle against drug cartels. The chapter finds that the respect for human rights was not an important preference of the government when it designed its security strategy. The chapter then shows that the militarization of the fight against drug trafficking has indeed had a negative impact on human rights in practice, and addresses the controversial issue of military jurisdiction over cases of violation of human rights presumably perpetrated by the armed forces. Again, the chapter finds that, in spite of the evidence of numerous violations of human rights and severe international criticism of military jurisdiction, the government's preference about the place of human rights vis-à-vis security has not changed. The chapter concludes with a reflection about the general social context—marked by real and perceived high levels of insecurity—within which security has been defined as a trump over human rights by the government of Felipe Calderón.

Setting out the strategy

President Calderón underlined the primacy of security within his government's agenda from the start. From the outset, it was clear that his approach to improving security would be based on giving state institutions more coercive tools to fight crime, while suggesting that due process rights (of suspected criminals) were *part of the problem*. So, in his 1 December speech he pledged to guarantee that laws "are an instrument to protect the rights of citizens and not routes to impunity for criminals."

Later on, the government presented the PND, which gravitates around five "guiding axes": rule of law and security; a competitive and job-generating economy; equality of opportunities; environmental sustainability; and effective democracy and responsible foreign policy.[5] The PND stressed the government's obligation to abide by the law and to guarantee the protection of the "life, property, freedoms and rights of all Mexicans." Overall, the PND included dozens of references to the promotion and respect of human rights through Mexico's foreign and domestic policy. A link between the rule of law and the respect of human rights was clearly and consistently acknowledged in the plan. But a clear connection between security and human rights was missing.

The PND identified organized crime and in particular drug trafficking as the key security challenge faced by the Mexican state: drug trafficking "as a manifestation of organized crime, challenges the state and turns into a strong threat to national security."[6] The PND clearly underlined the need to undertake institutional and legislative reforms that increase the coercive capacities of the state to tackle this threat. The plan explicitly called for a reform of the penal justice system, including the recognition of *arraigo* (the prolonged detention of suspects without charge), and greater capacity for public prosecutors to conduct house searches and to intercept personal communications. Human rights language within the PND's blueprint of the strategy to fight drug trafficking was scant. However, the PND did explicitly pledge that the army, the navy and the federal police would respect human rights in their fight against drug cartels.[7]

Reforming the penal justice system

During his administration, Vicente Fox had failed in an ambitious attempt to reform Mexico's penal justice system. His constitutional reform bill, presented to Congress in March 2004, included, *inter alia*: the creation of a single federal police; the introduction of oral and adversarial trials (in substitution of written and inquisitorial ones); the elimination of the value in court of confessions not made before a judge; and the constitutional enshrinement of the principle of the presumption of innocence. But, on the other hand, the Fox bill also proposed a series of measures that would result in the relaxation of due process guarantees in cases of organized crime.[8] The bill was not approved by Congress.

In March 2007, as he had proposed in the PND, President Calderón sent to Congress his own constitutional reform bill. The president's bill highlighted the rights of the victims of crime, but its main objective was to give public prosecutors more tools to fight organized crime. From a human rights perspective, the bill was particularly controversial because, in practice, it attempted to weaken due process guarantees in the investigation and prosecution of organized crime. Some of the more salient and controversial measures proposed by the bill were the constitutional recognition of the *arraigo* practice, and a disposition allowing public prosecutors to execute *arraigos*, searches and hearings of personal communications without prior judicial authorization in cases of organized crime. Similarly, the bill also proposed that the police could enter into a property without a judicial order or warrant, allegedly to "preclude the consummation of a crime or to protect the integrity of people." Calderón's reform bill did include some human rights language, though. It explicitly justified the *arraigo* practice, arguing that its use would be exceptional, and that therefore it did not contravene Article 9.3 of the International Covenant on Civil and Political Rights.[9] But, more surprisingly, the bill explicitly acknowledged a trade-off between security objectives and human rights, justifying measures that were "restrictive of fundamental rights" on the bases of the need to "protect society."[10]

From the outset, opposition parties in Congress criticized the bill, arguing that some of its dispositions would violate individual rights. In due time, even senators from the president's party—National Action Party, (Partido Acción Nacional, PAN)—recognized that the bill—in particular *arraigos*, property searches and hearings of personal communications *without judicial authorization*—violated constitutional rights. However, concurring with the president on the perceived need to give public prosecutors more tools to fight organized crime, and in particular on the usefulness of *arraigo* and other measures, senators from different parties reached a consensus that rested on the appointment of "control judges" (*jueces de control*), who would be able to act more swiftly in authorizing *arraigos*, searches and hearings of personal communications.[11]

In early 2008, after a painstaking legislative process, a quite different version of the constitutional reform bill was approved by Congress by an overwhelming majority.[12] In line with the "general spirit" of the original Calderón proposal, the new bill relaxed some due process guarantees for the investigation and prosecution of organized crime (which was vaguely defined as an organization "of three or more people, [established] to commit crimes in a permanent or reiterated fashion").[13] In addition, the *arraigo* practice and hearings of personal communications were formally and explicitly validated in the Constitution. In opposition to the Calderón proposal, however, the new legislation stated that *arraigos*, property searches and hearings of personal communications could not be mandated by public prosecutors, but only by "control judges," even in cases of organized crime. The reform bill revived Vicente Fox's 2004 proposal of transforming the penal justice system into an oral and adversarial one. The bill also included some clauses that were favorable to human rights—for example, "any evidence obtained through the violation of fundamental rights will be void" in court. It introduced explicitly the principle of the presumption of innocence and eliminated the judicial value of confessions not given in the presence of a defense attorney. Furthermore, it mandated that public security institutions should be guided by the principles of "legality, objectivity, efficiency, professionalism, honesty *and respect for human rights.*"[14]

In sum, the final version of the constitutional reform bill was the outcome of a bargaining process between political parties in Congress. For whatever reasons, the resulting bill took human rights a bit more seriously than the Calderón government had done so months before. Nevertheless, the constitutional reform to the system of penal justice affected the procedural bases for the protection of human rights in Mexico and was therefore strongly criticized by international NGOs and the UN Human Rights Council (HRC).[15]

The militarization of security

In her account of Fox's approach to the increase of drug trafficking-related violence, Laurie Freeman concluded that: "faced with rising violence, Mexico's inclination has been to deploy police and soldiers, in the hope that they will catch criminals and their presence will have a deterrent effect."[16] Fox's security approach was consistent, in this sense, with that of the last three Institutional Revolutionary Party (PRI) presidents Miguel de la Madrid, Carlos Salinas and Ernesto Zedillo, who—as discussed in Chapter 2 of this book—gradually militarized Mexico's public security institutions, particularly in relation to the fight against drug cartels.

The militarization of Mexico's security apparatus has been characterized by

> the expansion of the antidrug role of the military as an institution into domestic law enforcement responsibilities, and the appointment of military personnel (whether on active duty, on leave, or retired) to posts inside civilian law enforcement institutions such as the police and attorney general's office.[17]

The Calderón government followed to the extreme this militarization of the security strategy.[18] According to Eduardo Medina Mora (Mexico's attorney general from December 2006 until late 2009), Calderón had decided that a surge in military involvement in the war against drugs was necessary since July 2006 (before the outcome of the 2006 presidential election had been finally determined).[19] Indeed, within a few days of his inauguration as president of Mexico, Calderón sent thousands of troops to a good number of states, including Michoacán, Guerrero, Baja California, Durango, Chihuahua, Sinaloa, Veracruz, Tamaulipas and Nuevo León. In May 2007, President Calderón created the *Cuerpo de Fuerzas de Apoyo Federal* (Corps of Federal Support Forces), a special task-force to support civil authorities in public security functions (that is, the restoration of public order and the struggle against organized crime).[20] From the outset, the military assumed a leading role in every aspect of the war on drugs. Not only did the armed forces eradicate illegal crops as it had traditionally done; it also led intelligence activities, conducted raids and house-to-house searches, operated roadblocks, engaged in heavy gun battles, detained and interrogated suspects and seized drugs and weapons.

Historically, counter-drug efforts in Mexico have been characterized by the violation of human rights. Before the Calderón period, international NGOs had documented a broad catalogue of cases of arbitrary detention, disappearance, torture and executions perpetrated against suspects by the police but also by the military.[21] Not surprisingly, as this presidential period has evolved, abundant evidence about the negative consequences for human rights of the militarization of security has surfaced.[22] As can be seen in Table 5.1, the number of complaints against the Defense Ministry (Secretaría de la Defensa Nacional, SEDENA), received by the National Commission for Human Rights, the CNDH, has multiplied dramatically during the Calderón period, particularly in 2008 and 2009. In 2008 and the first half of 2009, the CNDH received more complaints against SEDENA than any other agency, including the Mexican Institute for Social Security and the attorney general's office, which used to be number one in this respect. In 2008, SEDENA also took the lead in complaints regarding torture and in precautionary measures issued by the CNDH—it was denounced in 19 torture complaints (90 percent of the total number of torture complaints registered by the CNDH in the year) and received a massive 399 precautionary measures (86 percent of the total number of precautionary measures issued by the CNDH in the year).[23] It is true that not all the complaints against SEDENA received by the CNDH are related to its involvement in the struggle against organized crime. In this respect, the Mexican government reported to the UN Human Rights Committee that from 1 December 2006 until 31 August 2009, the CNDH had received 1,836 complaints against SEDENA specifically related to its participation in the fight against organized crime.[24] As can be seen in Table 5.1, the total number of complaints against SEDENA for the period 2007 to 2009 is 2,521. In any case, and conceding the accuracy of the figures given by the government to the UN Human Rights Committee, 1,836 is a very significant number of complaints.

In addition to the number of complaints registered by the CNDH against SEDENA, it is important to take a look at the number of recommendations it has produced. In the 2007 to 2009 period, the CNDH issued 38 recommendations against SEDENA about situations related to the military's role in security activities.[25] As can be seen in Table 5.2, this is 24 percent of the total number of recommendations issued by the CNDH during 2008 and 2009, and 32 percent of the total number of recommendations issued in 2009. This stands in sharp contrast with the number of recommendations issued against SEDENA during the previous seven

TABLE 5.1 Complaints registered by the CNDH against SEDENA (2000 to June 2009)

Year	Total number of complaints	Complaints against SEDENA	Percentage of total
2000	4,473	116	2.6
2001	3,626	114	3.1
2002	3,184	105	3.3
2003	3,518	180	5.1
2004	3,914	143	3.7
2005	5,294	186	3.5
2006	5,475	182	3.0
2007	5,244	367	7.0
2008	6,004	1,230	20.0
January–June 2009	2,956	924	31.0

Source: Compiled by author with information from CNDH 2009.

years. It is worth noting, furthermore, that the bulk of the recommendations issued against SEDENA in the 2007 to 2009 period are related to cases that took place precisely in states and/or cities in which the military had been actively involved in the government's security strategy—particularly the state of Michoacán and the city of Ciudad Juárez, Chihuahua.

Even if previous under-reporting or current over-exposure could be at play, the increase in complaints and recommendations is impressive.

TABLE 5.2 Total number of CNDH recommendations and recommendations against SEDENA (2006–2009)

Year	Total number of recommendations	Recommendations against SEDENA	Percentage of total
2000	37	3	8.0
2001	27	1	3.7
2002	49	0	0.0
2003	52	3	5.8
2004	92	2	2.2
2005	51	3	5.9
2006	46	0	0.0
2007	70	3	4.0
2008	67	10	15.0
2009	78	25	32.0

Source: Compiled by author with information from CNDH website, online, available at: www.cndh.org.mx/recomen/recomen.asp.

Indeed, all these figures suggest strongly that the military has been perpe-
trating more violations of human rights after they were given a key role in
the fight against drug cartels in Mexico by the Calderón government. At
the very least, the figures do show that the military has perpetrated numerous violations of human rights during the first half of the Calderón
period.[26] The president's militarized security strategy has had a quite
negative impact on human rights in Mexico.

The dispute over military jurisdiction

Nobody would dare to deny that the Mexican state has the obligation to
tackle the huge security challenge presented by organized crime, in particular drug trafficking organizations. Human Rights Watch, for example,
has acknowledged that

> The need to improve public security is clear. Mexico is facing power-
> ful drug cartels that are engaged in violent turf battles, an influx of
> sophisticated weapons, a large number of kidnappings and executions
> in several Mexican states, and shocking forms of violence including
> beheadings.[27]

Most people would also agree that, given the levels of corruption and the
weak coercive capacities of police forces at all levels of government, military involvement in the struggle against drug cartels is necessary, at least
in the short term. The debate has therefore recently turned towards the
issue of military jurisdiction. In general terms, the argument is that if
military involvement is inevitable, then we should focus on eliminating an
important facilitator of the violation of human rights—the impunity generated by military jurisdiction.

Article 57 of the Code of Military Justice establishes that criminal cases
that involve military personnel as the presumed "active subjects" fall under
the jurisdiction of the military penal justice system. From the perspective
of international NGOs and intergovernmental organs specialized in human
rights, this is problematic, to say the least. In this respect, Human Rights
Watch has underlined that the cornerstone of Mexico's human rights shortcomings within the struggle against drug cartels is military jurisdiction
over cases of violation of human rights presumably perpetrated by the
armed forces. "An important reason such abuses continue is that they go
unpunished. And they go unpunished in significant part because most cases
end up being investigated and prosecuted by the military itself."[28] Human
Rights Watch has indeed provided strong evidence to show that SEDENA
has "routinely failed to hold those responsible for the abuses accountable."[29]
In other words:

The consequence of exercising military jurisdiction over these cases has been almost absolute impunity for transgressors. According to information provided to Human Rights Watch by the Interior Ministry, during the three years of the Calderón administration, military courts have only convicted one military officer for a human rights abuse: a soldier who was sentenced to nine months in prison for opening fire at a military checkpoint and killing a civilian.[30]

The Human Rights Council of the UN has also raised concerns about the issue of military jurisdiction in Mexico. In this respect, the HRC made the following recommendations:

- ensure that the primacy of the civil legal system prevail over military judicial process across the entire territory;
- extend the jurisdiction of civil courts in cases involving violations of human rights by the military;
- follow-up on the Recommendations of the Committee against Torture and the Office of the UN High Commissioner for Human Rights to empower civil courts to try offenses against human rights, in particular torture and cruel, inhuman or degrading treatment committed by military personnel, even when it is claimed that they were service-related;
- grant jurisdiction to its civil authorities/courts over the acts/human rights violations committed by members of armed forces when performing law enforcement functions;
- review the relevant legal provisions to ensure that all offences committed against human rights by military forces may also be submitted to civil courts.[31]

In a similar sense, in a recent ruling (*Radilla-Pacheco v. Mexico*), the Inter-American Court of Human Rights underlined that "in the face of situations that violate the human rights of civilians, under no circumstances can military jurisdiction operate." It mandated that "the [Mexican] state shall adopt, within a reasonable period, legislative reforms necessary to make article 57 of the Code of Military Justice compatible with the related international standards and the American Convention on Human Rights."[32]

The military jurisdiction issue was also introduced in the human rights agenda by US Congress, in the framework of the Merida Initiative. Congress conditioned the distribution of 15 percent of the Merida funds to a number of human rights measures to be taken by Mexico, including that "civilian judicial authorities investigate human rights violations allegedly perpetrated by federal police *and* military forces."[33]

In spite of the criticism by different international actors, the Mexican government staunchly defended military jurisdiction. Mexico readily accepted all the recommendations made in the evaluation by the HRC of the UN, except for specific recommendations, including those related to military jurisdiction mentioned above.[34] The government responded to the HRC that its National Human Rights Program purports to "promote reforms about the procurement and administration of military justice that comply with the international human rights commitments adopted by Mexican state." In addition, the government informed that the Code of Military justice was in the process of being "harmonized" with international standards with the objective of "making *even more transparent* the [penal] proceedings within military tribunals and enhancing the participation of the victims." The Mexican government also argued that, through the military penal justice system, "Mexico continues to investigate with detail the facts that presumably constitute violations of human rights perpetrated by members of the armed forces," underlining that the system operates "under the universal principles" that define due process.[35] In an equally apologetic way, though more confrontationally, President Calderón reacted to Human Rights Watch's 2009 report "Uniform Impunity." He argued that the military institutions efficiently prosecuted army abuses and challenged critics to give evidence of

> any case, just one case, where the proper authority has not acted in a correct way, that the competent authorities have not punished anyone who has abused their authority, whether they be police officers or they be soldiers or anyone else.[36]

In sum, the Calderón government rhetorically justified the current scheme of military jurisdiction and, in practice, did not give clear signs that suggested its meaningful reform.

Conclusion: security as trump

The protection of human rights did not figure within the government's preferences in the design of its security strategy. Human rights have been clearly affected during its implementation. From the outset of the Calderón administration, it was clear that upholding human rights was not an important concern in the design of the security approach. The Calderón administration considered explicitly that "fundamental rights" had to be restricted in order to "protect society" from organized crime. In the same sense, the very decision to militarize the struggle against drug cartels suggests that when the Calderón government defined its strategy to fight insecurity it did not give too much weight to human rights considerations. The consequent negative impact on human rights in practice should not be surprising. Since its conception and design, the Calderón approach to security—centered on greater coercion capacities and framed in terms of a military confrontation—was destined to produce negative consequences for human rights.

In spite of some sporadic and inconsistent human rights language in the PND, the strategy was not conceived and designed to explicitly attempt to strike a balance between security and human rights. In a similar sense, the Calderón government has not sought such a balance in the implementation of its security strategy. The growing evidence of violation of human rights, and the consequent criticism by national and international advocates of human rights, have been met with an inconsistent discourse about a commitment to human rights on the part of the government, in general, and the military, in particular.[37] The army and more recently the navy have even created human rights units within their bureaucratic structures, and as the heat of national and international criticism has increased, their human rights rhetoric has further intensified. But the core of the strategy has not been changed; Calderón's preferences regarding security vis-à-vis human rights remained constant. There were no signs that the government was willing to reconsider its position in respect to *arraigos*, and it remained unclear whether it would yield to international pressures regarding military jurisdiction. All along, security was understood in limited terms as the increase of the coercive capacities of the state. All along, it was a trump over human rights.

Different international NGOs and intergovernmental bodies specializing in human rights strongly criticized this trade-off between security and human rights in Mexico. The situation was also condemned by human rights organizations in Mexico, which made efforts to document the magnitude of the violations of human rights and strongly condemned both the *arraigo* practice and military jurisdiction.[38] But, this reaction by national and international actors did not influence more than the definition of the government's preferences in a significant way.

Comparative research about countries that experience transitions from authoritarian rule has found that processes of regime change bring consequences for institutional security arrangements. Previous schemes that efficiently controlled crime—or at least generated a general perception thereof—break down or are dismantled by the new post-authoritarian governments, before new arrangements are put in place. This, in turn, results in the growth of crime rates and/or a social perception of rising insecurity. So, either if post-authoritarian governments fail to deliver security or if a perception of failure emerges (due to more visibility and over-reporting, for example), security concerns gain salience within the public agenda. Real or perceived insecurity generates a collective feeling of anger and/or fear which in turn facilitates the emergence of demands for coercive measures—*la mano dura*, strong hand.

This is what some authors have called "the dynamics of public outrage"—angry and fearful societies demand coercive measures to control crime and are willing to ignore or tolerate violations of human rights. In addition to favoring simplistic solutions, angry and fearful societies often adopt desires for revenge. Animosity for rights defenders, polarization and demonization of presumed criminals also tend to emerge. In short, the mobilization of coercion by governments strongly resonates with social anger and fear.

The preferences of governments in post-authoritarian countries that experience social anger and fear in relation to security could hardly be constituted in isolation from, let alone opposition to, such "dynamics of public outrage." It could only be expected that any government that would attempt to pursue a human rights-oriented approach to security would face tremendous challenges. Therefore, "this is a challenge that is rarely met" in practice.[39] Quite to the contrary, there is plenty of evidence from case studies that shows that social anger and fear related to perceptions of insecurity are prone to political manipulation by governments and other actors. "Law and order" or "tough on crime" rhetoric is therefore not only almost inevitable but politically profitable for governments under social contexts characterized by some form of "the dynamics of public outrage."[40]

Evidence suggests that Mexico has been experiencing a process similar to "the dynamics of public outrage." According to figures collected by the Center of Research for Development (CIDAC), the homicide rate in Mexico during 2006, 2007, and 2008 was *lower* than ten years before (see Table 5.3 below). Even so, according to CIDAC, the homicide rate is very high for international standards—only 15 countries currently have higher homicide rates than Mexico.[41]

According to Mitofsky Consulting, 20 percent of Mexicans reported in 2007 and 2008 that they or someone in their family had been victims of crime in the three months previous to the poll; the figure rose to 24 percent in 2009.[42] The National Survey on Insecurity, conducted by the Citizens' Institute on Insecurity Studies (ICESI), reported that in 2007 and 2008 13.1 percent of the respondents to the survey or somebody in their household had been victims of crime.[43]

These figures do not show that crime and violence have increased in Mexico after the transition, but they do demonstrate that crime and

TABLE 5.3 Homicides for every 100,000 habitants in Mexico

Year	Number of homicides	Year	Number of homicides
1996	13.6	2006	9.3
1997	15.8	2007	11.1
1998	15.5	2008	10.6

Source: Centro de Investigación para el Desarrollo A.C. Índice de Incidencia Delictiva y Violencia 2009, August 2009, CIDAC (www.cidac.org).

violence are a very real problem in the country. This reality is reflected in and perhaps magnified by public perceptions. Survey data show that most Mexicans feel insecure. According again to Mitofsky Consulting, in 2005 and 2006 almost 25 percent of the population perceived insecurity to be Mexico's main problem; the economic crisis came second, perceived as the main problem by around 18 percent of the population. As of 2007, the economic crisis became of greater importance for more Mexicans, but insecurity continued to be the more pressing issue for 22.4 percent of the population in 2007, 19.9 percent in 2008, and 16.9 percent in 2009. It is noteworthy that during this period more people listed insecurity as their key concern than those who had unemployment as their number one problem.[44]

According to ICESI's National Survey on Insecurity, in 2004 54 percent of the population perceived that the state they lived in was insecure. The number rose to 59 percent in 2007, and to 65 percent in 2008. Similarly, in 2004, 40 percent of the population perceived that their municipality was insecure; in 2007 the figure reached 44 percent, and 49 percent in 2008. In 2007 40 percent of the respondents perceived that crime had increased in their municipality during the previous year; 48.6 percent thought so in 2007, and 58.5 percent in 2008.[45]

From a different perspective, Mitofsky Consulting reported that in 2007 65 percent of the people surveyed said to be "very afraid" of being the victim of armed robbery, and 62.9 percent were "very afraid" of being kidnapped.[46] In 2008, fear fell to 58 percent in respect of armed robbery, and to 51 percent in relation to kidnapping.[47]

In sum, during the last couple of years of the Fox presidency and the first three years of the Calderón government, crime and violence were a real problem in Mexico. Either because insecurity had in fact increased, or because crime and violence had just become more visible, a very large proportion of the population felt very insecure in Mexico.

This picture is complemented by an enormous lack of trust in police forces, as referred to in Chapter 4 of this book. According to ICESI's National Survey on Insecurity, only 15 percent of the population trusted local preventive police, and only 18 percent trusted local investigative police. Although federal investigative and preventive police had greater degrees of trust—31 percent and 29 percent respectively—the fact was that a vast majority of Mexicans did not trust law enforcement agencies, as also shown by surveys by Mitofsky Consulting and Colectivo de Análisis de la Seguridad con Democracia (Collective Security Analysis with Democracy, CASEDE).[48] The anger and fear that might be caused by real and perceived insecurity might also, then, be magnified by a feeling of vulnerability in the face of crime.

In this context of real and perceived insecurity, as shown in Table 5.4 below, a vast majority of Mexicans approved measures based on the mobilization of coercion.

TABLE 5.4 Approval of coercive measures in Mexico (2007 to 2009)

Type of measure	Percentage of people that "agree" or "partly agree"		
	2007	2008	2009
Increase prison time	94.8	95.1	96.6
Enrollment of military within police	73.3	80.3	79.6
Death penalty	74.8	76.7	76.6

Source: México Unido contra la Delincuencia and Consulta Mitofsky, Encuesta Mitofsky de Percepción Ciudadana sobre la Seguridad en México, August 2009 (online, available at: http://mucd.org.mx/secciones/informate/142).

Similarly, public opinion continued to approve one of the elements of Calderón's approach to security that has had more consequences for human rights—military involvement in the struggle against drug cartels. ICESI's 2009 National Survey on Insecurity reported that 86 percent of the population agreed with the implementation of the military-led operations against organized crime.[49]

In March 2009, the Survey on National Security, conducted by Analysis CASEDE, reported that 54 percent of the population agreed strongly and 31 percent were inclined to agree with the use of the military to fight drug trafficking. By August 2009 those figures had changed to 42 percent and 33 percent, respectively.[50] In the same line, Mitofsky Consulting reported that in 2007 84 percent of the population supported military involvement in the fight against organized crime. The figure dropped to 83 percent in 2008, and to 74 percent in 2010.[51]

In sum, even if these figures declined in the course of the past three to four years, a vast majority of the population continued to be in favor of the militarization of the government's security strategy.

In a context of real and perceived insecurity, the Mexican public has come to demand or at least approve an approach to security based on the strengthening and the mobilization of the coercive capacities of the state. Given the population's low trust in police forces, it is not surprising that one of the key features of this coercion-based approach to security rests on the militarization of security tasks.

No data is available to directly know if this means that people approve the (resulting) violation of human rights. We can infer, however, that given the support for coercive measures and military involvement in security activities, and since there are no explicit demands by a significant proportion of the population about the respect of human rights in the struggle against organized crime, many people in Mexico do approve (or at least tolerate) the violation of human rights for the sake of greater security.

Indeed, the preferences of the Calderón government have been shaped within a context that clearly and strongly favors security and neglects human rights. In such conditions a toxic conception of security has been, perhaps inevitably, constructed as a trump.

Notes

1 Laurie Freeman, *Troubling Partners: The Mexican Military and the War on Drugs* (Washington, DC: Latin America Working Group, 2002), 8–9.
2 Ibid., 11–12.
3 Online, available at: http://quetzalcoatl.presidencia.gob.mx/prensa/?contenido= 28316.
4 See James Cavallaro and Mohammad-Mahmoud Ould Mohamedou, "Public Enemy Number Two?: Rising Crime and Human Rights Advocacy in Transitional Societies," *Harvard Human Rights Journal* 18 (2005), 139–165; International Council on Human Rights Policy, "Crime, Public Order and Human Rights. Draft Report for Consultation" (Switzerland, 2003); James A. Piazza and James Igoe Walsh, "Transnational Terror and Human Rights," *International Studies Quarterly* 53: 1 (2009), 125–148; Clifford Shearing, "Crime, Rights and Order: Reflections on an Analytical Framework," Working Paper presented at the Review Seminar of the Crime, Public Order and Human Rights Project, Carnegie Council on Ethics and International Affairs (New York, October 2002); David Forsythe, "American Policy toward Enemy Detainees in the War on Terrorism," in David Forsythe, Patrice C. McMahon and Andrew Wedeman, eds., *American Foreign Policy in a Globalized World* (New York: Routledge, 2006), 193–214; Sonia Cardenas, *Conflict and Compliance. State Responses to International Human Rights Pressure* (Philadelphia, PA: University of Pennsylvania Press, 2007), 76–83.
5 Online, available at: http://pnd.presidencia.gob.mx/.
6 Ibid., section 1.4.
7 Ibid., sections 1.8 and 1.11.
8 See Human Rights Watch, *Lost in Transition. Bold Ambitions, Limited Results for Human Rights under Fox* (New York, 2006), 127–130.
9 Article 9.3 of the International Covenant on Civil and Political Rights states that:

> Anyone arrested or detained on a criminal charge shall be brought promptly before a judge or other officer authorized by law to exercise judicial power and shall be entitled to trial within a reasonable time or to release. It shall not be the general rule that persons awaiting trial shall be detained in custody, but release may be subject to guarantees to appear for trial, at any other stage of the judicial proceedings, and, should occasion arise, for execution of the judgment.

10 Secretaría de Gobernación, Subsecretaría de Enlace Legislativo, "Oficio con el que se remite la siguiente iniciativa: Proyecto de Decreto por el que se reforman diversos artículos de la Constitución Política de los Estados Unidos Mexicanos," 9 March 2007 (oficio no. SEL/300/1153/07).

11 Andrea Becerril, "No aprobará el PRD iniciativas del ejecutivo," *La Jornada* 8 May 2007; Andrea Becerril, "Algunas propuestas del Ejecutivo sobre justicia violan la Constitución: senador," *La Jornada* 1 July 2007; Claudia Guerrero, "Impulsa Senado juez de garantía," *Reforma* 18 June 2007; Comisión Permanente del Congreso de la Unión, Press Release no. 2007/234, 6 June 2007; Gabriel León, "Aprueba la Iglesia católica que el Ejército participe en la lucha contra el crimen," *La Jornada* 27 July 2007.

12 The bill was approved by the Chamber of Deputies on 26 February 2008, with 462 votes in favor, six against and two abstentions. On 6 March 2008 in the senate the bill obtained 75 votes in favor and 25 against. Online, available at: http://sitl.diputados.gob.mx/dictamenes_ld.php?tipot=&pert=0&init=55.

13 Diario Oficial de la Federación, "Decreto por el que se reforman y adicionan diversas disposiciones de la Constitución Política de los Estados Unidos Mexicanos," (18 June 2008), 6.

14 Ibid. (my emphasis).

15 José Miguel Vivanco, Letter to President Felipe Calderón, 5 March 2008 (online, available at: www.hrw.org/en/news/2008/03/05/letter-president-felipe-calder-n); José Miguel Vivanco, Letter to President Felipe Calderón, 1 June 2008 (online, available at: www.hrw.org/en/news/2008/06/01/letter-president-felipe-calder-n); Amnesty International, "Reforms to the Criminal Justice System: Steps Forward, Steps Backward," 7 February 2008 (AMR 41/004/2008) (online, available at: www.amnesty.org/es/library/asset/AMR41/004/2008/es/e435ea19-d5a9–11dc-8429-e9042f8eb6c4/amr410042008eng.html); Human Rights Council, Universal Periodic Review, Report of the Working Group on the Universal Periodic Review Mexico, 5 October 2009 (A/HRC/11/27), paragraph 94.

16 Laurie Freeman, *State of Siege: Drug-Related Violence and Corruption in Mexico. Unintended Consequences of the War on Drugs* (Washington, DC: Washington Office on Latin America, 2006), 20.

17 Laurie Freeman and Jorge Luis Sierra, "Mexico: The Militarization Trap," in Coletta A. Youngsters and Eileen Rosin, eds., *Drugs and Democracy in Latin America. The Impact of US Policy* (Boulder and London: Lynne Rienner, 2005), 277. See too Sigrid Arzt, "The Militarization of the Procuraduría General de la República: Risks for Mexican Democracy," in Wayne A. Cornelius and David A. Shirk, eds., *Reforming the Administration of Justice in Mexico* (Notre Dame, IN: University of Notre Dame Press, 2007), 153–174; David A. Shirk and Alejandra Ríos Cázares, "Introduction: Reforming the Administration of Justice in Mexico," in ibid., 21–22. Adam Isacson defines "militarization" as the "over involvement of the armed forces in aspects of governance other that external defense." Adam Isacson, "The US Military in the War on Drugs," in Youngers and Rosin, *Drugs and Democracy in Latin America*, 177.

18 See Maureen Meyer and Roger Atwood, *Reforming the Ranks: Drug Related Violence and the Need for Police Reform in Mexico* (Washington, DC: Washington Office on Latin America, 29 June 2007); and Stephanie Hanson, *Mexico's Drug War* (New York and Washington, DC: Council on Foreign Relations, 28 June 2007). According to a 2009 publication by Human Rights Watch, the government has deployed 40,000 officers (military and federal police) to fight organized crime throughout the country. Human Rights Watch, "Mexico: Calderón

Denies Military Impunity: Available Evidence Denies President's Statements," 10 August 2009. Online, available at: www.hrw.org/en/news/2009/08/10/mexico-calderon-denies-military-impunity.

19 Manuel Roig-Frainza, "Calderón's Offensive against Drug Cartels: Use of Mexican Military Increasingly Criticized," *Washington Post* 8 July 2007.

20 Diario Oficial de la Federación, "Decreto por el que se crea el Cuerpo Especial del Ejército y Fuerza Aérea denominado Cuerpo de Fuerzas de Apoyo Federal," 9 May 2007, 2–3.

21 Freeman and Sierra, 266–270, 287–291; Human Rights Watch, *Military Injustice: Mexico's Failure to Punish Army Abuses* (New York, 2001).

22 For some high-profile cases see Comisión Nacional de los Derechos Humanos, Recommendation 38/2007, 21 September 2007; 39/2007, 21 September 2007; 40/2007, 21 September 2007.

23 Comisión Nacional de los Derechos Humanos, "Informe de Actividades 1999–2009," Vol. 2. (Online, available at: www.cndh.org.mx/lacndh/informes/tomo_II.pdf).

24 Human Rights Committee, "Replies to the List of Issues (CCPR/C/MEX/Q/5) to be Taken Up in Connection with the Consideration of the Fifth Periodic Report of Mexico (CCPR/C/MEX/5)," 5 January 2010 (CCPR/C/MEX/Q/5/Add.1), paragraph 91.

25 The recommendations do not state explicitly and systematically whether or not the violations took place within the framework of the military's participation in the struggle against drug trafficking. The identification of the 38 recommendations was made by the author, on the basis of an analysis of the content of all the recommendation issued against SEDENA. The recommendations against SEDENA not included are related, for example, to cases of negligence or discrimination in the provision of health and medical services by the military.

26 The written press has also reported numerous cases of military abuses perpetrated in the framework of the struggle against drug cartels. The Miguel Agustín Pro Juárez Human Rights Center identified and analyzed 101 such cases. Centro de Derechos Humanos Miguel Agustín Pro Juárez, *¿Comandante supremo? La ausencia de control civil sobre las Fuerzas Armadas al inicio del sexenio de Felipe Calderón*, (Mexico City, 2009), 21–30.

27 Human Rights Watch, *Uniform Impunity: Mexico's Misuse of Military Justice to Prosecute Abuses in Counternarcotics and Public Security Operations* (New York, 2009) 1.

28 Ibid., 3.

29 José Miguel Vivanco, Letter to Dr. Plascencia Villanueva, Chairman of the Mexican National Commission of Human Rights, 28 January 2010 (online, available at: www.hrw.org/en/news/2010/01/28/letter-dr-plascencia-villanueva-chairman-mexican-national-commission-human-rights#_ftn2).

30 Ibid. See also Human Rights Watch, Letter in Response to Interior Minister of Mexico, Fernando Francisco Gomez-Mont Urueta, 20 November 2009 (online, available at: www.hrw.org/en/news/2009/11/20/letter-response-interior-minister-mexico-fernando-francisco-gomez-mont-urueta).

31 Human Rights Council, Universal Periodic Review: Report of the Working Group on the Universal Periodic Review. Mexico, 5 October 2009, paragraph 94.

32 Corte Interamericana de Derechos Humanos, "Caso Radilla Pacheco vs. Estados Unidos Mexicanos," ruling of 23 November 2009, paragraphs 272–277 and 342 (online, available at: www.corteidh.or.cr/casos.cfm).

33 House, Supplemental Appropriations Act, 110th Congress and 2(a), 2008, HR 2642. In July 2009, growing reports of human rights violations by the Mexican military in the fight against drug traffickers raised some expectations that the US Congress could withhold over US$100 million of the Merida Initiative funds. Steve Fainaru and William Booth, "Mexico Accused of Torture in Drug War: Army Using Brutality To Fight Trafficking, Rights Groups Say," *Washington Post* 9 July 2009; David Brook, "Retendrá EU apoyo antinarco; evalúa respeto a las garantías," *La Jornada* 14 July 2009; Alfredo Méndez, "Hay que ganar la batalla a criminales, pero con respeto a la ley: John Morton," *La Jornada*, 19 July 2009; Kenneth Roth, "Letter to Secretary of State Hillary Clinton," 13 July 2009 (online, available at: www.hrw.org/node/84417). The funds, however, were eventually released by Congress. NGOs have continued to insist that the human rights clauses of the Merida Initiative have to be taken seriously and funds retained. See José Miguel Vivanco, "Memorandum for Senator Patrick Leahy. State Department Report on Mexico and the Merida Initiative Human Rights Requirements," 10 September 2009 (online, available at: www.hrw.org/en/news/2009/09/10/memorandum-senator-patrick-leahy); Washington Office on Latin America and Centro de Derechos Humanos de las Mujeres, "Memo to US Congress: Complaints Filed by Women of Human Rights Violations Related to the Fight against Drug Trafficking in the State of Chihuahua have Grown," 27 January 2010 (online, available at: www.wola.org/ index.php?option=com_content&task=viewp&id=1046&Itemid=8).

34 Human Rights Council, paragraph 94.

35 Human Rights Council, "Informe del Grupo de Trabajo sobre el Examen Periódico Universal. México. Adición. Opiniones sobre las conclusiones y/o recomendaciones, compromisos voluntarios y respuestas presentadas por el estado examinado," (A/HRC/11/27/Add.1) paragraphs 12–14 (online, available at: www.upr-info.org/-Final-outcome-.html).

36 Human Rights Watch, "Mexico: Calderón denies Military Impunity".

37 See Alejandro Anaya Muñoz, "Security and Human Rights in Mexico: Do Pressure from Above and Argumentation have anything to do with it?," *Documento de Trabajo* no. 177 (División de Estudios Internacionales, CIDE, 2008).

38 See Centro de Derechos Humanos Miguel Agustín Pro Juárez, ibid.; Red Nacional de Organismos Civiles de Derechos Humanos, "Todos los Derechos Para Todas y Todos," September 2009 memorandum (on file with the autho~ Washington Office on Latin America and Centro de Derechos Hum~ las Mujeres, ibid.; No más abusos.org (an NGO that monitors m;'· against civilians). Monitoreo sistemático de abusos milit~ (online, available at: www.nomasabusos.org).

39 International Council on Human Rights Policy, Human Rights," 22. For an account of efforts tc approach to security in Brazil, and their limited su "Políticas de Seguridad Pública en Brasil: Tentativa Democratización Versus la Guerra contra el Crimen," *SU.*

de Derechos Humanos no. 5 (2006), 137–155; Luiz Eduardo Soares and Miriam Guindani, "La tragedia brasileña: la violencia estatal y social y las políticas de seguridad necesarias," *Nueva Sociedad* no. 208 (2007), 56–72.

40 See International Council on Human Rights Policy, "Crime, Public Order and Human Rights," 39–40.

41 Centro de Investigación para el Desarrollo (CIDAC), "Índice de Incide Delictiva y Violencia 2009," August 2009 (online, available at: www.cidac.org.)

42 México Unido contra la Delincuencia and Consulta Mitofsky, "Encuesta Mitofsky de Percepción Ciudadana sobre la Seguridad en México," August–October 2007; October 2008, and August 2009, all online, available at: http://mucd.org.mx/secciones/informate/142.

43 ICESI, "Sexta encuesta nacional sobre inseguridad: resultados principales, 2009" (online, available at: www.scribd.com/doc/19333447/Encuesta-Nacional-Sobre-Inseguridad-62009).

44 Consulta Mitofsky, "Monitor Mitofsky. Economía, Gobierno y Política, May 2010" (online, available at: http://72.52.156.225/Default.aspx).

45 ICESI, "Sexta encuesta nacional," 2009.

46 México Unido contra la Delincuencia and Consulta Mitofsky, "Encuesta Mitofsky de Percepción Ciudadana sobre la Seguridad en México," August–October 2007 (online, available at: http://mucd.org.mx/secciones/informate/142).

47 México Unido contra la Delincuencia and Consulta Mitofsky, "Encuesta Mitofsky de Percepción Ciudadana sobre la Seguridad en México," October 2008 (online, available at: http://mucd.org.mx/secciones/informate/142).

48 ICESI, "Sexta encuesta nacional," 2009; Consulta Mitofsky; Colectivo de Análisis de la Seguridad con Democracia (online, available at: www.seguridadcondemocracia.org/biblioteca/segnalagosto09.pdf).

49 ICESI, "Sexta encuesta nacional," 2009.

50 Colectivo de Análisis de la Seguridad con Democracia, "Encuesta de Seguridad Nacional," March 2009 (online, available at: www.seguridadcondemocracia.org/biblioteca/seguridadnacional3.pdf); "Encuesta de Seguridad Nacional," July–August 2009 (online, available at: www.seguridadcondemocracia.org/biblioteca/segnalagosto09.pdf).

51 México Unido contra la Delincuencia and Consulta Mitofsky, "Encuesta Mitofsky de Percepción Ciudadana sobre la Seguridad en México," January 2008 (online, available at: http://mucd.org.mx/secciones/informate/142); ibid., "Encuesta Nacional sobre la Percepción de Seguridad Ciudadana en México," April 2010 (online, available at: http://mucd.org.mx/assets/files/pdf/encuestas-mitofsky/2010/abril10.pdf).

PART III

...and Abroad

6

DRUG TRAFFICKING AND UNITED STATES–MEXICO RELATIONS

Causes of Conflict

Jorge Chabat

Since 1969, the governments of Mexico and the United States have experienced several instances of conflict related to drug trafficking. These conflicts did not, however, directly influence the volume of drugs produced for, or transported to, the United States from Mexico, as some might suspect.[1] In fact, these conflicts took place at moments when the trafficking of drugs to the United States was not particularly high.[2] What are the reasons? Why, in light of the specific efforts of the governments of both Mexico and the United States to reduce the likelihood of conflict resulting from drug trafficking during the decade of the 1990s—such as the High Level Contact group— did these conflicts continue to contaminate the bilateral agenda? From this perspective, what are the mechanisms these countries can use so that the drug trafficking conflicts do not worsen the image of Mexico in the United States and complicate the bilateral rapprochement in other areas of trade? How much do these conflicts owe to the political willpower of both governments? What is the relation with other variables, such as the production and transit of drugs, the war against drugs, corruption, internal legitimacy, or the electoral landscape in Mexico and the United States?

To answer these questions, this chapter analyzes the bilateral conflicts related to drugs, mainly since 1969, their causes, and how they are resolved or ended. This analysis will seek to identify the variables that provoke these conflicts, examine to what extent the conflicts were inevitable, as well as the impact they had on the bilateral relations.

The first Operation Intercept: learning to read the neighbor

During the first decades of the twentieth century, drug trafficking was not a problem of large magnitude in relations between Mexico and the United

States. While there were some occasional frictions—such as the demands of the United States for better cooperation that even caused the resignation of the Mexican secretary of the interior in 1941—it was certainly not a priority item on the bilateral agenda, nor did it contaminate the negotiation of other issues.[3] Nevertheless, this changed in the 1960s. Drug use in the United States grew significantly in this decade, and the Nixon government declared a full-frontal war on drug trafficking. This required greater collaboration in the fight against marijuana and heroin production in Mexico. However, the response of the Díaz Ordaz government was unsatisfactory, and the Nixon administration decided to implement a direct measure of pressure to force the Mexican government to engage more decisively in combat: 1969's Operation Intercept.

This operation consisted of exhaustive searches of vehicles entering the United States through the Mexican border, in order to find illicit drugs. While this effort was not effective in the detection of drugs, it did change the attitude of the Mexican government, which seemed not to have understood that combating drug trafficking was such a priority for the US government. So, after two weeks of Operation Intercept, Díaz Ordaz's government decided to cooperate fully with Washington and tried to change the negative image that may have existed in US public opinion by announcing Operation Cooperation to replace Operation Intercept. As a result of this new policy, in the following years the production of heroin and marijuana in Mexico was significantly reduced, and Mexico stopped being the main provider of both drugs for the US market.

While Operation Intercept was a sign of cold diplomatic conduct, in the end it did not cause a major conflict. It even led to the implementation of Operation Condor in the late 1970s, one of the few successful examples of a country being able to effectively reduce drug production in its territory through police and military combat. Certainly though, the drugs that no longer entered the United States through Mexico were quickly replaced by drugs from Asia and Colombia. In the final analysis, the conflict had been caused by miscommunication between the governments of Mexico and the United States. While this would be avoided in the future, the 1980s were to show that conflict between the two countries had other sources too.

The assassination of Enrique Camarena: corruption as an explanation for the conflict

As a result of the financial crisis of 1982, the US government started to doubt one of the supposed pillars of the "special relationship" with Mexico that had been constructed during the 1950s: the capacity of the Mexican government to maintain stability within its own territory. These doubts increased in the following years, resulting from the fact that each Mexican election generated more post-electoral conflicts. Additionally, since the early 1980s, Operation Condor's battle against drug trafficking lost its momentum and effectiveness, and Mexico began again to be an important supplier of marijuana and heroin for the American market. Mexico also became a transit country for the cocaine from South America that began arriving into the United States.[4] It is in this context that the main drug trafficking conflict in the history of the bilateral relation in recent times occurred: the abduction and murder of an agent of the US Drug Enforcement Administration (DEA), assigned to Guadalajara, Enrique Camarena.

Camarena was abducted when leaving the US Consulate in Guadalajara in February 1985. Two weeks after this event, and without finding the body of the DEA agent, the US government decided to implement the so-called Second Operation Intercept, which once again sought to detect illegal drugs in vehicles entering US territory from Mexico. This measure was obviously a form of pressure from Washington on the Mexican government to expedite investigations into the kidnapping of the US agent. A couple of months after his disappearance, Camarena's body was found in the state of Michoacán, adjoining the state of Jalisco where the narcotics agent had been kidnapped, murdered and initially buried.

The Camarena "affair" clearly reflected the role of Mexican corruption as a generator of the conflict between both countries. Jack Lawn, who was Director of the DEA when Camarena was murdered, when talking about this incident in 1992 declared that:

> [The] confidence that exists in the international police community, that permits us to operate in other countries and to collaborate with our counterparts in every place of the world, did not function in the Camarena case, due to the corruption of some members of the police institutions that were partly responsible for his abduction and his murder.[5]

The murder of Camarena did indeed lead to a period of prolonged frictions that lasted until 1986. In April of that year, the US Embassy decided unilaterally to suspend the issuing of visas to Mexican citizens until the month of August.[6] The pretext used by the US government was the possibility that a terrorist attack by Libya would occur, but very probably this decision was a reflection of the deterioration of the bilateral relationship and a way to pressure to Mexico to provide a greater contribution to the fight against drug trafficking and greater alignment to the politics of Washington. The issue of drug trafficking continued to generate conflict between the two countries. It was the theme of the accusations that some officers made to the Reagan administration against the Mexican government in the so-called Helms hearings in May 1986. In these hearings, sponsored by the Leader of the Subcommittee of Foreign Affairs of the

Senate, the Republican Senator of North Carolina, Jesse Helms, the Mexican government was criticized for the lack of transparent elections, for corruption and for the involvement of Mexican authorities in drug trafficking. The government of De La Madrid responded to the Helms hearings with a demonstration by government bureaucrats on the main square of Mexico City, in defense of "sovereignty."

The Camarena affair also led to the development of unilateral actions by the DEA. It backed the 1986 kidnapping of a Mexican citizen, René Verdugo Urquídez, who had allegedly participated in the killing of the DEA agent.[7] The government of Miguel De la Madrid did not want to escalate the conflict, and decided not to publicize the kidnap. However, the DEA orchestrated another kidnapping in 1990, also a repercussion of the murder of Camarena. On 2 April of that year, the DEA hired Mexican police to kidnap the Jaliscan-based doctor, Humberto Alvarez Machain, who had also allegedly participated in the interrogation of Camarena.[8] This time, the government of Salinas de Gortari did protest at the kidnapping, but otherwise avoided the issue as this might have harmed the negotiation of the North American Free Trade Agreement (NAFTA) with the United States and Canada.

The abduction of Alvarez Machain resulted in the United States Supreme Court authorizing the kidnapping of those who attack US federal officials abroad.[9] This in turn led to a rather symbolic rejection of anti-drug aid from Washington by the government of Salinas for that year. Additionally, the Mexican government pressed the United States to sign a bilateral agreement prohibiting cross-border abductions, which was signed but not ratified by Washington.[10] In the end, Alvarez Machain was released in 1992 for lack of evidence against him. The relationship between the two governments improved substantially in subsequent years, largely through the interest of both countries in protecting NAFTA. According to a memorandum by the US Department of Defense, there was a direct relationship between the adoption of NAFTA and the efforts to combat drugs in the Mexican government: "As such, NAFTA's pending approval probably will continue somewhat to influence President Salinas's policy decisions on drug issues vis-à-vis the United States."[11]

It is worth mentioning that largely because of the Camarena case the US government decided in 1986 to establish the so-called certification process, eventually suspended in 2002 because of the constant friction it generated with Mexico and several other Latin American countries. Nevertheless, despite the annual threat of decertification, the process was useful: it improved diplomatic relations with Mexico by providing it with arguments supportive of its goodwill in the fight against drug trafficking. This was possible because the criteria used for certification were based more on the efforts by countries producing or transiting drugs than on the results.

These criteria were:

- a budget for fighting drug trafficking;
- seizure of shipments and eradication of crops;
- police and military casualties in the war on drugs;
- the number of arrests;
- institutional and legal reforms to strengthen institutions responsible for combating drug trafficking;
- signing of agreements;
- acceptance of US cooperation, as well as the presence of DEA agents in Mexico.

The use of these indicators allowed for the dismantling of the case of those in the United States who for one reason or another were interested in criticizing the Mexican government. Unlike what happened in countries like Colombia, which were decertified on several occasions, the interdependent relationship with Mexico prevented the use of sanctions—even in years in which there was sufficient grounds to do so, as in 1997 when the Mexican "drug tsar" was arrested for having ties to drug trafficking.

As a result of the drug certification process, each year the Salinas government aimed to arrest a notorious drug lord prior to the announcement of the certification result—on 28 February—in order to facilitate the White House's approval of Mexico. Ernesto Zedillo's government continued with a strategy that only came undone in early 1997 when that year's intended catch, the leader of the Juárez cartel, Amado Carrillo, fled 20 minutes before federal forces arrived at his sister's wedding.

As part of the logic of closer collaboration between the two countries, in 1990 the Northern Border Response Force was established—also known as Operation Falcon—which increased aerial surveillance to prevent the flow of drugs from Central and South America through Mexican territory.

The Gutiérrez Rebollo scandal and the issue of narco-governors

In March 1996, the governments of Mexico and the United States agreed to create the High Level Contact Group, composed of officials from both countries, in order to prevent diplomatic crises resulting from the issue of drug trafficking. This mechanism functioned until the start of the Fox government and facilitated cooperation on anti-drug efforts between the two countries. However, despite the efforts of both governments to isolate the conflict, in 1997 bilateral relations deteriorated again as a result of the arrest of the Commissioner of the National Institute to Combat Drugs, General Gutiérrez Rebollo. Accused of having ties to Amado Carrillo, Gutiérrez Rebollo was arrested on 18 February—timing that could not have been worse. This scandal, while showing a significant degree of collaboration between the two governments (in some versions, the information on Gutiérrez Rebollo was provided by Washington), also reintroduced US distrust of Mexican authorities and the traditional concerns about corruption in Mexico. At the same time it generated great concern in the White House, as Gutiérrez Rebollo had sensitive information that he presumably would have been providing to Amado Carrillo.

A few days after the scandal, on 23 February 1997, the *New York Times* published an article accusing the Institutional Revolutionary Party (PRI) governors of Sonora and Morelos, Manlio Fabio Beltrones and Jorge Carrillo Olea, of involvement in drug trafficking, on the basis of intelligence reports.[12] This article had a profound impact on Mexican public opinion and of course complicated the bilateral relationship. Although there were no major legal consequences, Carrillo Olea resigned his governorship after announcing the involvement of his police chiefs in a web of kidnapping in Morelos. In the end, the governments of Mexico and the United States succeeded in handling the crisis and the accusations were toned down. Nevertheless, this scandal showed that the absence of conflict around drugs not only depended on the goodwill of both governments or on levels of corruption in Mexico, but also on external actors able to generate friction.

In this context, in 1997, the Zedillo government intensified what it had started the year before: the extraditions of Mexican citizens accused of drug trafficking.[13] The extraditions increased steadily from that point on, accelerating following the 2001 ruling of the Mexican Supreme Court which declared that they were not unconstitutional. This helped to improve the image of Mexico in official circles in Washington. At the same time, the Mexican government began training Mexican police with the help of experts from the FBI and the DEA; the Department of Defense participated in the training of Mexican military in combating drug trafficking.[14] President Zedillo also agreed for US planes and ships to have access to Mexican ports and airports.[15] According to journalists, his government tolerated the carrying of weapons in Mexico by DEA agents, despite the fact that Mexican law forbids it.

Operation Casablanca: unilateralism and distrust

The mistrust of the Mexican authorities can be seen in Operation Casablanca of May 1998, which was developed by the DEA and the Treasury Department to uncover banks engaged in money laundering. The operation was initiated in 1995 by these agencies without the knowledge of the Mexican government.[16] In 1998, the operation was made public, and this sparked angry protests from the Mexican government which even threatened to seek the extradition of the DEA agents participating in it. However, over the months, Mexican anger dissipated and both governments dealt with this conflict through the High Level Contact Group.

In the end, 150 people were arrested, US$100 million were seized, and over 100 Mexican bank employees were indicted in Mexico but not extradited. In this case, it is clear that the conflict was caused by the unilateral action of two US agencies, the DEA and the Treasury Department, which had decided to carry out this operation without consulting the Mexican side, probably due to their mistrust of the Mexican authorities.

Violence on the United States-Mexico border and the Merida Initiative

Since assuming the presidency of Mexico, Vicente Fox focused his anti-drug strategy on the capture of the kingpins of the major drug trafficking cartels. Thus, Fox arrested the leader of the Gulf Cartel, Osiel Cárdenas, the leader of the Tijuana cartel, Benjamin Arellano Félix, and the leader of the Colima cartel, Adan Amezcua, as well as some other important leaders, such as "June" of the Gulf Cartel. As expected, these arrests pleased the US government and the drug issue ceased to be as conflictual as in previous decades. Indeed, the two governments went on to consider means of collaboration that would have been unthinkable a few years before, such as the establishment of an FBI school in Mexico to train Mexican police.[17] This atmosphere contributed to the suspension of the drug certification process in 2002.[18] The relationship between the two countries on the issue of drug trafficking was so good in those years that the American drug tsar, John P. Walters, congratulated the Mexican government for its efforts in combating drugs, and suggested in mid-2002 that Mexico was an "example" and that the United States should copy the Mexican strategy.[19]

However, despite the cordial atmosphere between the two countries during the early years of the Fox government, Mexico's own strategy for fighting drugs had an unintended consequence: the disruption of the existing balance between drug cartels and the start of a war between the Gulf Cartel and the Sinaloa cartel, which dramatically increased the execution-style killings between the warring cartels. This increase in violence was concentrated initially in a city on the border between Mexico and the United States, a key crossing point for trade in illegal drugs: Nuevo Laredo, Tamaulipas. The violence in the city soon began to worry the US government to such a degree that on 26 January 2005, the US ambassador to Mexico, Tony Garza, sent a letter of protest to the foreign secretary of Mexico, Luis Ernesto Derbez, in which he complained that: "the growing struggle between elements of the drug cartels has resulted in dramatic increases in murders and kidnappings."[20] According to Garza, the high level of violence "has resulted in increased risks for thousands of US citizens who visit or will pass through the border region every day. A greater number of murdered and kidnapped Americans in recent months confirm this." At the same time though Garza sought to minimize the impact on bilateral relations and focused his criticism on the local Mexican authorities:

> I am concerned that the inability of local law enforcement to cope with the battle between drug crime, kidnappings and violence in general have a negative effect on trade, tourism and trade between our borders, which are vital to the prosperity of the region.

Finally, the US ambassador congratulated President Fox for his statements of concern about the phenomenon and "hoped that this commitment will make a difference at state and local level."

Garza's protest caused some uneasiness with the Mexican government and even led to some nationalist statements reminiscent of past decades. For example, the secretary of the interior, Santiago Creel, said that "we cannot accept external meddling in situations which concern only Mexicans ... We know our assets and our problems; we do not need anyone from outside to lecture us."[21] However, despite the tough language of the Mexican government, just days later Garza and Derbez were meeting to iron out differences.[22] The result was a joint communiqué that symbolically solved the conflict.

Faced with an increase in violence on the northern border, the Fox administration decided to implement a combined police–military operation called "México Seguro." This was four days after the newly appointed Director of Police of Nuevo Laredo, Alejandro Domínguez Coello, was assassinated seven hours into the job. In the initial phase of the program, the Federal Preventive Police (PFP) and the army took control of eight towns affected by the violence resulting from drug trafficking, in the states of Tamaulipas, Sinaloa and Baja California. Despite this program, the wave of violence continued and there were incidents in other cities in the states of Michoacán and Guerrero. Given the limited benefits of the program, two months later the president acknowledged that he had failed to attain the expected results and ordered in reinforcements. The wave of violence in Nuevo Laredo and other cities continued to generate friction with the United States in the second half of 2005 and in 2006. There are even rumors of a raid on US territory by Mexican drug traffickers dressed as soldiers in early 2006. "México Seguro" was renamed "Northern Frontier Project" on 15 March 2006, but the violence generated by drug trafficking continued to escalate until mid-2007. Then it began a decline, following police and military operations by President Calderón's new government, and probably as a result of an agreement between drug trafficking gangs to reduce the violence.

In this context of increased violence in Mexico, according to journalism sources and sources within the US government, discussions of a regional security initiative began in May 2007, bringing together the United States,

Mexico and Central America for the purpose of addressing the threat of organized crime. According to a newspaper in Texas, Mexico and the United States were negotiating a plan to substantially increase aid to fight drug trafficking. This "regional security initiative" would also include Central America and proposed to fight other forms of organized crime, such as the "*maras*."[23] Some officials called the initiative Plan Mexico, in obvious reference to Plan Colombia developed by the United States and Colombia in the early years of the twenty-first century. Subsequently, the chargé d'affaires of the US government in Honduras, James Williard, said that in two months the governments of Mexico, Guatemala, Honduras and the United States would have a regional security plan to combat trafficking in drugs, humans and weapons, as well as the "*maras*" in Central America. According to Williard, President Bush proposed this plan to President Calderón and President of Guatemala Bergua on his tour of the region in March that year.[24] In this context, on the eve of the inter-parliamentary meeting between the United States and Mexico in Austin, Texas, in June 2007, US Congressman Silvestre Reyes said that the Mexican government had requested US assistance on a scale similar to Plan Colombia to combat organized crime.[25] As was to be expected, this announcement brought strong criticism from the Mexican political opposition of the Calderón government. Reyes then said the agreement being negotiated was not comparable to Plan Colombia, as it did not include the participation of US troops.[26]

After nearly a year of negotiations, agreement on regional security was finally reached in June 2008 and was named the Merida Initiative, after the city of Mérida where Presidents Bush and Calderón initially negotiated the agreement, and to avoid comparison with Plan Colombia. The Merida Initiative included US$1.4 billion in equipment to Mexico for a period of three years, and an additional amount for Central America. One of the greatest obstacles to the adoption of this initiative was the mistrust expressed by the US Senate about possible human rights abuses in Mexico, and the insistence of that legislative body in setting up monitoring mechanisms on this issue. Even so, the approval seemed to indicate that the traditional distrust of Mexico based on past corruption cases had finally been overcome and that a new stage of unreserved collaboration in combating drug trafficking had been entered.

Corruption cases: return to mistrust?

The approval of the Merida Initiative created a cordial atmosphere in the bilateral relationship. However, this was suddenly clouded by the announcement, in October 2008, that the attorney general for Mexico had discovered that a network of senior officials from the assistant attorney general's office for the Specialized Investigation of Organized Crime (SIEDO) had been bought by the cartel of the Beltrán Leyva brothers.[27] This investigation, called Operation Cleanup, soon involved the attorney for SIEDO, Noé Ramírez Mandujano, arrested in November 2008 on suspicion of receiving bribes from the Beltrán Leyva brothers' cartel.[28] Operation Cleanup also implicated officials from the Ministry of Public Security, including the commissioner of the PFP, Victor Gerardo Garay Cadena. What was striking in these corruption scandals was that, unlike what happened in the case of Camarena and Gutiérrez Rebollo, the bilateral relationship did not appear to be significantly affected. In fact, both President Bush and President-elect Barack Obama showed their support for the fight against drug trafficking by the Calderón government.[29]

Despite this formal support, since 2008 some sectors of the US government and the media began to show their concern about violence in Mexico and the advance of organized crime, to the degree of talking about a possible "failed state," sometimes comparing the country to Afghanistan.[30] These criticisms certainly reflected a real concern about the situation in Mexico. However, this atmosphere of alarm did not impact the policies of the White House towards the Calderón government during the Obama administration.

Finally, though, the conflicts of recent decades between Mexico and the United States have shown that US pressure has not helped much to solve the problems of Mexico. From this perspective, it is feasible to expect that, despite the corruption scandals that sometimes generate the temptation to return to the era of distrust toward Mexico, the United States will decide to increase cooperation with Mexico, especially in what appears to be the Achilles heel of the Mexican anti-drug fight: the corruption generated by drug trafficking.

The causes of the conflict

By recounting the moments of tension between Mexico and the United States over the past four decades around the issue of drug trafficking, we have found the following the causes:

- communication problems between the two governments (Operation Intercept I);
- corruption of Mexican police forces (the murder of Camarena, the Gutiérrez Rebollo case);
- the distrust that exists in some sectors of the US government toward the Mexican authorities, driven largely by cases in which Mexican corruption was evident (Operation Casablanca, kidnappings of Alvarez Machain and Verdugo Urquídez);
- the unilateral action of US government agencies, fuelled by mistrust of the Mexican government (Operation Casablanca, the kidnappings of Alvarez Machain and Verdugo Urquídez);

- the impact of non-governmental actors, such as the press (the narco-governors scandal);
- the unintended consequences of Mexican anti-drug policies (violence at the border).

Curiously, the historical causes of conflict resulting from drugs have nothing to do with the flow of drugs into the United States, but rather with the impaired operation of bureaucracies of both countries, whether it is their performance in meeting their daily assigned duties or in communication with their counterparts across the border.

Additionally, some of the disputes around drugs are related to the overall climate of bilateral relations and its deterioration for other reasons: post-electoral conflict, financial crisis, Mexican foreign policy and illegal migration flows from Mexico to the United States, and the pressure from US public opinion on those issues. But that is only part of the explanation. Certainly, the conflicts of the 1980s, especially in the aftermath of friction over the Camarena case, actually can be seen in that context. However, in times where the bilateral relationship was generally very good, as in the 1990s, there were strong conflicts over drug trafficking, even though certification was granted to Mexico automatically each year. This suggests that the capacity of the drug trade to generate conflict in the bilateral relationship is more related to the phenomenon itself and the problems of bureaucracies in managing it and is, therefore, structural rather than cyclical. Therefore, conflicts are only somewhat dependent on the goodwill of governments and much more dependent on the dealings of governments with drug trafficking. This is confirmed when we analyze the effectiveness of the mechanisms deployed by the two governments to deal with drug conflict.

The responses to conflict: much will, few results

The responses implemented by both the United States and Mexico to reduce friction around drugs may be classified as follows:

- defensive nationalistic statements and symbolic actions by the Mexican government (the Camarena case, the abduction of Alvarez Machain, Operation Casablanca, violence at the border);
- the creation of bureaucratic mechanisms to improve communication between the two governments in order to prevent crises (High Level Contact Group);
- implementation of spectacular measures by Mexico to improve the image of the Mexican authorities before US public opinion (the arrest of drug lords, extraditions, mass dismissals of corrupt policemen, the abolition of the National Institute to Combat Drugs);

- the development of collaborative anti-drug programs by both countries (Operation Falcon, Mexican police training by the FBI, the Merida Initiative);
- the cover-up of information about friction between the two countries involved in drug smuggling (the abduction of Verdugo Urquídez);
- silence and exclusion of information generated by the conflict (the narco-governors case).

Generally speaking, we can identify conflicts that were caused by the actions of governments, or by responses to these actions, or by non-governmental actors. In the latter case, the governments have tried to coordinate their responses and fundamentally, have tried to neutralize the conflict in the eyes of public opinion, though without necessarily resolving the underlying causes. In the case of conflict caused by one of the two governments, the responses have tried to address the roots of the problem, but have not always been very effective. In the case of the first Operation Intercept, the response of the Mexican government had a strong impact on the root of the conflict and secured an outcome that went beyond rhetoric. However, in the Camarena case, the results were mixed. While eventually some of the alleged perpetrators of the crime were arrested, such as the drug trafficker Rafael Caro Quintero, the investigation did not include everyone involved, which in turn led to unilateral actions by the DEA. Certainly, as a result of this conflict, the Salinas government initiated some internal reforms, such as the creation of the National Institute to Combat Drugs; captured some drug kingpins such as Miguel Angel Félix Gallardo; and sought to avoid the escalation of conflicts, such as over the abduction of Alvarez Machain. With respect to Operation Casablanca, there was not really any particular way to defuse that conflict: both governments simply let it cool down, and the Mexican government held noisy protests in order to save face with what was clearly a sign of mistrust and enmity by the DEA and the Treasury Department.

In the case of violence on the border since 2005, the Fox administration did not do much. As mentioned, the response to the increase in drug executions was the development of a police–military operation called México Seguro. However, the levels of violence continued to rise. Interestingly, the US government decided not to publicly protest at the violence, even when the levels of drug executions began reaching historic levels. This may be due to the Calderón government's decision to make the US government co-responsible for the problem by asking for aid to fight drug trafficking and other threats, leading to the Merida Initiative, and the interest of Washington in supporting the new Mexican government that took office while having problems of legitimacy.

The offensive against drugs, initiated by the Calderón government in early 2008, probably facilitated the passing of the Merida Initiative, although it also generated a further increase in the levels of violence after the curve of drug executions had begun to go down in the second half of 2007. Unlike the Fox government, Calderón's strategy against drugs has damaged the operational structure of the cartels, which has accelerated their fragmentation and therefore has also generated a dramatic increase in drug-related violence from 2008 on. The Calderón government hoped that this strategy would weaken the drug cartels in the medium term, as happened in Colombia after the dismantling of the Medellín and Cali cartels in the mid-1990s. This reduced the levels of conflict with the United States, but not the flow of illegal drugs into the country. In fact, Washington's readiness to grant aid of US$1.4 billion to Mexico in the Merida Initiative suggested that confidence in Mexico had increased, despite the corruption scandals of senior police chiefs, including the drug tsar, and despite loud criticism on the part of some US government offices and media of the Mexican government. However, the Achilles heel of this strategy is corruption, which if not successfully controlled by the Calderón government might result in the re-emerging of the friction of the 1980s and 1990s.[31]

Conclusion

As we have seen, the issue of drug trafficking has led to many conflicts between Mexico and the United States since the late 1960s. These conflicts have been directly related to the collateral damage of the fight against drug trafficking, such as corruption and violence, and not with the volumes of drugs going from Mexico to the United States. Although during the last two decades governments have sought to create a mechanism to cushion the effects of these conflicts and eventually to prevent them, they have not been entirely successful. "Solutions" that were implemented to resolve the friction between the two countries have served primarily to generate the image that the problems have disappeared, and to show a willingness to cooperate. However, recounting the confrontation between Mexico and the United States on drug trafficking during the last decades shows that international cooperation is not enough. Nor are institutional reforms or spectacular operations against drug trafficking sufficient. Everything indicates that the key to reducing conflict between Mexico and the United States on the issue of drug trafficking is the ability of the Mexican government to curb corruption in the forces fighting the phenomenon.

Most of the confrontations in recent years have been related in one way or another with this problem and the spiral of distrust it has generated. Certainly, reducing Mexican corruption does not eliminate the possibility of conflict—the drug violence can also lead to conflict—but it is clear that high levels of corruption in the Mexican anti-drug forces opened the door for those in the United States looking to criticize the Mexican government for different reasons, and even alienated certain sectors in the United States, both inside

TABLE 6.1 The United States and Mexico: conflicts, causes and responses related to drug trafficking (1969–2008)

Conflicts	Causes	Responses
Operation Intercept (1969)	• Bad communication and lack of effectiveness on the part of Mexico in the fight against drug trafficking	• Operation Cooperation • Operation Condor
Assassination of DEA agent Enrique Camarena (1985)	• Corruption in the Mexican government: complicity with drug traffickers	• Pressure by the United States: Operation Intercept II, Helms Hearings, US visa suspensions, kidnapping of Verdugo Urquidez and Alvarez Machain, creation of certification process • Mexican negotiation, calls for sovereignty, arrest of Rafael Caro Quintero • Demonstrations backed by the Mexican government • US–Mexican agreement to suspend kidnappings • Operation Falcon (Northern Border Response Force) (1990) • Creation of the National Institute to Combat Drugs by the de Salinas de Gortari government (1993) • Reforms of the penal and fiscal law in Mexico (1993) • Creation of the High Level Contact Group (1996) • Federal Law against Organized Crime in Mexico (1996) • Creation of the Special Unit against Organized (UEDO) (1996)

Gutiérrez Rebollo Scandal (1997) Narco-governors case (1997)	• Corruption of the Mexican government: the monitoring mechanisms did not work • Role of the media • Mexican corruption	• Arrest of General Gutiérrez Rebollo • Reorganization of DEA agency in Mexico • Extraditions of Mexican drug traffickers to the United States • Authorization for US boats and planes to use Mexican installations • Training of Mexican police by the FBI • Rhetoric-based response by Mexico • Refusal by Mexico to hand over Mexican laundered currency
Operation Casablanca (1998)	• Lack of confidence in Mexican authorities • Corruption of Mexican bankers.	• Protests of the United States for the levels of violence • Negotiation of the Merida Initiative. • "Operation Cleanup" by the Mexican government
Violence in Mexico and on the Mexican–US border (2005–2008) Corruption in the office of the attorney general for Mexico and the Ministry of Public Security (2008)	• Strategy of Fox to arrest drug leaders • Frontal war against drugs by the Calderon government • Corruption of Mexican police forces	• Open support of the US government for the Mexican fight against drugs • Warnings about a Mexican "failed state" in certain sectors of US government and public opinion

TABLE 6.2 Drug production in Mexico (metric tons of marijuana, opium and heroin produced annually and captured metric tons of cocaine per year[1])

Year	Marijuana	Estimated heroin	Estimated opium	Captured cocaine
2006	15,500	13	110	21
2005	10,100	8	71	30
2004	10,440	9	73	27
2003	13,500	12	101	21
2002	7,900	5	58	12
2001	7,400	7	71	30
2000	7,000	2	21	18
1999	6,700	4	43	33
1998	8,300	6	60	22
1997	8,600	5	46	34
1996	11,700	–	54	23.6
1995	12,400	–	53	22.2
1994	5,908	–	60	22.1
1993	6,283	–	49	46.2
1992	7,795	–	40	38.8
1991	7,775	–	41	50.3
1990	19,700	–	62	48.5
1989	30,200	–	66	38.1
1988	–	–	67	15.4

Source: Department of State, *International Narcotics Control Strategy Report*, online, available at: www.state.gov/p/inl/rls/nrcrpt/2008.

and outside government. Of course, there will always be voices in the United States with an interest in putting pressure on Mexico and in intervening in national politics, but the existence of high levels of corruption is an open invitation to these pressures. The future of the relationship between Mexico and the United States is directly linked to the ability of Mexican institutions to build capacity and strong accountability in security and other areas. When that happens, there will be little room for opportunistic pressures from some sectors of society and the US government—and for nationalist rhetoric from Mexico. If Mexico succeeds in effectively combating corruption, the conflict over the drug trade that has so far been unavoidable, will cease to be.

Notes

1 Richard Craig argues the following:

> The tone of the relationship has depended on the participation of Mexico in the illicit drug market of the United States, especially with respect to heroin and cocaine. The larger the participation of Mexico, the greater the

pressure from Washington. The larger the pressure, the higher the level of political confrontation between Mexico and United States on the issue of drugs in particular, and in bilateral relations in general. Conversely, when the indicators of participation in the market are good, so are the relations to a greater or lesser extent.

(Richard Craig, "Operación intercepción," *Foro Internacional* 22:2 (1981)).

2   Jorge Chabat, "Drug Trafficking in US–Mexican relations: What you See is what you Get," in Bruce M. Bagley and William O. Walker III,, eds., *Drug Trafficking in the Americas* (New Brunswick: Transaction Publishers/North–South Center, 1994).

3   William O. Walker III, *Drug Control in the Americas* (Albuquerque: University of New Mexico Press, 1989), 79–80.

4   On the context of the deterioration of bilateral relations in the 1980s, see Wayne Cornelius, "México/EU: las fuentes del pleito," *Nexos* no. 118 (October 1987), 25–35.

5   Dolia Estévez, "El Narcotráfico, amenaza a la Seguridad Nacional Mexicana," *El Financiero* 25 February 1992.

6   J. González et al., "El impacto de las Audiencias Helms en la relación bilateral," *Carta de Política Exterior Mexicana*, CIDE, 6: 2 (April–June 1986), 8.

7   Elaine Shannon, *Desperados* (New York: Penguin Books, 1989), 347–357.

8   On the abduction of Alvarez Machain, see Jorge Chabat, "Mexico's Foreign Policy in 1990: Electoral Sovereignty and Integration with the United States," *Journal of Interamerican Studies and World Affairs* 33: 4 (Winter 1991), 1–25; Ellen L. Lutz, "State-Sponsored Abductions: the Human Rights Ramifications of Alvarez Machain," *World Policy Journal* 9: 4 (Autumn–Winter 1992), 687–703. For the Mexican government's perspective on the case, see Secretaría de Relaciones Exteriores, *Límites de la Jurisdicción Nacional. Documentos y Resoluciones Judiciales del caso Alvarez Machain*, 1992.

9   See "Excerpts From Supreme Court's Decision on the Kidnapping of Foreigners," *New York Times* 16 June 1992.

10   Maria Celia Toro, "La gobernanza internacional: una propuesta para gestionar la globalización," September 2003. Online, available at: www.ceri-sciencespo.com/archive/sept03/artmct.pdf.

11   Defense Intelligence Agency, "Untitled Memorandum," 1 December 1992, (photocopy). According to Jorge G. Castañeda, it is possible that from the mid-1990s, drug traffickers concluded that because of pressure from the United States the Salinas government decided to break with the implicit agreement with the drug barons. See Jorge G. Castañeda, *Sorpresas te da la vida* (Mexico: Aguilar, 1994), 157–173.

12   Sam Dillon and Craig Pipes, "Drug Ties Taint 2 Mexican Governors," *New York Times* 23 February 1997.

13   México, Procuraduría General de la República, "La lucha de México contra el narcotráfico (Reducción de la Oferta)," May 2000.

14   Toro, "La gobernanza internacional."

15   Jorge Chabat, "Mexico: The Security Challenge," in Jordi Diez, ed., *Canada and Mexico's Security in a Changing North America* (School of Policy Studies, Queen's University. Kingston, Montreal: Queen's-McGill University Press, 2006).

16 According to some news sources, Mexican authorities were informed from the start of Operation Casablanca, but this was denied by the Mexican government. Moisés Sánchez Limón, "Lozano Gracia supo del inicio de la Operación Casablanca," *La Crónica de Hoy* 4 June 1998.

17 Ricardo Sandoval, "Fox Pushes FBI School for Mexican Federal Police," *Dallas Morning News* 20 May 2001.

18 "Anuncian fin de certificación antidrogas," *Reforma* 14 November 2001.

19 Maribel González, "Copiará EU política antidrogas de Fox," *Reforma* 14 August 2002.

20 "Letter by Ambassador Antonio O. Garza," *El Universal* 27 January 2005.

21 Juan Arvizu Arrioja, "Contesta Creel a Garza enérgicamente," *El Universal* 14 May 2005.

22 "EU y México suavizan diferencias," BBC Mundo.Com, 30 January 2005. Online, available at: http://news.bbc.co.uk/hi/spanish/latin_america/newsid_4220000/4220907.stm.

23 "Negocian México y EU plan contra narcotráfico: *Dallas Morning News,*" *El Universal* 10 May 2007.

24 Horacio Jiménez, "Frente multinacional contra narco, migración y 'maras,'" *El Universal* 23 May 2007.

25 Claudia Guerrero, "Pide FCH a EU 'reproducir' Plan Colombia," *Reforma* 8 June 2007.

26 Jorge Vega, "Niega México pedir 'Plan Colombia' contra el narco," *Organización Editorial Mexicana* 10 June 2007, online, available at: www.oem.com.mx/laprensa/notas/n307477.htm.

27 Carlos Benavides and Francisco Gómez, "Compró el narco a jefes de la SIEDO," *El Universal* 27 October 2008.

28 Gustavo Castillo García, "Detienen a Noé Ramírez por supuestos nexos con el *cártel* de los Beltrán Leyva," *La Jornada* 21 November 2008.

29 Sergio Javier Jiménez, "Obama respalda lucha antinarco de Calderón," *El Universal* 13 January 2009; Sergio Javier Jiménez, "Ratifica Bush apoyo en lucha anticrimen," *El Universal* 14 January 2009.

30 See US Joint Forces Command, "The Joint Operating Environment 2008," November 2008, online, available at: www.jfcom.mil/newslink/storyarchive/2008/JOE2008.pdf; Jesse Bogan and Kerry A. Dolan, "The Next Disaster," *Forbes* 22 December 2008.

31 The 2009 Drug Report of the State Department places great emphasis on the problem of Mexican corruption:

> All of this progress, however, comes against a backdrop of continuing high levels of corruption and turmoil within Mexico's security and judicial bodies. Corruption throughout Mexico's public institutions remains a key impediment to successfully curtailing the power of the drug cartels.
>
> (US State Department, "2009 International Narcotics Control Strategy Report," 27 February 2009, online, available at: www.state.gov/p/inl/rls/nrcrpt/2009/#.)

7

MEXICO'S WAR ON TERRORISM

Rhetoric and Reality

Athanasios Hristoulas

Mexican foreign policy has gone through dramatic changes in the last decade. A critical defining factor here was the 9/11 terrorist attacks on the United States that took place in 2001. Given Mexico's geographic proximity as well as its economic dependence on the United States, the country's leaders had to adapt to the post-9/11 security needs of their much more powerful economic partner. Indeed, leaders in all three North American Free Trade Agreement (NAFTA) countries recognized that changes had to be made in the way goods, services and people cross their shared borders.

This chapter examines some of these changes and how Mexico has implemented them. The central argument is that, although publicly, Mexico's leaders have repeatedly argued that they want to be "good" allies in the war against terrorism in North America, the implementation of said policies has been lacking. There is, in other words, a disconnect between the rhetoric and practice of Mexican security policy. A number of factors contribute to this disconnect: corruption; the capacity of the Mexican government to respond to the threat; interagency competition; and the abuse of nationalism by politicians for personal political capital. This stands in sharp contrast to the situation that presents itself along the Canada–United States border. There, authorities are much more likely to put their "money where their mouth is."

The chapter begins by outlining why Mexico is considered a security challenge by certain sectors of the US government and public opinion. The media have portrayed the disorganized and porous nature of the border between the United States and Mexico as a serious threat to national security. To date, there is absolutely no evidence that this is the case. The chapter then moves on discuss the "rhetoric" in Mexican foreign policy: in other words, the declaratory statements on the part of Mexican authorities.

It then contrasts this with the "reality" of cooperation by American and Mexican security forces. Finally, the chapter compares and contrasts the United States–Mexico experience with those of Canada and the United States. Although problems exist between Canada and the United States with respect to how to deal with the terrorist threat, the long tradition of security cooperation between the two countries has made it easier for them to work together.

Why worry about Mexico?

Why is Mexico perceived as a threat? The US concern with respect to Mexico is that the country *might* represent a terrorist threat in the near future. Mexico does not have a large Muslim community where Islamic terrorists can easily "blend in" as is the case in multicultural Canada. Yet the fear is that Al Qaeda and other terrorist organizations might somehow reap the benefits of corruption, inefficiency, and archaic investigation techniques present in Mexican immigration, customs and public security forces. A second concern is that terrorist organizations will create strategic alliances with other criminal agents such as drug dealers and *polleros* in order to gain easy access into the United States.[1] A third concern is the porous nature of Mexico's southern border with Guatemala. A final concern is the ability of drug cartels to corrupt and weaken Mexican institutions and the capacity of these institutions to respond to the terrorist threat. While in the immediate post-9/11 context both Mexico and Canada were perceived as potential platforms for a terrorist attack, this has to some extent changed due to a slow but apparent recognition in the United States that current levels of violence in Mexico are the most urgent problem, and that the United States itself shares some of the responsibility for this through the easy availability of US weapons.

In response to these fears, both Canada and Mexico signed border agreements with the United States (Canada in late 2001 and Mexico in early 2002). Both agreements outline bilateral mechanisms with regard to border infrastructure to secure the flow of goods and people. The agreements also placed special emphasis on the twin principles of coordination and information-sharing as critical components of a secure common border.[2] Equally important was the meeting between George Bush, Paul Martin and Vicente Fox in Waco, Texas in March of 2005 which resulted in the signing of the now defunct Security and Prosperity Partnership. In its own words, the partnership was "a trilateral effort to increase security and enhance prosperity among the three countries through greater cooperation and information-sharing."

At a more general level, the Conference Board of Canada has argued that North American security can entail some or all of these three elements.[3] The first is the enhancement of border efficiency by exploiting more intelligent methods of processing border examinations for both people and cargo. This most basic form of *continental* security would turn the frontiers between Canada and the United States, and Mexico and the United States, into "smart" borders.[4] The second element involves rethinking the way borders are conceived to begin with. Here the law enforcement agencies of the three countries would work more closely together away from the physical frontiers to reduce the need for inspection at the borders themselves. The Conference Board refers to this strategy as moving away from the *Maginot line* of defense mentality to a *defense in depth* philosophy.[5] A third potential scenario involves the harmonization of immigration and refugee policy, customs clearance, and even national and public security policy in order to remove border inspections altogether. This "Fortress North America" scenario would also include common visa requirements.[6]

Mexico's response to 9/11: the rhetoric

After the initial stumble when President Fox failed to offer condolences at once after 9/11, Mexico took steps to politically demonstrate its solidarity with the United States following the terrorist attacks. For example, in October of 2001, President Fox stated that Mexico

> considers the struggle against terrorism to be part of the commitment of Mexico with Canada and the United States to build within the framework of the North American free trade agreement a shared space of development, well being and integral security.

Later that year, Jorge Castañeda, the then foreign secretary, said: "Mexico would favor a continental approach to border security issues, extending a North American partnership that already operates at a trade level."[7] In the same speech, Castañeda signaled that the Mexican government would prefer to take perimeter security "as far as possible, but that depends on the Canadians and the Americans."

The Mexican government saw continental and border security as offering multiple opportunities in the areas of trade, security, migration and even social development. Similar to Canadian concerns, Mexico worried that enhanced security at the border would hurt free and open trade between the United States and Mexico. But Mexico's interests went beyond simply trade. Mexico's strategy had been one of *issue linkage*, or the attempt to trade security for other types of benefits. An initial issue linkage directly related to the expansion of NAFTA to include other non-trade related issues. When Carlos Salinas signed NAFTA in the early 1990s, his administration argued that the trilateral trade agreement would result in an improvement in the standard of living of all Mexicans. Two administrations later, Vicente Fox was under tremendous domestic pressure to deliver on those promises. In the months following the terrorist attacks he repeatedly argued that as long as Mexico was a place where 40 percent of the population made less than US$2 a day, US borders would never be secure. The answer he had in mind was enhanced regulation at the border—rather than the criminalization that threatens to blur the distinction between undocumented workers and criminals and terrorists.

Thus, although open and free trade was Mexico's immediate concern in enhancing security cooperation, a possible migration deal designed to regulate rather than criminalize it was not far from the minds of Mexican decision makers at the time. The hope on the part of those decision makers was that by giving the Americans what they wanted in security terms there would be positive spill-over effects in other areas of concern to Mexico.

Mexico's response to 9/11: the reality

However, Mexico has had trouble keeping up, both politically and operationally with the changes occurring in North America. There is, in other words, a disconnect between Mexican rhetoric and action. Taking the twin border agreements signed late 2001 between Canada and the United States and early 2002 between Mexico and the United States as an example, first and foremost, it goes without saying that the Canada–United States version is much more comprehensive in nature. Those areas of the Canada–United States border agreement which focus on harmonization and cooperation—such as pre-clearance, joint training and exercises, integrated intelligence, and the Integrated Border Enforcement Teams (IBETs)—simply do not appear in the Mexican–US version of the agreement.[8]

Second, even though the Mexican–US accord is more modest in its objectives, there has been tremendous difficulty in implementing the various parts of the agreement. For example, whereas in the case of the Canadian–US agreement, almost all of the 32 points have been implemented or are in the process of being implemented, the Mexican–US counterpart has stalled. Of the 22 points in the Mexican–US agreement, there has been no progress whatsoever in seven of the critical areas. These include: secure railways, combating fraud, contraband interdiction, electronic exchange of information, screening of third country nationals, and visa policy consultations (see Tables 7.1 and 7.2).

A further four interrelated factors combine to lead to the conclusion that Mexico faces an upward battle in its effort to become a reliable partner in the war against terrorism within the context of North America. The first is the institutional corruption which permeates almost all sectors of Mexico's political life. Corruption, to begin with, is particularly rampant in the country's National Migration Institute (the agency responsible for immigration control). At the central airport in Mexico City, cases of people entering the country illegally by paying off migration officials are rampant.

Rumors have it that there exists a scaled payment mechanism which corresponds to the illegal's country of origin, with for example Brazilians paying less to enter illegally than Iraqis. Equally important is the anarchic situation at the country's southern border. Undocumented migrants of all sorts trying to cross the border from Guatemala face an unprotected and shallow river crossing. The uncontrolled nature of the border between Mexico and Guatemala has led to the evolution of professional, illegal river-crossing entrepreneurs. They can get away with this because there are literally no migration officials on either side of the border.[9]

Corruption, of course, characterizes not only the National Migration Institute but, as amply discussed throughout this book, permeates the country's police forces, its military, government officials and even politicians. Corruption is indeed a fact of life for all Mexicans from all walks of life. This is not to say that corruption does not exist in the United States. Transparency International has ranked the United States at 7.2 on a scale of one to ten where ten means a complete lack of corruption.[10] Mexico however, scores 3.5, which suggests that the problem is *systemic* rather *isolated*.[11] The problem is major and affects the state's capacity to function properly. It weakens government agencies which in turn are not able to comply with their objectives. The net effect is that, to some extent, the Mexican state has begun to collapse. From all the factors discussed in this chapter, it should be emphasized that corruption is the most serious challenge facing Mexico today.

The second obstacle, which is strongly related to the first, is the *capacity* of the Mexican government to respond to the perceived threat. Beyond the fact that Mexico is a developing nation and by definition has less capacity than its other two North American partners, the US-driven criminalization of certain transactions (narcotics and labor markets) has radically altered the nature of corruption in Mexico and has also magnified the size of this problem, weakening in turn the institutional capacity of the state. The criminalization of these transactions rests at the heart of the problem of corruption and ultimately explains the difficulties recurrently faced in United States–Mexico efforts at law enforcement cooperation.

Corruption in Mexico is fundamentally driven by the drug trade, and the drug trade is in turn propelled by a widely promoted and enforced US policy: that of conceptualizing the drug trade as a threat to US national security. This has essentially externalized and placed the burden of the drug trade on other states such as Mexico and Colombia, when in fact, it should also be viewed as an internal US public health consumption problem. Moreover, the price of drugs has increased dramatically because of this externalization policy which in turn has made it a highly profitable endeavor for those willing to participate in the illicit market, further contributing to the corruption problem. Indeed, it has been estimated that at least 250,000 Mexicans are involved in the drug trade, with profits approaching US$5 billion annually.[12]

Third, looking at interagency competition, the last six years of President Fox's administration were characterized by intense political infighting between different ministries. Combined with the fact that the Mexican Congress was (and still is) deeply divided, this led to a situation where the country's leaders simply could not make any decisions of a substantial manner. The implications of this problem are fairly obvious: much of the decision-making structure of the state is heavily permeated by this personal and institutional competition. Indeed, President Fox essentially muddled through his presidency without taking many active decisions at all.

A classic example of this is the case of Mexico's National Security strategy after the 2000 general election. When President Fox came into office, he tried to formalize the national security agenda of the country. He did this by creating the nation's first National Security Presidential Advisor. The move signaled an attempt to develop a coherent national security doctrine rationalizing the different agencies in charge of intelligence. At last count they included: the Center for Investigation and National Security (Centro de Investigación y Seguridad Nacional, CISEN); Naval Intelligence; Army Intelligence; the attorney general's office (PGR); the Federal Preventive Police (PFP); and finally, the Federal Investigation Agency (Agencia Federal de Investigación, AFI).

The president's policy failed because the National Security Advisor chosen, Adolfo Aguilar Zínser, was extremely unpopular with the above agencies (he had previously been a senator from a left-leaning party). Indeed, Zínser's access to the intelligence community was purposely limited not only by CISEN (who did not want him there because they saw him as a direct threat), but also by other intelligence agencies. Ultimately, the National Security Advisor left for a diplomatic post in New York and more significantly, the president decided that no replacement was needed. Thus, political infighting between the above noted agencies as well as Fox's disinterest in the subject essentially doomed any real restructuring of national security doctrine and intelligence services. The net effect of the National Security Advisor fiasco was that no clear mandate for Mexico's intelligence agencies was created. The overlapping and competing activities of different intelligence agencies, as well as an uncoordinated intelligence structure, undermines decision making. Information collected by different agencies is jealously guarded, and no centralization mechanism exists that can synthesize and consolidate intelligence.

A further example includes the open and public dispute between Jorge Castañeda as foreign secretary and Aguilar Zínser, now in his role as Mexican ambassador to the United Nations. This dispute focused on Mexico's position vis-à-vis the war against Iraq. While Castañeda was willing to entertain the idea of supporting the United States, Ambassador Zínser adamantly opposed the move and openly criticized not only the United States, but the Mexican Foreign secretary as well. The drama was played out on Mexican national television and even solicited a clarifying request by the US State Department on "who was running the show." What was abundantly clear to all observers was that Fox was politically paralyzed by the dispute between his two civil servants.

In some cases, inter-agency competition is a good thing because it allows for checks and balances and innovation. However, the case of Mexico goes much further, to the point where inter-agency competition actually inhibits decision making. The classic example of this is the inter-ministerial rivalry between the Mexican navy and army. During the Fox administration, the Mexican navy (Secretaría de Marina) took a much more open attitude towards cooperation with the United States in security matters. On the other hand, the Mexican army (Secretaría de Defensa Nacional) pursued a more traditional and isolationist policy. This led to repeated and public confrontations between the respective ministries.

If Mexican officials have a hard time dealing with one another, the situation along the northern border is even worse. Few, if any, mechanisms for cooperation and communication exist between the authorities of both countries. For the most part, pre-clearance has stalled. Further, smart border technology, which was first implemented along the Canada–United States border in 1996, has stalled along the Mexico–United States border. In the specific case of Nogales, Arizona and Nogales, Sonora (twin cities along the Mexico–United States border), US authorities have already implemented the infrastructure for a fast lane connecting the two cities, but Mexican officials have refused to allow the border crossing to be opened. The reason for the delay is telling in nature. Because Mexican federal authorities were dragging their feet on the fast border lane crossing between these two cities, state and local authorities in Sonora decided that they would take matters into their own hands, and assisted US officials in the construction of a "fast" lane. However, Mexican authorities in Mexico City refused to allow its use, stating that border crossings were a federal not a local or state matter. In the meantime, citizens on both sides of the border had to suffer the inconvenience of conventional border crossings which ordinarily take at least one to three hours because Mexican local, state and federal authorities could not coordinate.

The situation becomes even more troubling when one looks at the relationship between Mexican officials of all types and the US border patrol: both Mexican and US officials have deeply entrenched problems over trust. Little communication and information-sharing exists between the two sides.

> US law enforcement officials often find themselves in frustrating situations, unable to deal with the inefficiency that often characterizes Mexican officials, while Mexican authorities are overly sensitive to US

unilateralism, and lack the technical expertise to foment the kinds of cooperative mechanisms that exist along the Canada–US border.[13]

The end effect is that no "security confidence" exists along the US–Mexican border. As argued by David Shirk,

> Bi-national cooperation is typically focused on reducing cross border interagency irritants and misunderstandings rather than on coordinated operations, and—while occasionally stronger at the local level of inter-agency cooperation—tends to vary from place to place and time to time.[14]

In one incident in 2003, US border officials, in an attempt to repatriate an undocumented Mexican elderly woman who had somehow miraculously crossed into the US border from Sonora, requested help from Mexican authorities. As they were unresponsive, a US border patrol officer made the mistake of crossing into Mexican territory to help the old woman. He was greeted at gun-point by a squad of Mexican officials and arrested. It took almost a full day of intensive work by the US consul to have the officer released.[15]

The final obstacle is the use of nationalism and sovereignty by Mexican political actors in order to pursue their own personal agendas. The bilateral Merida Initiative serves as an indicative example. The plan provides for US assistance to Mexico to fight drug cartels. From an orthodox perspective that can be no bad thing, and the rejection of that aid gives rise to the incredulity expressed in the following:

> While President Felipe Calderón's government has pursued US assistance, opposition politicians have argued the aid package would violate Mexico's sovereignty and polls show most Mexicans oppose the help. Calderón's political opponents have railed against the aid package, many to make political hay.[16]

Another anecdote is telling. In 2003, a gang of youths on the Mexican side of the border were regularly robbing a train on the outskirts of Nogales bound for the United States. After multiple thefts, US authorities requested the assistance of Mexican local and state authorities who were more than eager to participate in the joint operation. However, after a number of weeks, members of the Mexican Federal Congress in Mexico City accused the participating Mexican officers of being traitors, claiming that they were assisting US authorities in their attempts to violate the sovereign integrity of Mexico. Fearing political backlash, the joint operation was halted. The problem of course, had nothing to do with sovereignty and territorial integrity, but rather the blatant attempt of a Mexican Congressperson to gain political capital. The end result was the continued operation of the gang of thugs in the name of Mexican national sovereignty. These kinds of events, common along the Mexico–United States border, do not paint a particularly positive portrait with respect to the future of security cooperation.

Canada, the United States and their shared border

This stands in sharp contrast to the Canada–United States post-9/11 relationship. Particularly since the arrival of the new Conservative Stephen Harper government, Canada took upon itself the task of demonstrating to American policy makers and public opinion alike that Canada was in fact a good ally of the United States with respect to the fight against terrorism.

First and foremost, the Harper administration extended Canada's military presence in Afghanistan until at least 2014, overturning the previous Liberal government's promise to bring the troops back home by the beginning of 2007. Canada had 2,200 troops in Afghanistan, engaged primarily in combat missions alongside US and other NATO troops.

With specific reference to North America, and in light of the North Korean nuclear tests, Harper's government reopened the national debate on whether or not Canada would participate in the US ballistic missile defense program—once again, something that the previous Liberal governments had rejected as not being in the country's national interest. Should Canada participate in missile defense, this would require a renegotiation of the bilateral Canada–United States North American Air Defense (NORAD) treaty established in 1958.

NORAD monitors and tracks human-made objects in both countries' airspace. It is also tasked with the prevention of attacks on North American targets by airplanes, missiles or space vehicles. The NORAD commander is chosen by and is responsible to both the Canadian prime minister and the US president. NORAD is located at the Peterson Air Base in Colorado Springs, Colorado.

The 9/11 attacks produced a structural change in NORAD's organization. It was incorporated in the US Northern Command (NORTHCOM), whose mission is to dissuade, prevent, and confront threats directed against the United States, its territories and interests within its area of responsibility. This includes airspace, land and maritime assets as well as the continental United States, Alaska, Canada, Mexico and waters extending out to 500 nautical miles such as the Gulf of Mexico. Canada's role within NORTHCOM is to assist in the defense of airspace as stipulated in NORAD. It is important to note that NORTHCOM is not considered a threat to Canadian sovereignty. Indeed, because NORAD is now part of NORTHCOM, most observers agree that any renegotiation of the treaty would eventually result in closer military cooperation between the two countries not only with respect to air, but also coastal and territorial defense. According to the Canadian Department of Foreign Affairs web site, "the Canadian government will further develop Canada–United States cooperation in other areas, involving other departments, including cooperation on maritime security … and with regard to border issues."

Canada and the United States had also implemented the IBETs program the length of 23 points along the US–Canadian border. This bi-national program permits five security agencies to exchange information and to work together on a daily basis with local, state and provincial authorities. These agencies cooperate on matters such as national security, organized crime and other crimes committed along the Canada–United States border. The agencies involved in the IBETs program include the Royal Canadian Mounted Police (RCMP); the Canadian Border Service Agency (CBSA); US Customs and Border Protection; the US Bureau of Immigration and Customs Enforcement; and the US Coast Guard.

Canada has also located four Integrated National Security Enforcement Teams (INSETs) in the urban centers of Toronto, Montreal, Vancouver and Ottawa. The INSETs increase Canada's ability to collect, share and analyze intelligence gathered by different Canadian security agencies. The INSETs include the RCMP, the CBSA, Citizenship and Immigration Canada (CIC), the Canadian Security Intelligence Service (CSIS), and other local and provincial authorities.

Canada has also taken some steps to change its immigration and refugee policies. Bill C-11 for example, intends to limit access to appeals on the part of rejected refugee claimants and at the same time make it easier to deport individuals whose specific requests for asylum have been rejected. With respect to terrorist activities specifically, the government introduced Bill C-36, which provides for additional resources and police powers to identify and punish terrorists and terrorist support groups. More specifically, the bill makes it illegal to raise funds on behalf of terrorists, allows the government to seize assets of terrorist organizations, and expands the police authority to pursue suspected terrorists.[17]

This does not mean that Canada and the United States have not had bilateral problems in the months and years following the terrorist attacks. The US media has portrayed Canada as a hotbed for terrorist activity. Special emphasis has been placed on Canada's refugee laws, which purportedly allow terrorists to operate within the country with relative ease. As many as 30,000 refugees enter Canada every year, and unlike other industrialized countries Canada does not detain refugee claimants until their status can be determined. Under Canadian law, refugees are allowed to move freely until their court appearance, and as many as 10,000 individuals have not appeared for their hearings in recent years. US officials and especially the US media have criticized these policies as allowing terrorists and terrorist organizations to operate within the country with relative ease.

Indeed, Ward Elcock, the former Director of CSIS, recognized this in a report submitted to parliament when he argued: "the related policies concerning refugees and immigrants make Canada particularly vulnerable to terrorist influence and activities."[18]

However, Canadian officials are quick to respond that none of the 9/11 terrorists entered the United States from Canada. More importantly, Canada received approximately 37,000 refugees in 2001.[19] Of them, 13,000 requested entry to the country from US territory.[20] Clearly problems exist, but the United States is not without blame here. For Canada then, the issue is not so much the existence of terrorists in Canadian territory, but rather, the somewhat ill-begotten US perception that the country might somehow represent a terrorist threat.

Second and probably more importantly, Canada has been slow in dealing with known terrorist groups operating within the country. The case of Ahmed Ressam, the so-called millennium bomber captured by US customs and immigration officials trying to cross over to the United States from Canada with a trunk-load of explosives, has served as the rallying point with respect to criticisms against the country in this regard. Ressam, an Algerian, lived in Montreal for five years as a political refugee even though a Canadian judge had ordered his deportation from the country because he had falsified travel documentation. Yet he was able to move around the country with relative ease because, as the country's law enforcement agencies admitted, they simply do not have the resources to track down individuals who have been ordered deported.[21]

It is this specific area where concerns on the part of US officials seem most warranted because, unlike refugee law—which most Canadians would vehemently defend even in light of 9/11—the under-funding of security agencies is to blame. In the report cited above, Elcock stated that: "with perhaps the singular exception of the United States, there are more international terrorist groups active in Canada than any other country in the world," and that the Counter-Terrorism Branch of CSIS was investigating the existence of over 50 terrorist organizations and 350 individuals for links to terrorist groups. Among the most active groups, Elcock listed Hezbollah, Hamas, the Provisional IRA, the Tamil Tigers and, the Kurdistan Workers Party (PKK). None of these groups directly target Canadian interests, rather they use Canada as a "venue of opportunity" to "support, plan or mount attacks elsewhere."[22]

Further, Canada has even begun to be an important source of marijuana for the US drug market. Indeed, US officials

> are very concerned about an upward trend in seizures, which have increased 259 percent since 2001. Both countries also recognize that, despite their best efforts, law enforcement seizes only a portion of marijuana smuggled across the border, although this is true for all

illicit activities. Law enforcement reporting indicates that most southbound seizures are in bud form, which generally has higher potency levels than other forms of marijuana.[23]

Conclusion: ending the blame game?

Some problems over security, then, do exist between the United States and Canada—but they should not be exaggerated. Overall the cooperation is not only intense and smooth; it has progressively deepened. It clearly sets the benchmark against which Mexico's relationship with the United States is judged. On any count, Mexico faces an uphill battle in its efforts to be a good ally in the war against terrorism. Although the political will to participate exists, in terms of actual policies the response has been muted. Alternatively, when there has been a response, it has been incoherent and tainted by corruption.

US decision makers recognize that it is in their interests that Mexico "work better." The dysfunction of Mexico's security institutions affects not only the war against terror, but also increases the bilateral insecurity caused by the illegal drug trade, especially along the border regions of the two countries. Cognizant of this, in 2008 US Congress authorized the sum of US$1.4 billion in bilateral and multilateral aid for professionalization and modern equipment for Mexico and Central America. Referred to as the Merida Initiative, funding was to be made available for:

- inspection equipment, ion scanners and canine units;
- technologies to improve and secure communications systems that collect criminal information in Mexico;
- technical advice and training to strengthen the institutions of justice in Mexico;
- helicopters and surveillance aircraft to support interdiction activities and rapid response of law enforcement agencies to Mexico.

The aid package was considered a turning point in Mexico–United States relations. To begin with, it was the first time the United States had provided such a substantial sum of military and police assistance to Mexico. Moreover, the level of cooperation between Mexican and US authorities, specifically in the area of training, was unprecedented. Further, this was the first time that Mexico had specifically requested funding for security sector reform. For example, the initiative reserved US$73.5 million for judicial reform, institution-building, human rights and rule-of-law issues.

The Merida Initiative was designed to go a long way in helping Mexico deal with many of the above outlined problems. For example, increased positive interaction between the two countries was to help alleviate some of the nationalist fears endemic in Mexican public opinion. It was also to go a long way in helping different agencies across the border work more closely together. Enhanced professionalization of Mexican security forces would likely alleviate some of the friction generated by inter-institutional rivalry. Finally, professionalization would help fight corruption and therefore enhance the capacity of the state to act appropriately in the face of threats.

In many ways then, the Merida Initiative was a "no-brainer" for both Mexico and the United States. Yet there have been significant delays in the disbursement of the funds. The General Accounting Office (GAO) found that as of the summer of 2010, only 9 percent of the Merida Initiative funding had been distributed to Mexico.[24]

> The reasons for the slow pace of delivery are multiple. The GAO notes problems in several areas including an insufficient number of staff to administer the program, delays in negotiations of interagency and bilateral agreements, slow and cumbersome procurement processes, and turnover among government officials.[25]

Understandably, this frustrated Mexican decision makers, with President Felipe Calderón raising the issue with top US law makers in a meeting in 2009.

As outlined in this chapter, Mexico has a long way to go, but US policy makers can help by making sure that bilateral mechanisms designed to improve the security sector in Mexico are fulfilled. The Merida Initiative ought to go a long way in helping Mexico modernize its security apparatus. Yet the question remains whether or not both sides would really fulfill their end of the bargain.

TABLE 7.1 Canada–United States smart border action plan: explanation and status

Basic points	Explanation	Status as of early 2008
1. Biometric identifiers	Common standards for biometrics	Since January 2004, US authorities check all persons going into the country with biometric identifiers
2. Permanent resident cards	Common standards to implement fraud-resistant cards in both countries	Presently, they are implemented in both countries: the Canadian card is considered one of the most fraud-resistant documents in the world
3. Single alternative inspection system	Continue with pilot program (NEXUS) with two-way movement of pre-approved travelers	Now operative at several ports: • Douglas/Peache Arch • Pacific Highway/Blaine • Boundary Bay/Point Roberts • Sarnia/Port Huron • Windsor/Detroit • Fort Erie/Buffalo
4. Refugee/asylum processing	Ensure that applicants are thoroughly screened for security risks and share information on refugee and asylum claimants	Significant progress on a Statement of Mutual Understanding; Canada implementing changes to its legal code with regards to refugees
5. Managing of refugee/asylum claims	Negotiate a safe third-country agreement to enhance the management of refugee claims	Already signed a safe third-country agreement whose main purpose is family-reunification
6. Visa policy coordination	Joint review of respective visa waiver lists and share look-out lists at visa issuing offices	Common visa policies for 144 countries

7. Air pre-clearance	Resume past programs	In-transit preclearance project in Vancouver; seeking Congressional approval for immunity for Canadian customs agents in the United States
8. Advance passenger information/passenger name record	Share advance passenger information	Share advance passenger information and passenger name records (API/PNR) on high-risk travelers
9. Joint passenger analysis units	Joint units at key international airports	(Pilot project) joint passenger analysis units at the Vancouver and Miami international airports.
10. Ferry terminals	Review customs and immigration presence and practices	Marine benchmarking exercise completed; beginning implementation
11. Compatible immigration databases	Develop jointly an automated database	Discussions begun
12. Immigration officers overseas	Increase number of Canadian and US immigration officers at airports overseas and enhance joint training of airline personnel	More officers at different offices in both countries
13. International cooperation	Undertake technical assistance to source and transit countries	Both Canada and the United States have provided assistance to third countries
14. Harmonized commercial processing	Establish complementary systems for commercial processing. FAST program (free and secure trade)	FAST program established in: • Blaine/Pacific Highway • Sarnia/Port Huron • Windsor/Detroit • Fort Erie/Buffalo • Queenston/Lewiston • Lacolle/Champlain
15. Pre-clearance	Integrated approach to improve security and facilitate trade in truck/rail cargo	Talks in progress

continued

Basic points	Explanation	Status as of early 2008
16. Joint facilities	Creation of small, remote joint border facilities	Have agreed to consider certain common points: • Calais, ME/St. Stephen, NB • Easton, ME/River de Chute, NB • Monticello, ME/Bloomfield, NB • Vanceboro, ME/St. Croix, NB • Morses Line, VT/Morses Line, QC • North Troy, VT/Highwater, QC • Walhalla, ND/Winkler, MB • Northgate, ND/Northgate, SK • Hanna, ND/Snowflake, MB • Opheim, MT/West Poplar River, SK • Nighthawk, WA/Chopaka, BC • Porthill, ID/Rykerts, BC
17. Customs data	Sign the Agreement on Sharing Data Related to Customs Fraud	Extended scope of information with some new plans
18. Intransit container targeting at seaports	Jointly target marine intransit containers arriving both countries	Created joint targeting teams at five marine ports: Vancouver, Montreal, Halifax, Newark and Seattle
19. Infrastructure improvements	Joint improvements in key border points	New funding will support FAST and NEXUS
20. Intelligent transportation systems	Deploy interoperable technologies.	Piloting the Automatic Identification System (AIS) on the St. Lawrence Seaway
21. Critical infrastructure protection	Bi-national threat assessments on trans-border infrastructure	Agreed on a Joint Framework for United States–Canada Cooperation on Critical Infrastructure Protection and established a Bi-national Steering Committee

22. Aviation security	Finalize Federal Aviation Administration–Transport Canada agreement	Recognition of both national security standards
23. Integrated border and marine enforcement teams	Expand IBET/IMET to other areas of the border	Operations in the 14 geographical areas for the deployment or enhancement of Integrated Border Enforcement Teams (IBETS)
24. Joint enforcement coordination	Coordination of law enforcement	Continue with Project North Star
25. Integrated intelligence	Joint teams to analyze and disseminate information and intelligence	Integrated National Security Enforcement Teams in Canada; they also participate with the US Foreign Terrorist Tracking Task Force (FTTTF) in Washington
26. Fingerprints	Implement the Memorandum of Understanding to supply equipment and training in this matter	Awaiting implementation
27. Removal of deportees	Address legal and operational challenges to joint removals	Continuing cooperation in removing individuals to source countries. Presently, five joint operations
28. Counter-terrorism legislation	Bring into force legislation on terrorism	Both countries implemented new legislation 2001–2002
29. Freezing of terrorist assets	Exchange advance information.	Working process in place to share advance information
30. Joint training and exercises	Increase dialogue and commitment for training and exercise programs	To culminate into the full-scale TOPOFF II (counter-terrorism exercises) in May 2008

Source: compiled by the author.

TABLE 7.2 Mexico–United States border partnership action plan: explanation and status

Basic Points	Explanation	Status as of early 2008
1. Long-term planning	Develop and implement a long-term strategic plan that ensures a coordinated physical and technological infrastructure that keeps pace with growing cross-border traffic	US$1.4 million feasibility study for infrastructure projects in Mexico
2. Relief of bottlenecks	Develop a prioritized list of infrastructure projects and take immediate action to relieve bottlenecks	Initial FAST (free and secure trade) lane was opened in El Paso/Juárez
3. Infrastructure protection	Conduct vulnerability assessments of trans-border infrastructure	The Mexico–United States Critical Infrastructure Protection Framework for Cooperation has branched out into six sector-specific working groups (transportation, energy, telecommunications, water/dams, public health and agriculture)
4. Harmonize port of entry operations	Synchronize hours of operation, infrastructure improvements, and traffic flow management at adjoining ports of entry on both sides of the United States–Mexico border	Implementing sound risk management principles and harmonized processing at ports of entry
5. Demonstration projects	Establish prototype smart port of entry operations	Completed at major ports of entry
6. Cross-border cooperation	Revitalize existing bilateral coordination mechanisms at the local, state and federal levels	They mainly work through binational commissions as the Border Environmental Cooperation Commission, and the Mexico–United States Critical Infrastructure Protection Framework for Cooperation

7. Financing projects at the border	Explore joint financing mechanism to meet the main development and infrastructure needs	Sistema de Transferencia Electrónica de Fondos Internacionales (Automated Clearing of International Funds, TEFI) has been created in Mexico
8. Pre-cleared travelers	Expand the use of the Secure Electronic Network for Traveler's Rapid Inspection (SENTRI)	Five SENTRI lanes have been established
9. Advanced passenger information	Establish a joint advance passenger information exchange mechanisms for flights between Mexico and the United States and other relevant flights	An Advanced Passenger Information System (APIS) with Mexico is to be operational in the next few months
10. NAFTA travel	Explore methods to facilitate the movement of NAFTA travellers, including dedicated lanes at high-volume airports	No major advances
11. Safe borders and deterrence of alien smuggling	Reaffirm mutual commitment to the Border Safety Initiative and action plan for cooperation on border safety, established in June 2001; expand Alien Smuggling and Trafficking Task Force	Expanded partnerships with the private sector such as the Business Anti-Smuggling Coalition and the Customs–Trade Partnership Against Terrorism
12. Visa policy consultations	Continue frequent consultations on visa policies and visa screening procedures	No major advances
13. Joint training	Conduct joint training in the areas of investigation and document analysis to enhance abilities to detect fraudulent documents and break-up alien smuggling rings	Strategies aimed at training to prevent migrant deaths and to strengthen border safety
14. Compatible databases	Develop systems for exchanging information and sharing intelligence	Implement an Advance Passenger Information System to improve and expedite screening of air travelers

continued

Basic Points	Explanation	Status as of early 2008
15. Screening of third-country nationals	Enhance cooperative efforts to detect, screen, and take appropriate measures to deal with potentially dangerous third-country nationals	No major advances
16. Public/private-sector cooperation	Expand partnerships with private sector trade groups and importers/exporters to increase security and compliance of commercial shipments	Major Entrepreneurial Workshop in San Francisco, California to discuss business opportunities in the region
17. Electronic exchange of information	Continue to develop and implement joint mechanisms for the rapid exchange of customs data	No major advances
18. Secure in-transit shipments	Continue to develop a joint in-transit shipment tracking mechanism and implement the Container Security Initiative	Cooperative efforts in securing in-transit shipments
19. Technology sharing	Develop a technology sharing program to allow deployment of high technology monitoring devices such as electronic seals and licence plate readers	Non-intrusive inspection equipment at major ports of entry (POE) has been implemented
20. Secure railways	Continue to develop a joint rail imaging initiative at all rail crossing locations on the United States–Mexico border	No major advances
21. Combating fraud	Expand the ongoing Bilateral Customs Fraud Task Force initiative to further joint investigative activities	No major advances

*Source: compiled by the author.

Notes

1 Literally speaking a *pollero* is someone who transports and sells chickens. *Polleros* is a term referred to those paid individuals who assist Mexican migrants to cross the border. They employ trucks similar to those used for chickens. Further, people are packed in the trucks like cattle.

2 "Security and Opportunity at the US–Canada Border," White House website 28 June 2002, online, available at: www.whitehouse.gov/news/releases/2002/06/20020628.html.

3 "Border Choices: Balancing the Need for Trade and Security," in *Conference Board of Canada*, 2001, 3–5, online, available at: www.conferenceboard.ca/pubs/borderchoices.10.01.pdf.

4 Ibid., 3.

5 Ibid., 4.

6 Ibid., 5.

7 "Mexico would Support Shift to Security Perimeter with US and Canada," *Canadian Press* 2 February 2002, online, available at: www.cp.org/english/hp.htm.

8 According to Royal Canadian Mounted Police web page, online, available at: www.rcmp.ca/security/ibets_e.htm, the IBETs program

> is a multi-faceted law enforcement initiative comprised of both Canadian and American partners. This bi-national partnership enables the five core law enforcement partners involved in IBETs to share information and work together daily with other local, state and provincial enforcement agencies on issues relating to national security, organized crime and other criminality transiting the Canada/US border between the Ports of Entry (POE).

9 The information presented in this part of the chapter is based on visits conducted by the author to the border region.

10 Transparency International, online, available at: www.transparency.org/policy_research/surveys_indices/cpi.

11 Ibid.

12 Sergio Aguayo, *El Almanaque de Mexico: 2008* (Mexico: Aguilar, 2008).

13 Andrew Cooper and Athanasios Hristoulas, "Relating to the Powerful One: Security and Efficiency at the Borders," paper presented at the Conference Relating to the Powerful One: How Canada and Mexico View Their Relationship to the United States, Weatherhead Center for International Affairs, 5–6 May 2003.

14 David Shirk, "Law Enforcement and Public Security Challenges in the US–Mexican Border Region," *Journal of Borderland Studies* 18:1 (Autumn 2003), 7.

15 Story recounted to author by US Consul in Nogales Sonora, 6 May 2006.

16 Jeremy Schwartz, "US Plan for Drug War Has Some in Mexico Worried," 14 October 2007, online, available at: www.coxwashington.com.

17 "Canadian Anti-Terrorism Act Tabled: New Powers to Fight Terrorism," in *Canada On Line*, 2001, online, available at: www.canadaonline.about.com/library/weekly/aa101701a.htm.

18 Ward Elcock (Director of the Canadian Security Intelligence Service), *Submission to the Special Committee of the Senate on Security and Intelligence*, Ottawa, 24 June 1998, online, available at: www.csis-scrs.gc.ca/eng/miscdocs/kelly_e.html.
19 Allan Thompson. "Flow of Refugees at Heart of Deal," *Toronto Star* 26 October 2001.
20 "Canada Bound Asylum Seekers Housed in New York Refugee Shelter," *Associated Press* 27 June 2002.
21 See "Canada's Importance," *Boston Globe* 1 October 2001.
22 "Report of the Special Senate Committee on Security and Intelligence," *Senate of Canada Committee Reports*, 1999, online, available at: www.parl.gc.ca/36/1/parlbus/commbus/senate/com-e/secu-e/rep-e/repsecintjan99part1-e.htm.
23 Public Safety Agency of Canada, online, available at: www.publicsafety.gc.ca/prg/le/bs/uscabdta-en.asp#a06.
24 Eric Olson, "GAO Report Finds Merida Initiative Needs Better Performance Measures," Woodrow Wilson Center for International Scholars: Mexico Institute, 2010, online, available at: www.wilsoncenter.org/topics/docs/GAO%20Merida%20Initiative%20Report%20Analysis%207.22.pdf.
25 Ibid.

8

THE MESOAMERICAN DILEMMA

External Insecurity, Internal Vulnerability

Raúl Benítez and Arturo Sotomayor

Mesoamerica comprises the geographic, political and cultural space that covers Mexico, Guatemala, Belize, Honduras, El Salvador, Nicaragua, Costa Rica and Panama.[1] It is a macro-region, with great ethnic and linguistic diversity yet with a cultural unity based on something that Paul Kirchoff defined more than six decades ago as the Mesoamerican complex—a geographic space that developed similar political, religious, irrigation and farming systems, and even architectural styles.[2]

Of all the sub-regions of Latin America, the Mesoamerican region today is probably the least militarized and also the least controversial in terms of conventional security. Military spending per capita is the lowest of the hemisphere, and territorial conflicts between states are rare. This is the result of the peace processes initiated in the 1990s in El Salvador, Guatemala and Nicaragua, which have resulted in disputes being resolved through diplomacy and negotiation, and even by relying on international courts. As a result, the region does not depend on a military balance of power. On the contrary, Mesoamerican security is defined by non-conventional threats, but these are damaging the emerging democracies and regional integration in profound ways. This is mainly due to porous borders, little governmental oversight, predominant mafias, criminal networks, human trafficking and institutionalized corruption.

In Mesoamerica one can identify what experts like Barry Buzan have called a regional security complex; this refers to a group of states whose concerns and perceptions about security cannot be independently or unilaterally analyzed or resolved.[3] This security complex has three essential characteristics.

First, the main source of threats in Mesoamerica is *internal* in character, driven by socio-political conflicts that take place within states. As opposed to the Southern Cone, the Mesoamerican area is not confronted with the classic security dilemma. This term, often used in the study of International Relations, refers to a situation in which a state, intending to increase its security by raising its military spending, provokes almost automatically the perception of insecurity on part of its neighbors, who in turn are forced to respond in kind by augmenting their military arsenal. At the core, the dilemma is that for the most part regional and international security is constantly undermined by arms races, conflict spirals and constant military conflicts. Rather than guaranteeing their national security, the states affected by this dilemma are constantly expecting war.[4] This particular dynamic, which persists in Latin American interstate relations, particularly in countries such as Chile and its neighbors, is non-existent in Mesoamerica. On the contrary, Mesoamerican security relations are determined by what Brian Job has called the "insecurity dilemma." In other words, the major vulnerability of the region is not caused by external insecurity, but rather by the lack of internal security in which different actors perceive their personal and collective security as constantly threatened by public and private agents located within the state, and not in neighboring countries.[5] Therefore, the problem of assuring internal order and public security subordinates the efforts of cooperation and integration, causing a dilemma for the region where internal insecurity persists, with detrimental effects for foreign relations.

Second, security in Mesoamerica has become an *intermestic* matter, whose causes are national but whose effects are transnational; where the actions of a single government cannot resolve this dilemma, and the inaction of states in dealing with the matter leads to a profound deterioration in security. Public order issues, which once would have been classified as merely internal, often literally overflow state borders, causing insecurity, distrust and suspicion between neighboring countries.

Third, while there is a regional security complex, it is not possible yet to talk about a Mesoamerican security community. The existence of such a complex does not facilitate, in itself, the emergence of a pluralistic and transnational security community, composed of sovereign states whose populations have solid expectations of a peaceful change. According to Karl Deutsch and his followers, in a community defined as such, the armed forces no longer have the function of intimidating or dissuading, but rather of protecting states against external aggression.[6] Mesoamerica is far from forming a community of this type, in part because the military sectors have not fully accepted the supremacy of civil control, and because there are few incentives for increased regional cooperation through consultation and confidence-building mechanisms, similar to those that exist in the Southern Cone.

This chapter develops and presents evidence to validate all of these three hypotheses in relation to the Mesoamerican security complex. It does so mindful of the profound variations in forms and types of governments, state capacities, and economic and social development levels in Meso-america.[7] These variations are notable between consolidated democracies, like Costa Rica and Belize, and countries on the way to democracy, like Mexico, Guatemala, El Salvador, Nicaragua, Honduras and Panama. Disparities are also clear in differences in geographic sizes and state capacities. In spite of these important differences, all Mesoamerican countries share the three characteristics described earlier: public insecurity, intermestic challenges, institutional weaknesses and a complex that does not favor the emergence of a pluralistic security community. These shared characteristics justify an analysis that focuses on what Mesoamerica has in common, rather than on how individual countries vary.[8]

The Mesoamerican insecurity dilemma

In their analysis of international security, Brian Job and Mohammed Ayoob argued that the Third World is characterized by the "weak state" model, whose main features are the persistence of internal threats, institutional inefficiency, the absence of a cohesive society and a lack of popular legitimacy.[9] The result of this combination of factors is what Job calls the insecurity dilemma of the Third World, which is the incapacity of the state to monopolize the use of force and provide security for its inhabitants. The dilemma is that the external and regional environments permit the subsistence of these weak states, even while they are incapable of carrying out the minimum functions of a normal state, such as the protection of property rights and citizens. On this theoretical basis, one could advance the hypothesis that Mesoamerica suffers from this syndrome.

This situation persists despite the relative advance in matters of democratization, and the various peace accords agreed on in the decade of the 1990s, including the Framework Treaty on Democratic Security of 1995.[10] Unfortunately, these advances have been eroded by the deterioration of public and citizen security.[11] The first symptom of this dilemma is the generalized perception of internal insecurity. In effect, during the last decade, public security has become the central theme of the agenda of sub-regional security. This problem appears regularly in opinion polls as one of the main threats facing this area. The judgment of seriousness transcends social stratification, educational levels and geographic location. According to the well-known *Latinobarómetro* reports, in almost all the countries of the sub-region citizens have perceived the most important problem to be crime, followed by unemployment. Crime is related to several other phenomena, ranging from kidnapping, the growing use of arms, illegal human trafficking, narcotics, drugs and property. Without a doubt, the causes of crime are multiple, yet there is a general pattern that explains part of the regional insecurity dilemma. The entire Mesoamerican region has experienced authoritarianism, civil wars and armed insurgency, albeit in different historical moments in time and with different intensities. This resulted in the regional security complex and its diverse national doctrines. While in the last decades peace and reconciliation accords have been signed with various degrees of success, in almost all states worrying forms of political and societal violence, such as paramilitary groups and new types of crime, have reappeared. In general, the peace processes of Central America—including that of El Salvador, considered the most successful—failed to successfully re-integrate former insurgents in civil society or in politics. The effect was that a substantial part of society remained armed and the proliferation of light weapons remained high.

In cases like Guatemala, insecurity has been aggravated by the justifiable government decision to substantially reduce its military apparatus in order to strengthen the emerging democracy and to avoid military coups. However, the military structure that previously repressed also maintained public order, often outside the legal order. The military structure was not replaced by a ready police force with the capacity to confront the problems that are part of an armed society. What began as democratization and pacification processes ended up profoundly eroding the capacity of the state to monopolize the use of force and maintain public security in a society that is highly prone to armed violence.

The second syndrome of the dilemma can be seen in the institutional inability of the state to guarantee public security. This inefficiency is caused in part by the type of democratic transition, mainly characterized by the collapse of the old authoritarian system, and the difficulty of constructing an efficient and transparent democratic system. The armed and police forces, accustomed to acting without having to worry about accountability, were never trained to work in a democratic context. This institutional void was quickly exploited by organized crime, which was more successful in adapting and in formulating strategies to sidestep law and order. The most notable perverse effect has been the surge of hidden ad hoc powers—a coalition formed between some who were previously responsible for repression by the state and who were ousted during the transition, and organized crime.[12] This coalition has penetrated public institutions and affected the relation between citizens and government. According to one source, in Mexico the gravity of the situation a few years ago was such that the attorney general estimated that 80 percent of his personnel had been corrupted by drug trafficking.[13]

The erosion of public institutions caused by insecurity is patent in the justice apparatus, which has been overwhelmed in almost all the Mesoamerican countries. Further aggravating conditions, the number of private security agencies and companies has more than tripled in the region. The institutional weakness of the state and the inability of the government to effectively and efficiently monopolize the use of force have created a paradox where security, rather than being a public good, has been privatized. Many of these private agencies employ former military officers or retired police officers, and many of them, predominantly the police officers, have either been laid off as a result of corruption or have a criminal past. This system, which is lax in its use of arms and its personnel contracting policies, means that some of these agencies represent a real threat to public security.

In sum, the processes of democratization and pacification in the sub-region have been mostly accident-prone. Authoritarian regimes have been substituted by weak democratic states, which do not have the minimum level of institutionalization to guarantee the security of its citizens. While levels of state repression have been reduced substantially, levels of armed violence are much higher than those in the authoritarian age.

Regional security as an intermestic theme

The Mesoamerican sub-region is characterized by a rather divided picture of security. While there is relative calm in relations among states as a result of the relative absence of territorial disputes, this peace stands in stark contrast to increasingly organized and widespread violence within state borders. Compared with previous decades, one can observe an increase in and diversification of transnational violent actors. These include segments of the armed forces, the police, and guerrilla movements. The violence is carried out by private groups, who have networks that cross national borders. Therefore, in Mesoamerica it is increasingly important to adopt a broader concept of security—one that includes intermestic issues. This refers to issues that are traditionally considered to be domestic in nature but that have important regional and international components and repercussions. Typically, these issues tend to be quite complex because they produce alignments and coalitions among various transnational actors who have the capacity to destabilize countries and undermine their political, social and economic systems.

Probably the most remarkable phenomena that have prompted a true intermestic and transnational dynamic in Mesoamerica have been the growing internationalization of migration; the trafficking of drugs, persons and arms; and violence and organized crime. Peter Andreas and Ethan Nadelmann argue that the internationalization of these issues, previously considered to be national or legal issues, requires a much more sophisticated explanation than one of growing transnational organized crime in an era of globalization.[14] The internationalization of crime is the result of a number of factors, including the power of the United States, the expansion of inter-state cooperation in matters of intelligence and policing, as well as normative changes that have modified the notion of both what constitutes normal behavior and what falls outside of the norm. We now analyze the three intermestic and transnational issues that affect the Mesoamerican security complex.

Migration

Migration in the sub-region has been transformed into a real security issue. One of the factors that most accelerated the process of transnationalization has been the intervention of the United States and the effects of 9/11. The effect of the terrorist attacks in New York, Washington and Pennsylvania was to securitize migration. Illegal migration from Mesoamerica to the United States was quickly transformed into a security issue for Washington and thus went from being a tolerated practice to a criminalized one. Bureaucratically, post-9/11 US policy modified the administrative apparatus that previously dealt with the issue of migration (the border patrol) and created a new bureaucracy (the Department of Homeland Security) which has been much more conservative in its approach and less willing to cooperate with countries in the south.[15] The transformation of the issue of migration into a national security concern for the United States seems to be due to the sometimes erroneous association between illegal migration and the movement of terrorist groups through these migration flows. This has led to the implementation of unilateral practices on the part of both federal and state governments in the United States. Among them, the most controversial has been the construction of a wall between Mexico and its neighbor to the north. This has certainly eroded bi-national cooperation.

On a Mesoamerican level, the securitization of the migration theme has had an important, if less well-known, effect. Mexico has been forced to gradually adjust its own migration policies vis-à-vis its Central-American neighbors, adopting practices and restrictions that aim to limit human trafficking to the north, such as visa policies and the deportation of people with "controlled nationalities"—mainly from the Middle East, Asia, as well as Central America and Colombia. Thus the immigration issue has been also securitized for Mexico, creating a source of friction between it and the governments of Central and South America.

Starting in 2001, Mexico's Interior Ministry, through the National Migration Institute, designed "Plan South" in order to "strengthen the monitoring and control of migration flows between the Isthmus of Tehuantepec towards the southern border."[16] However, the Mexican–Guatemalan border has been vulnerable to the corruption of officials on both sides by organized criminal networks. The fact is that the new security requirements have led the United States to build a new security relationship with Guatemala, which has become more complex due to the type of transnational actors involved.

Drug and arms trafficking

Drug trafficking is an old problem that has affected the Mesoamerican region since the 1980s, but the negative effects have recently been exacerbated. Similar to migration, drug trafficking has undergone a transformation as a result of changing policies and practices of the United States. The anti-drug policies of the United States have a large number of undesired effects, which include calls for involving the military in the war against drugs. The unintended effect has been, paradoxically, the growth of corruption in all institutions involved in controlling drugs. Moreover, this policy undermines the construction of democratic institutions.[17]

The traffic in firearms, purchased legally in the United States but illegally traded in the region is another source of interstate tension in Mesoamerica. In Guatemala alone there are more than 500,000 illegal weapons, not registered by the state but acquired on US soil. In El Salvador 224,600 illegal arms have been estimated, of which 147,581 are registered. Meanwhile, in Honduras, it is suspected that there are more than 400,000 unregistered firearms, compared to 88,337 registered.[18] Without doubt, this phenomenon contributes to the Mesoamerican security dilemma and undermines public security in the region.

The trafficking in weapons is possible due to relatively porous borders and the absence of a mechanism for control of small arms. The US government does little to prevent the smuggling of weapons to the south and lacks effective regulation of production and sales, while the states in Mesoamerica have few resources to prevent it. In 2001, the United States blocked an international initiative, promoted by several Central American countries, which would have created a binding agreement to limit the international trafficking of such arms.

The inefficiency on the side of Mesoamerica in changing the preferences of the United States is essentially a problem of collective action. The Mesoamerican countries do not possess the capital or the political organization necessary to construct a lobbying group able to influence the legislative process of US Congress. In contrast, a small number of groups, such as the National Rifle Association, have abundant resources to pressure members of Congress to maintain the status quo on the sale of light weapons. The result is a security scenario adverse for the region: organized crime and drug trafficking merge with the trafficking of arms.

Crime and violence

Irregular criminal groups clearly reflect the transnational dilemmas of Mesoamerican security. The best known are the *maras* whose origin can be traced to the urban areas of Los Angeles, where in the 1980s some Central American immigrants, displaced by civil wars, began involving themselves with local gangs.[19] Over time, these immigrant groups returned to their countries of origin in Central America, either by forced deportation or because the conflicts had ended. In the region, they established their own network of gangs and expanded in numbers, replicating illegal practices and establishing ties to criminal groups in the United States, Mexico and Central America. Probably the main threat that these groups represent is their association with drug traffickers, as well as their capacity to disrupt public order.

The *maras* have been a serious problem for public security in El Salvador, Honduras and Guatemala. These are three countries where the perception of public insecurity is the highest, and where the state tends either to have the least presence, or to resort to repression to maintain public order. In these countries, the number of *maras* has even exceeded the number of police officers and armed forces.

Armed forces, and the difficult road towards a Mesoamerican security community

Mesoamerica is a relatively de-militarized region. By demilitarization, two things are understood. First, there is little inter-state conflict in the region, although there are occasionally disputes over unresolved border issues.[20] Second, demilitarization includes both the reduction of military spending and the reduction of the military apparatus. In fact, in Mesoamerica, the defense budget is relatively low, especially when contrasted with other regions in the world. Some countries in the area have even eliminated their military altogether and have zero military spending, such as Costa Rica and Panama. Certainly, in comparison with the rest of the world, Mesoamerica is one of the few regions where military spending has been maintained at relatively low levels. This can be interpreted as a result of the success of the peace processes of the 1990s.

The sum of these two facts—the relative absence of interstate conflicts and the decline of military spending—may contribute to the expectations of the citizens of the region in developing solid expectations of peaceful change in the way predicted by security community theory. Karl Deutsch defined a security community as a group of persons integrated though formal and informal institutions who have developed strong expectations about peaceful change.[21] Contemporary scholars have broadened this concept in several ways, adding that the community becomes pluralistic when, in a transnational region, the role of the armed forces is not to dissuade or intimidate, but rather to protect the states against an external aggression. The absence of conflict permits countries to find mutually beneficial solutions, in turn encouraging a basis for a security community.

Yet the data on military spending is insufficient to clearly identify the emergence of a pluralist security community. First, there is no positive reorientation of military spending. In other words, the budget that used to be spent on the armed forces is not transferred towards programs of poverty eradication, or to strengthening the state. Social and income inequality in Central America (with the exception of Costa Rica) is still very high. At the same time, there has been an erosion of state capacity in providing security to its citizens, by not allocating sufficient resources for the construction of efficient and democratic law enforcement. These points question the assumption that demilitarization, or the reduction in military spending means, *ipso facto*, better quality of life, greater social spending and a more effective state.[22]

Despite the reduced military spending in the region, then, there is little information on why tax money is spent on defense, and even less information on the resources involved. The Mesoamerican problem here lies in weak budgetary transparency, where data is available but the elements to analyze and report on the spending processes are lacking or inadequate at best. Mexico is an illustrative case of the relationship between the unequal access to information and accountability.

The governments of Vicente Fox and Felipe Calderón instituted significant increases in the budget for public safety. But while there is a national law of public transparency, and an awareness of the amounts of military spending, it is unknown how priorities and resources are assigned; how additional funds are allocated; who takes management decisions; and what is done before approving the budget in Congress. The cost of the anti-narcotics campaign remains a mystery to most Mexicans. Even more paradoxical is that the information related to foreign military assistance or the purchase of equipment is not usually disclosed and made public by domestic sources, but instead by donors or sellers (such as the United States, France, Britain or Israel) or by private organizations abroad that report data on arms exports and imports (such as Jane's Military, Military Balance, or the National Security Archive). There are also gaps in budget rationalization where the underlying reasons or the justifications of budget allocations are unknown. So, the problem lies not only in the amount of information available, but also in its quality. This is, in greater or lesser degree, also the case in Central American countries.

The absence of interstate armed conflict does not imply that the population in the Latin American sub-region perceives the military as less important. Rather, public support for the armed forces and the use of the military to impose law and order remains high. In almost all of Latin America, with the exception of countries like Argentina, Chile or Uruguay, the answer to organized crime or public demonstrations has been militarization. The ruling élites have recurrently called on the army to occupy militarily the *favelas* and the slums. In fact, in almost all countries of the region the armed forces have a constitutional and legal mandate to maintain public order.

Using the military to deal with internal security challenges the very notion of a pluralistic security community, in which the military should have a smaller role in regional integration efforts, forcing it to focus its energies on external affairs and foreign missions. The effect is that instead of reducing the problem of regional insecurity, military intervention is worsening it. In countries where the armed forces are involved in anti-drug operations, institutional corruption and impunity have increased. In those countries where soldiers are in charge of policing, there has been a growth in complaints of human rights violations and abuse of authority. In both cases the result has been the reverse of what was intended: crime rates, drug and public insecurity have increased, despite military intervention.[23]

The military sector in Central America, unlike its counterpart in South America, has not wholly accepted civilian control. This translates into military autonomy and a conditional support for democracy. There are, in fact, some hot spots that have serious implications for regional security. Mesoamerican countries have different ministries responsible for formulating defense policy, and so the degree of control exercised by civilians over the military varies depending on who holds the defense portfolio. Theoretically, the main functions of a defense ministry should be to centralize defense policy; standardize guidelines; establish criteria for organizing the armed forces; create the budget for the financial resources allocated to the defense sector; serve as mediators between the armed forces and society; and coordinate the participation of the different forces with other government ministries, according to the countries' respective Constitutions. However, the defense ministries in Latin America carry out their functions unevenly, as few defense portfolios are in the hands of civilians who effectively set military policy.[24] The establishment of civilian defense ministries has been difficult in Central America. In Nicaragua, the civilian ministry of defense has failed to consolidate itself institutionally, as the armed forces are not hierarchically subordinate to this institution. In Honduras, the civilian ministry of defense is also weak. In Guatemala and El Salvador, portfolios of defense are managed by civilians, but the high command is staffed by senior officers.

The Mexican case is probably the least institutionalized and has the least ministerial control. Defense policy is formulated through the use of the old authoritarian system, in other words, directly by the military ministries under the secretary of defense—army and air force—and the secretary of the navy. The forces are not integrated within a single ministry and civilian control other than that of the president, the chief of the armed forces, is nonexistent. The democratization process has not changed the institutional structure of the defense sector in Mexico. In fact, it is possible to assert that there was more civilian control over the armed forces, albeit not democratic civilian control, during the authoritarian era, when the Institutional Revolutionary Party (PRI) exercised its hegemony over the armed forces, than there is now, as the military is not accountable to either ruling party.

In Mesoamerica there is weak civilian control over the armed forces because civil society has shown itself to be apathetic, indifferent and not very committed to issues of defense policy. Society has a positive perception of the military, but expresses little interest in issues of security and defense. Centers of strategic studies are directed by the same military institutions, and there are few citizens with knowledge of war, peace and security. The social effect of this indifference is a lack of critical thinking. The lack of confidence in, and respect for, the civil authorities on the part of some Mesoamerican military sectors is in turn not surprising. Other militaries, such as the Mexican armed forces, are deeply skeptical of civilian authorities.[25]

One of the elements that defines civilian participation in the formulation of defense policy in Latin America is the drafting of the so-called White Papers on Defense, in which the doctrine, missions, budgets, equipment and geopolitical considerations in each country are defined. This mechanism allows for an increase in public transparency and contributes to an environment of trust with neighboring states. In Mesoamerica, white papers have been published, in consultation with civil society, in Guatemala, Honduras and Nicaragua.[26] El Salvador and Mexico have also made their respective white papers public. However these were written without public consultation, which can be seen as an indicator of the weak accountability that affects relations between civilians and military.[27]

The problem of the lack of civilian control is local, but its implications are regional. The theoretical premise of a pluralistic security community is based on the assumption that civilians and politicians are responsible for formulating security policies. In Mesoamerica, on the contrary, the policies of national and regional security remain formally and de facto in the hands of the military, usually the least progressive and most nationalistic of actors.

Conclusion

In Mesoamerica, the transition to democracy, the peace processes, and the processes of demilitarization have been slow, weak and have had mixed results. These are non-consolidated democracies, supported by weak institutions, subject to setbacks. The main obstacle to security is that the countries of the region lack the institutionalism and the professionalism necessary to ensure the security of their newly initiated citizens. The levels of state repression have been substantially reduced. However, there has been an increase of social violence, which has caused an insecurity dilemma, one where the source of threats comes from the within states themselves.

Additionally, the borders have become weakened and overwhelmed, whether caused by the passage of illegal goods and people or uncontrollable criminal activities, and there exists little government capacity to monitor and impose order. These problems have resulted in states that traditionally were protected from the insecurity dilemma, such as Costa Rica, becoming defenseless against such symptoms. Thus, issues of national security today have regional effects.

The biggest obstacle is that these transnational and intermestic problems have prompted a complex reaction by various coalitions of actors, whether they are bureaucracies, advocacy groups, drug traffickers or gang members, all of whom have a considerable lead vis-à-vis the Mesoamerican states' capacity to respond. This advantage is not just financial; it also includes a considerable ability to adapt to the new dynamics of security. The traditional governmental actors in the region are weak when confronted with these sudden changes. Far from improving the regional security complex, the intermestic issues and transnational actors have deteriorated it.

Similarly, study of the regional security agenda reveals the perverse effects caused by US policies in Central America, although these are perhaps not intended. It is difficult to characterize the behavior of Washington as a benevolent hegemon, willing to bear the costs of regional peace and distribute collective goods such as security. On the contrary, its behavior is more erratic and atypical of a hegemonic power. Far from improving the Mesoamerican security complex, Washington's interventions (or lack of thereof) make it worse. In more ways than one, Washington is responsible, directly or indirectly, for the activation of many of the transnational and intermestic actors challenging Mesoamerican states.

The lack of progress in terms of civilian control over the armed forces hinders the construction of a pluralistic security community. So too does the lack of regional leadership. The potential role of regional power would fall on Mexico, which has previously mediated peace processes and used active diplomacy in the creation of a nuclear-free zone in Latin America. Yet Mexico of late has shown a lack of interest in the region, as witnessed in the lapsing of Vicente Fox's 2001 Plan Puebla Panama—a plan that was to have linked the southern states of Mexico to Central America.

In the absence of an active regional power it is difficult to organize, coordinate and align positions on regional integration in order to consolidate a Mesoamerican security community. What currently exists is fragmented integration, where some countries are more economically and commercially integrated with the United States; where security policies are semi-tailored to the preferences of the north, but carry setbacks for democratic institutionalization and civilian control. This has led some experts to identify the emergence of a paradigm of hemispheric security that is both irregular and inconsistent. It is similar to a puzzle where the pieces of the partnership are added slowly, with the puzzle lacking a defined form or outcome.[28]

Notes

1 Geographically, Panama is not a part of Mesoamerica, but the integration processes of the Central American isthmus make it strategically close to

Mesoamerica, though its geopolitical and geoeconomic situation is distinct and determined by the Panama Canal on one hand and the border with Colombia on the other.

2 See Paul Kirchoff, *Escritos Selectos: Estudios mesoamericanistas* (Mexico City: Universidad Nacional Autónoma de México, 2002).

3 Barry Buzan, *People, States, and Fear: An Agenda for International Security Studies in the Post-Cold War Era* (Boulder, CO: Lynne Rienner, 1991), 105–115.

4 Robert Jervis, "Cooperation Under the Security Dilemma," *World Politics* 30: 2 (1978), 186–214.

5 Brian L. Job, "The Insecurity Dilemma: National, Regime, and State Securities in the Third World," in Brian L. Job, ed., *The Insecurity Dilemma: National Security of Third World States* (Boulder, CO: Lynne Rienner 1992), 17.

6 Karl Deutsch, *Political Community and the North Atlantic Area* (Princeton, NJ: Princeton University Press, 1957); Emmanuel Adler and Michael Barnett, *Security Communities* (New York: Cambridge University Press, 1998), 1–65.

7 Daniel Matul, "Condiciones estructurales, inequidad y exclusión como fuente de conflicto en Centroamérica: explorando los vínculos," in Andrés Serbín, ed., *Paz, conflicto y sociedad civil en América Latina y El Caribe* (Barcelona: CRIES, Icaria Editorial, 2007).

8 Gabriel Aguilera Peralta "Sísifo revisado: Conflictos y conflictividad en Centroamérica," in ibid.

9 See Mohammed Ayoob, *The Third World Security Predicament* (Boulder, CO: Lynne Rienner, 1995), 15.

10 Francine Jacome, ed., *Seguridad Democrática en Centroamérica. Logros y limitaciones en Costa Rica, Panamá, Guatemala y El Salvador* (Caracas: CRIES, 2004).

11 See Ricardo Córdova y Orlando Pérez, "La agenda de seguridad en Centroamérica hacia el siglo XXI," in Joseph S. Tulchin, Raúl Benítez Manaut and Rut Diamint, eds., *El Rompecabezas. Conformando la seguridad hemisférica en el siglo XXI* (Buenos Aires: Prometeo Libros, 2006), 233.

12 Susan Peacock and Adriana Beltrán, *Poderes ocultos en la Guatemala post conflicto. Grupos armados ilegales y las fuerzas detrás de ellos* (Washington, DC: Washington Office on Latin America, 2005).

13 Jane's Sentinel Security Assessment Central America and the Caribbean, "Mexico: Security," (London: Jane's Military Review, 2007). Online, available at: www.janes.com.

14 Peter Andreas and Ethan Nadelmann, *Policing the Globe: Criminalization and Crime Control in International Relations* (New York: Oxford University Press, 2006), 7.

15 See Christopher Rudolph, *National Security and Immigration: Policy Development in the United States and Western Europe since 1945* (Stanford, CT: Stanford University Press, 2006).

16 Instituto Nacional de la Migración, Secretaría de Gobernación, Mexico, *Plan Sur*, 5 July 2001.

17 See Coletta A. Youngers and Eileen Rosin, eds., *Drugs and Democracy in Latin America: The Impact of US Policy* (Boulder, CO: Lynne Rienner, 2005), 9–10.

18 Eugenia Zamora Chavarría and Ana Nancy Espinoza, eds., *The Face of Urban Violence in Central America* (San José, Costa Rica: Fundación Arias-United States Institute of Peace, 2005), 32.

19   See Win Savenije, "La Mara Salvatrucha y el Barrio 18st," *Foreign Affairs en Español* 4: 2 (April–June 2004).

20   See Jorge Domínguez, *Boundary Disputes in Latin America* (Washington, DC: United States Institute of Peace, 2003), 1–44, online, available at: www.usip. org/pubs/peaceworks/pwks50.html); Aguilera Peralta, "Sísifo revisado," 61.

21   Deutsch, 98.

22   This hypothesis is defended by Oscar Arias, former president of Costa Rica and Nobel Peace Prize winner, who has initiated the agenda to reduce and eliminate the armed forces in the region.

23   See Gastón Chillier and Laurie Freeman, *El Nuevo Concepto de Seguridad Hemisférica de la OEA: Una Amenaza en Potencia* (Washington, DC: Washington Office on Latin America, 2005).

24   Raúl Benítez Manaut, "Los ministerios de defensa: un enfoque estructural," document published by la Red de Seguridad y Defensa de América Latina (REDSAL), Buenos Aires, 2005, online, available at: www.atlas.resdal.org.ar/atlas-ministerios.html.

25   David Pion-Berlin, "Introduction," in David Pion-Berlin, ed., *Civil–Military Relations in Latin America: New Analytical Perspectives* (Chapel Hill: University of North Carolina Press, 2001), 1–35.

26   In these three countries, the auditing of the white papers and the organization of the consultation forums were an important role of the United Nations Development Fund.

27   In the Mexican case, the two ministries for military affairs, Defense Ministry (Secretaría de la Defensa Nacional, SEDENA) and the Navy Secretariat (SEMAR), have edited their white papers separately, making clear there is no joint doctrine between them beyond a desire to guard their fiefdoms. The papers are kept in great secrecy.

28   Tulchin, Benítez Manaut and Diamint, eds., *El Rompecabezas*.

CONCLUSION

Authoritarian Evolution

Paul Kenny and Mónica Serrano

In the Introduction we met two very different broad ideas about security failure. The first is the dominant idea, the idea of the failed state agenda. It presides in the world of policy briefs, strategic papers, country warning reports and intelligence assessments—and it augurs ill. The threats faced by weak states are awesome—global criminal networks, insurgencies, terrorists. These are trans-national enemies operating from the outside, and they aim to come in, take control of and overthrow the state. They thus pose a threat to international order. Not only is securitization a justified response to them by the state and its international allies; it is the only possible response. The threatened state must put itself on maximum security alert. This means that it must undertake militarization—the military's openly active involvement in public order policies, as well as in the wars on drugs and terror. The assistance the state receives from its key international allies will be predominantly in the form of transfers bolstering military capacities and responses. Both the state's own efforts and this assistance will save it from failing.

We argue against this idea and aim to rein in talk of state failure. Our starting point is an observation: while it calls itself "state failure," the agenda has nothing to say about states: everything hinges on the exogenous threats to them. From our perspective, things are exactly the other way round. The Mexican state doesn't confront a drug insurgency aiming to overthrow it. The Mexican state faces coalitions of individuals—some of them extremely powerful and violent—whose ultimate ambition is to pay taxes to the state, to be able to issue Treasury-registered receipts to their hotels' customers, to receive a state subsidy for their agricultural businesses.[1] This enemy wants the state to function for it, needs its collusion and protection, aspires to shape its electoral and legislative processes. This enemy is also nestling within the state's economic, political and social orders. Our focus, then, is upon the state's institutions and capacities—and this is what we denote by security failure, a failure of the state to provide internal and external security. This is such a serious failure that we find it tragic that the securitizing agenda should completely misrepresent the true challenge, and waste enormous resources on the wrong "war." As for militarization, it increases violence and further undermines the state—pushing it towards "failure."

Those are the battle-lines. In this chapter we expand on our core claim that to take seriously the threat of organized crime to Mexico the diagnosis ought to begin with the state. So, where the failed state agenda only sees an inert victim-state, security failure focuses on the agency of the state—its struggle and change in interaction with the threat. The survival of the Mexican state is not in question, but its evolutionary path has very much become a question now. Once again, that is, pressing security problems have emerged not from a vacuum, but in a political frame.

We have two threads through this chapter. We first resume the narrative thread from 2008. Then we test its consonances with the precedent of Colombia. We also return to the political–theoretical dialogue about state failure that, in the Introduction, we saw to be unfinished, in order to get some paradigmatic sense of how the Mexican state's evolution could change it. In conclusion we posit that, while authoritarian shoots can be detected at an early stage of germination, the challenge of Mexico's security failure can be cast more bracingly. A challenge to the country's young democracy, it ought to be realized that it can only be resolved by more democracy.

To begin with, though, we unpack just why authoritarian evolution concerns us more than the failed state agenda for Mexico, as expressed by President Calderón:

> The duty is to fight crime, particularly organized crime, otherwise they will take control of the important parts of the government or important parts of the country. So we'll act on time to fix the problem. The alternative doesn't exist.[2]

The state crisis: 2006

"Important parts of the government, or important parts of the country": no Mexican president since possibly Santa Anna in the 1830–1840s has talked like that. The Mexican state *is* in some kind of crisis. Quite what crisis, though, depends on the point of view.

In the years since 2006 the shaping narrative of the crisis has been the president's, and his ability to get it across is no doubt why he for so long carried the public with him. The narrative was as follows. When he assumed the presidency he realized that the presence of organized drug crime in the country was far greater than known—the cancer, in his image, had metastasized. President Calderón deduced that organized crime had, at the least, been tolerated by his predecessors. He was left with no alternative but to start waging the fight of the state against organized crime.

Critics of the administration's security policy have tended to depart from that narrative. One can see why. It invites criticism with its picture of rash improvisation—a president of just ten days sending out thousands of soldiers to make a show of force, but with no longer-term comprehensive strategies in place, no goals, no exits. The critics make points that we shall echo, but the shaping narrative of the state's crisis does not seem to us to be the right place to start from. That place is instead the election year of 2006.

The 0.58 percent margin of Felipe Calderón's victory was a matter of 233,831 votes.[3] The evidence is overwhelming that the narrow gap was overcome thanks to the impact of a negative TV campaign targeting Andrés Manuel López Obrador through 2006.[4] Fair practice in other democracies, Mexico's electoral legislation prohibits negative propaganda in campaigns. The Electoral Tribunal ruled both that 25 percent of the "spots" transmitted had been negative—and that it was incompetent to judge their impact. The two highest-impact of all presented López Obrador as "a danger to Mexico."

"We had no other alternative," said President Calderón: "[it was impossible to] leave the country in hands of someone like him." President Fox joined in on the attacks on the same explicit basis. The tribunal judged that his interventions had jeopardized the validity of the election (but that it was incompetent to determine their precise influence).

The prospect of López Obrador's victory was cast as a state crisis; yet preventing it also brought one about. No conspiracy theories are required to affirm that very powerful actors and groups in the state coordinated against López Obrador; leading business associations also lent their voice for Calderón. The electoral rules and institutions were compromised, but most flagrantly of all, the election was securitized. There was no alternative to throwing everything at López Obrador because of the danger he represented. It was the same logic that had led to President de la Madrid's disqualification of Cuauhtémoc Cárdenas in 1988 when he declared that "he doesn't know how to govern."[5] Through 2006 a climate of fear was engendered about the harm a candidate of the left—another Hugo Chávez—would do to Mexico. *And yet* even with a candidate who played into the hands of his opponent, the fruit was a mere 0.58 percent.

President Calderón, as we saw in Chapter 2, used the military institution to defend his victory. And he sent it out with no objectives allowing for withdrawal. *Was* that incompetence? There is a case for concluding not. Against the current of critical opinion, that is, we see the military-strategic deficiencies of the Calderón years as certainly important, but ultimately secondary for the purpose of critique. The strategy was first and foremost to militarize. It wasn't improvised, but was a continuation of the electoral year's campaign. Engendering fear cut down the left, and built up the president. But that was the short term. In the longer, for those sectors for which the left's possession of power was unthinkable, 0.58 percent was not a comfortable margin. Permanent securitization was accordingly promoted. By 2010 the secretary of defense talked openly of the army remaining on the country's streets *for another ten years*.[6] Effectively, that was a contemplation of an indefinite de facto state of emergency.

The true story, then, had little to do with the legacy that the president discovered when he assumed office—everything to do with the future. From the very serious institutional crisis of 2006 emerged an opportunity to reconfigure the state on an authoritarian setting. This mutation would be justified by the war on crime.

President Calderón said: "It is a long path, it is true. It is a long path perhaps without many results in the short term or at least not spectacular ones. But is an effective path and, moreover, it is the only one there is."[7]

Early hits: the military institution

The risks in respect of the armed forces, especially the army, were serious. To politicize the military institution was enormously problematic. Indeed, the army's last great moment of crisis, at the start of 1997, had coincided with the decision of several retired generals and admirals to join the Democratic Revolution Party (Partido de la Revolución Democrática, PRD) opposition.[8] Fears of the armed forces' reaction had been in the air in 2000's election year, evaporating to all-round relief as they maintained a healthy distance from the electoral dynamics that produced the first government of alternation. Now, from 2006 onwards, the military high command would be forced to work in unprecedented closeness with the National Action Party (Partido Acción Nacional, PAN) government. Yet the army as a whole retained an old-style institutional and corporate identity. It retained its significant degree of autonomy, and even kept its own bank—at odds with the business culture of the PAN. It was also accustomed to working for governments with social policies to offer the rural environments in which it operated. The signs soon pointed to the relationship being under strain.

The armed forces were receiving an open-ended mandate, but one in no way driven by pre-existing policy consensus between them and civilians, other than the president and his advisors. The army was going out on a limb. Looking back, it had both a history of richly ambiguous relations with drug traffickers, and a problem with desertion so great that, in 2008, it could only aim to cut the number of deserters by 30 percent.[9] Looking ahead, it faced the subordination entailed by a new "partnership" with US agencies. While it was pushed to the front line of the war on drugs it faced the conditioning of US military aid to its human rights standards and their wider exposure to international scrutiny. The full-scale militarization of anti-narcotic policies gave the army much to lose. There would indeed be indications that the high command understood far better than the civilians how militarization could *weaken* the armed branch of the state.

Yet weakness also explained the acquiescence: the army in particular was strapped for resources. Its first gain in 2007 was accordingly budgetary—an approved 16 percent increase.[10] In the time-honored fashion described in Chapter 8, this bid was made by the secretary of defense on behalf of the army and air force; the secretary of the navy made a separate bid, from his separate ministry. This inter-service system was an inheritance from authoritarianism whose effect was to render civilian control of the armed branch of the state more difficult. But it engendered competition that the United States would soon exploit against the army.

The new framework for the Mexican military was established by the Merida Initiative. Heralded as an "urgent" aid package, it was composed largely of equipment (predominantly Bell and Black Hawk helicopters and surveillance aircraft) and training. The equipment would be held up, but not the intention of the initiative: to produce an immediate impact against "the threats of drug trafficking, transnational crime and terrorism."[11] On cue, by the start of 2008 the secretary of defense was committing the army and air force to 168 "high impact" operations against "the drug traffickers and other criminal organizations."[12] In spring 2007 the intention was announced to create the CFAF, the Federal Support Forces Corps. This was to be a 5,000-strong brigade of special forces, a mobile élite force at the direct command of the president.[13] By then the number of regular soldiers constantly deployed was 40,000–45,000, initially serving 40-day-long shifts.[14] Impact was being provided as requested.

But there was one thing the army was not prepared for—sustaining losses. The first occurred in May 2007, when five soldiers were ambushed and executed in Michoacán. The year's losses ended at 34. It may not have seemed a lot, but it was already the highest in living memory—above 2003's losses of 30, and 1989's losses of 32. The army had become accustomed to waging low-intensity counter-guerrilla operations while taking the most minimal of casualties in public.

As for the people killed by the military, the government didn't begin to release any information regarding this until 2008.[15]

Security sector war

As ever, militarizing the police only begged the question—what *was* to be done about the peculiar hybrid known as the police in Mexico? President Calderón was aware of the ambiguity involved in instructing the military to change its mission from protecting national security to protecting public security. His first proposal had thus been to create the special CFAF force by fusing the two principal federal police bodies, the Federal Preventive Police (PFP) and the Federal Investigation Agency (AFI), under military command.[16] This proved doubly impossible—the bodies wouldn't merge, and not under that command. The battles over institutional turf within the Mexican war on drugs were becoming fiercer.

The secretary of public security, García Luna, had been attempting to achieve a fusion of the country's police bodies under a single command since 2007.[17] In the abstract, this might have made sense; in the concrete, even if such a single police entity could be trusted to resist corruption, its formation would have meant depriving both the attorney general's office and the federal public ministry of their investigatory police. García Luna merged the AFI with the PFP, but de facto, without juridical ground. They then separated, but remained within the Secretariat of Public Security (SSP). García Luna then attempted to dismantle the body he had created, the AFI, in favor of the PFP which he now designated the federal police, to allow it greater spheres of operation. One of its first operations was to smash up the head offices of the AFI, in September 2008.

This was the context for the next major corruption scandal. In the autumn of 2008, and in the standard manner, it was reported that corruption had been discovered within a brand new institution, the Specialized Investigation of Organized Crime (SIEDO): six of its members were arrested, 35 dismissed, but the sensation was about Noé Ramírez Mandujano, SIEDO's head and so Mexico's drug tsar, from December 2006 to July 2008. He was arrested on suspicion of passing critical intelligence to the Sinaloa cartel for US$450,000 a month.[18]

Ramírez Mandujano wasn't alone—two former directors of Interpol in Mexico were also arrested.[19] Yet Ramírez Mandujano, who had argued for stiffer sentences against drug criminals, made an especially unlikely villain. Quite possibly he was a victim of those years' internecine bureaucratic battles.[20] SIEDO was within the assistant attorney general's office.

Meanwhile—and not perhaps coincidentally—another charge of corruption was being made. In the autumn of 2008 the parliamentary committee assigned to public security received a letter signed by 50 AFI officers denouncing the secretary of public security, García Luna, for collusion with Arturo Beltrán Leyva.[21] This was weeks after the arrest of García Luna's close associates and leading police directors, Edgar Bayardo and Gerardo Garay. They had been brought in to make statements at SIEDO. Garay was released; Bayardo turned state witness (and was assassinated in 2009).[22] President Calderón hastened to defend García Luna.[23]

The year of "state failure"

2008 was the year that the costs of the militarized policy became clear. These were not the economic costs—the public would learn the precise amounts of drugs seized, but not the funding figures of the government's campaign. Other costs couldn't be hidden.

In 2008 there were 52 military fatalities, including ten beheadings in Nuevo León. The impact was all the greater because of the political disaster of the year—the evidence that the militarization of the country was in step with a surge in criminal violence. Open-ended as the military mandate had been, it evidently wasn't supposed to produce this result. The conjunction with the year's corruption scandal suggests another context had come into play. The corruption had been discovered by an operation called *Cleanup*. It was a repeat of 2002's *Operation Cleanup*. Both had been launched at the request of the United States. President Fox had escaped with sending three sergeants to prison.[24] President Calderón, infinitely more active, paid a far heavier price. The arrest of his former drug tsar was proof, if proof were needed, that Mexico was "a failed state."

The real strategy of the administration looked very much like business as usual. The fissure within the Sinaloan federation had created a new war of alliances—the group headed by Joaquín Guzmán and Ismael Zambada versus Arturo Beltrán Leyva, his infamous executioner Edgar Valdez Villarreal, and the Zetas. If the government strategy was to be to pursue the most violent group, the choice wasn't the most difficult. Arturo Beltrán Leyva became the new enemy number one.

Having failed to dislodge his old associates in the north, Beltrán Leyva had reorganized and relocated. His "Cartel of the South Pacific" was based in the state of Morelos. As of January 2008, three operations to capture him there were launched. Each failed. While on the road from Morelos to Mexico City García Luna was allegedly threatened at gun-point by Beltrán Leyva not to stop his alleged protection.[25]

In the chaos after the Sinaloan federation's disintegration, Edgar Bayardo had sided with Beltrán Leyva. The result was that the former subject of Bayardo's protection—Ismael Zambada's brother, Jesús Reynaldo—was tricked into arrest on 21 October 2008.[26] Along with Jesús Reynaldo Zambada were his son and adopted son, and it was their testimony that led to the attorney general's arrest of Bayardo on 29 October. On 4 November the head of SIEDO, José Luis Santiago Vasconcelos, and the secretary of the interior, Juan Camilo Mouriño, were killed along with seven other people when their airplane mysteriously crashed. Ismael Zambada, it was said, had felt betrayed by his brother's arrest.[27] Besides holding the second most senior post in the administration, Mouriño was the president's closest ally, right hand man, and best friend. Mouriño's father publicly set the death of his son in the context of the war on drugs.[28]

The internecine war within the Sinaloan federation had led to the surge in violence; it had also, however, exposed the deeper patter of the violence. The criminals were desperate for the precious commodity of state protection not to go to their rivals. The upshot was that, quite visibly now, the state was not above the criminals' struggle. The criminal war consequently transmuted into a campaign of terror.

The terror: 2009

In 2009 there were 7,724 drug-related executions. This was a 21 percent increase on 2008.[29] Within a standard definition of armed conflict, 25 deaths are enough to raise the alarm—and not 25 deaths a day.[30] "We live among assassinations as in other countries people move among cinemas, theatres or museums," it would be written by the year's end.[31]

The new secretary of the interior, Fernando Gómez Mont, became the most vocal of mouthpieces for the administration's line that the press was exaggerating the violence. Mexico's homicides per 100,000 were way below Brazil's, Colombia's, El Salvador's, not to mention New Orleans'. The violence was "concentrated" in the municipalities of four states "only"—Guerrero, Durango, Sinaloa and (above all) Chihuahua.

In part, the government's line failed because it was caught in a blatant contradiction: now it wanted to minimize the violence, but before it had hailed it as an encouraging sign of criminal disorganization. More generally, the government's invitation to consider the violence in statistical abstraction was no match for another type of impact, one the government hadn't thought of—the media's. People weren't looking at abstractions. They were looking at the color photos of the pyre of 24 legs and 24 arms and 12 torsos of the federal policemen and policewoman tortured and executed by La Familia in July 2009.

The criminals weren't killing state representatives on a huge scale; they didn't have to: graphic barbarity was effective enough, as with the five soldiers whose decapitated heads appeared in the central plaza in Chilpancingo, the capital of Guerrero.[32] In this way the criminals conveyed their messages and spread panic, gaining a decisive propaganda edge over the government. In this way, indeed, they acted like terrorists.

Apart from the rising tide of violence, this was the most notable feature now. Time and again, the traffickers used terror to openly assert themselves. A form of blackmail, the terror was far from random; it was calculated on an ever more confident assessment of their strength.[33] The Beltrán Leyva brothers unveiled a huge sheet-like placard denouncing the protection being given, according to them, by the Commander of the Fifth Military Zone, General Felipe de Jesús Espitia, to the Sinaloa cartel—"How do you dare to call yourself 'general'?, vermin."[34]

This kind of affront was unimaginable before, when rules of respect and secrecy between traffickers and their colluders held. Now they could still profess respect for the president, while letting it be known that they considered themselves equal to any other of the state's representatives—through the power of their knowledge about corrupt functionaries, and their intimidating ability to kill any of them. The aim was to sap the state's authority and establish parity with it.

La Familia had been in the sights of the first troop deployment, to Michoacán. After murdering the 12 police, its leader Servando Gómez Martínez called on President Calderón for "dialogue" and a "pact," coolly affirming his right to both: "We know we are a necessary evil."[35]

The political war: 2009

The administration continued to act as if it believed that legitimacy was to be primarily defended by military means. In April 2009 President Calderón announced his intention to consider the enactment of states of emergency across the federation. The move would have widened the legal protections granted to the army. Politically, it was the first true test of support for the president's security policy. The PRI and PRD opposition joined together to denounce what they considered a move to widen the army's immunity. The country's bishops added to the severe criticism.[36] The proposal was withdrawn.

The government's frustration was vented in the May 2009 occupation of Michoacán. On 25 May, the governor, Leonel Godoy, started to hear reports of the movement of battalions of the army and convoys of federal police into his state.[37] Godoy's enquiries of the presidency, the attorney general's office, the army and the SSP all drew a blank. Early on 26 May, the federal forces swooped, arresting 30 mayors, local and state officials in their offices, homes, and on the street. They were taken handcuffed to the airport and flown away. The governor's palace was stormed by troops.

Most of the 30 were members of the PRD; Godoy was a former president of the party, one of its most senior figures. His half-brother, Julio César—a former mayor, businessman and now candidate for federal deputy—was known to be in the pay of La Familia. He was detained, and inexplicably released, whereupon he went into hiding.

The operation was a major bungle on every level. Leonel Godoy was one of the few at the top of the PRD who had overcome the party's ban on recognizing the president and had established working relations with his government.[38] Now, the attorney general's office leaked out *his* "friendship" with La Familia—then withdrew the smear. A taped telephone conversation was proof of Julio César Godoy's relationship with Gómez Martínez, yet it was only made public in October (leaked again), a month after the president personally stated that it existed. An impartial legal process did not appear to be on the president's mind. Leonel Godoy may have been tainted by association, but so too, for example, was the PAN governor of Morelos, Sergio Estrada Cajigal, who a few years back had taken as a girlfriend the daughter of a prominent local drug lord.[39] The final indignity of 2009's operation was also inevitable: the bulk of the arrested officials were eventually released for want of proofs of wrongdoing.[40]

There had evidently been a strong criminal–political nexus in Michoacán. Yet attacking it in a head-on military operation exemplified the problems with the government's strategy. Just as moving against one cartel always by default favored the others and hence compromised the state, so moving against one criminal–political nexus and not all of them was to be seen to be engaging in political persecution. This, of course, was how both the opposition parties interpreted things. They did so now without knowing that, late in 2010, President Calderón's sister—Luisa María Calderón Hinojosa—would emerge as the PAN's candidate to be governor of Michoacán.

From here dated both the opposition parties' determination for the army to return to barracks, and their adamant refusal to trust the president's security policy. The sequel was swift. In August 2009, after the army's budgetary restraints had held it back, the creation of the president's special force corps, the CFAF, was finally announced by the president and his defense secretary.[41] The CFAF, however, was not to exist, and the announcement was a protest. It emphasized with ill-concealed bitterness that the president did enjoy executive authority to create pretty much anything he liked in the armed forces. But budgets required Congress, and the opposition there paid the president back: it feared that the new corps would "serve the Government as an instrument of repression."

Through 2009 the general political paralysis deepened. Of 624 legislative initiatives presented to the Chamber of Deputies and Senate from the start to the finish of the year, eight (1.2 percent) were passed. Of the eight, six related to the budget that, if not passed, would have brought the country to a halt. That left one on health, the other on readjusting the clocks in winter.[42] It later turned out that to get the budget passed, Secretary of the Interior Gómez Mont had formally pledged that the PAN would not enter into electoral alliances with the PRD against PRI candidates for governor.

Paralysis ruled until one development shook everything up. Polls indicated that had there been elections at the end of 2009, the PRD would have received 10 percent of the vote, and the PAN 20 percent. That left the PRI set to win the December 2012 election with 31 percent.[43] It was a sharp rebuff to the president who, in June 2006, had crafted the alternatives open to the country as: the "danger or risk" of the PRD; the "corruption" of the PRI; and "the best option," the PAN.[44]

That the president continued to believe that its corrupt past would be the PRI's downfall had been shown when, early in the year, in the presidential residence of Los Pinos, he told its leaders to their faces that "it could be that the next time you come to Los Pinos you will have to sit down with a drug-trafficking president."[45] It had been a way of saying that if the PRI took Los Pinos, it would be as the party of drug trafficking.

After the poll results, the PRI replaced the PRD as the focus of the president's attention. Gómez Mont left the government, allowing his pledge to the PRI to reach its sell-by date. The year 2010 would see PAN–PRD coalitions scoring hits against the PRI in a number of governor elections, most notably in Oaxaca. Whether such an alliance could stop the PRI's leading presidential candidate, Enrique Peña Nieto, became the burning question.

The police breakdown

A world away, the decomposition of the police proceeded apace. At the lowest level were the country's 135,000 municipal police agents.[46] At best, these were trained to deal with public order violations—things like people urinating in public or dog waste being left on the streets. Any idea that they could confront convoys of traffickers armed to the teeth was not worth entertaining. People didn't. Instead, the common assumption held that the municipal police had become an infrastructure at the service of the criminals. When, for example, in 2009, some municipal police in Michoacán came to the aid of federal police agents under attack, they were automatically taken to be with the enemy and violently subdued.[47]

The general situation prompted García Luna, towards the end of 2009, to propose phasing out the municipal bodies and replacing them with a nationally standardized police force. It was a rational plan, but García Luna wasn't the right messenger. He was opposed by 17 out of 23 governors polled.[48]

In fact, García Luna had been given his first major setback when, at the end of 2008, the Chamber of Deputies removed from the Secretariat of Public Security its responsibility for the design of national public security legislation.[49] Then, in May 2009 the attorney general recovered command over the AFI, which fell under the remit of the newly created Federal Ministerial Police.[50] The attorney general's victory lasted two days. But García Luna lost ground to his stronger rival. General Del Real Magallanes moved into the secretariat to assume control of police strategy and intelligence—and of almost 40,000 police.[51] The military-identified federal police replaced the PFP.

These moves reflected the larger change in the scheme of things brought about by militarization. Its most eloquent testimony was the budgets. When the secretary of defense made his first bid during the Calderón administration, it was for an increase from 26,000 to 32,000 million pesos.[52] That was 2006–2007. By 2011 he was bidding for 50,000 million.[53] The army (and air force) were the budgetary lions.

Next came the SSP. But within the SSP military police were more trusted than federal police, and rewarded with more resources. The almost 40,000 military police were 75 percent of the total by 2009, leaving the rest divided between federal and state SSP police. In 2007 the SSP's budget had been 13,664 million pesos.[54] In 2011 it was 35,700 million.

In turn, the SSP was more rewarded than the PGR (attorney general's office). In 2000 the PGR received 11,700 million pesos; in 2011, 12,000 million.

In policing terms as conventionally understood, these priorities were devastating. To the PGR fell the investigation and prosecution of federal crimes—violent and serious crime. Its budgetary diet was the starkest proof that this did not fall within the administration's plan for organized crime. But not only that; by rights, the PGR ought to have been the senior of the SSP. Instead, after years of bureaucratic warfare, the SSP had become autonomous. It was easy picking now for the military command.

So too were the public security posts within the states and municipalities of the federation. Retired military men were thought to occupy two-thirds of these posts across the country by 2009.[55] The message was thus reinforced that the state had withdrawn trust from the police. The dangerousness of the vacuum being created was demonstrated late in 2009 when the new PAN mayor of one of the municipalities of Nuevo León, reputedly the richest in the country, announced that, given the extremity of insecurity there, he would be dealing with criminals and especially kidnappers by means of an extra-judicial force. In the press conference, he also announced that he knew of the death of the leader of a local kidnapping ring. Hours later the tortured bodies of the man and three others were discovered.[56] The mayor, it soon transpired, had reached an understanding with Arturo Beltrán Leyva. His assassins had also been conducting a "cleansing" of thieves, kidnappers and rapists in the state of Morelos.[57]

State authorities queued up to denounce the mayor, but Alejandro Marti, leader of the country's most important civilian movement for citizen security, expressed support.[58] The moment dramatized how the state's willful neglect of the police had made it lose ground to its enemies—political, not territorial ground.

The attorney general calculated that 449 police officers were killed between late 2006 and early June 2008.[59] No one could say how many of them were bona fide, but clearly some had been killed in the line of duty. One way or another, the losses to the federal police were on an upward trend: 63 in 2008; 75 in 2009; 91 in 2010.[60]

Armed forces at war

Beltrán Leyva could only hold out as public enemy number one so long; through 2009 the layers of his protection system began to peel away. First went a Mexico City federal police chief; then the "mafia" of municipal, ministerial, state and federal police bodies in Cuernavaca; and then the colonel and two majors of the Twenty-Fourth Military Zone in Cuernavaca who had synchronized their espionage surveillance technology against the army units pursuing Beltrán Leyva.[61] Arturo Beltrán Leyva was finally killed on 16 December 2009. He was reported to have been expecting a lunch guest, the chief of the Twenty-Fourth Military Zone, General Leopoldo Díaz Pérez whose headquarters was located just a few blocks from his Cuernavaca apartment.[62]

Such was the setting for a new downturn. The 2,400 soldiers around the corner hadn't been trusted for the final operation. Instead, the navy high command sent in marines. Beltrán Leyva's death looked every bit like an execution; his stripped corpse was then left covered in peso bills, for the benefit of the yellow press. A police badge was symbolically placed under the bills.

Savage as this was, the marines were still playing by the rules—killing Beltrán Leyva prevented him testifying about the many state officials he had corrupted. But the eruption of the marines in the center of the country signaled that new rules were also coming into place. These came from the United States. The DEA had first alerted the Mexican army that it had located Beltrán Leyva, yet the army's "refusal to move quickly reflected a risk aversion that cost the institution a major counter-narcotics victory." That was the judgment of US Ambassador Carlos Pascual.[63] It wasn't his only one. The marines' success put the Mexican army "in the difficult position of explaining why it has been reluctant to act on good intelligence and conduct operations against high-level targets."

Ambassador Pascual had been the first director of the Office of the Coordinator for Reconstruction and Stabilization—a coordinating agency within the US government created in 2004 to deal with state failure, on which Pascual had also published.[64] In Mexico he had wasted no effort in subtlety, taking questions in press conferences alongside García Luna, appearing on TV as well to claim credit for helping design Mexico's security strategies. After the killing of Beltrán Leyva—as revealed by Wiki-Leaks—the Ambassador praised the marines corps for "its emerging role as the key player in the counter-narcotics fight." The role was a punishment for the army. Special operations training had been given by Northern Command in Colorado to the unit that killed Beltrán Leyva, and more would go to the navy. Intelligence, over which US diplomats boasted they had a monopoly in Mexico, would henceforth go to the navy; the navy would operate on the army's land. Amongst other "strikes," marines hunted down a Zeta leader in Tamaulipas, and avenged the killing of a retired general in Nuevo León.[65]

The response to all this came within a year when secretary of defense Galván reported to the country's senators that the Merida Initiative had brought "no benefit for the country." The general was quoted as saying that "while Mexico works in combating drug trafficking in the United States they do nothing to control the demand for drugs or the traffic of arms."[66] Apparently, General Galván did not feel that he had any more explaining to do to the United States.

The outburst expressed a frustration that came from many sources. December 2009's defeat by the navy was only the most wounding symbol of a greater reality: the army was having a bad war. It had been the bureaucratic winner, but even that worked against it. The army had a structural problem. While its high command was attracted as ever by plans for the creation of élite units, the vast bulk of the army was made up by its rank and file. According to expert calculation, 60 percent of these had no education beyond primary school level.[67] That is, they came overwhelmingly from the rural poor. In 2006 a soldier's salary had been 4,474 pesos a month. For 2011, the intention was to increase it to 4,500.[68] Enough to make the army a valid option for young men facing unemployment in the countryside, this was still low. Yet 90 *percent* of the whole army and air force budget went on salaries.[69] This ought to have been at most 60 percent. Thus, the army was winning extra resources in an ever more desperate struggle to sustain almost 200, 000 soldiers, the bulk of whom were not sufficiently paid or equipped to keep any morale when it came to combat with the drug traffickers. The "physical and moral" erosion of his troops was accordingly the secretary of defense's overriding concern. The shift rotations that had been every six months went down to every three months.[70] Even so, as desertion continued to occur on a large scale, new battalions had to be formed—18 new ones in 2011.[71] The circle was vicious: the army was too big, but had to keep expanding to make up for its losses. By the time General Galván made his first bid with President Calderón the army had long ceased to be a fighting machine; its true fight was for survival.

As for fatalities, from December 2006–December 2009, there were 35 from the navy—and 120 from the army.[72] Two of the army's victims were retired generals, one shot in Quintana Roo in February 2009, the other tortured and killed by the Zetas in Monterrey in November 2009. Both had been fulfilling public security functions at municipal levels. The first, General Mauro Enrique Tello Quiñones, had previously been military commander of Michoacán and as such in charge of the government's first operation, in 2007. His assassination was planned by a former soldier.[73]

The political degradation of human rights

Militarization made human rights abuses by the army inevitable. As for any other armed force, its mandate and standard operating procedure was to use force against the enemy. Its deployment was both geographically irregular and constant—a matter of hitting trouble areas with high impact, then moving on. And its logic was to supplant both the police and their methods.

The effectiveness of the army was in considerable measure a function of the population's response to both it and the traffickers. In Tijuana, where the streets had been battlegrounds, the army was welcomed in. It returned the traffickers' fire, and replaced the state and municipal police. By the end of 2010 Tijuana businesses were running a promotion campaign for the city.[74] By contrast, in July 2009 the army encountered stiff local resistance in Michoacán. If, as in Ciudad Juárez, the violence increased its stay would prove precarious.

The picture on the ground was varied, then. But the human rights problem was constantly on the rise. Alejandro Anaya Muñoz has charted the trend in Chapter 5. Complaints filed by the National Commission of Human Rights against the Ministry of Defense went up from 182 in 2006 and 367 in 2007 to 1,143 in 2008, and 1,644 in 2009—an increase of 400 percent through the Calderón years.[75] Amnesty International documented cases of forced detentions, torture and executions by members of the armed forces, and feared they would become systematic.[76]

That was to fear on the wrong basis. The most tragic cases were random. *This* pattern started with the accidental killing of a family in June 2007.[77] Other children would be killed by soldiers, as would students and partygoers. There were two typical situations here. Jorge Mercado and Javier Arredondo, the students, had wandered into a gun-battle between traffickers and army on the doorstep of the prestigious Tec of Monterrey. Bryan and Martín Almanza, aged five and nine, were killed at a checkpoint on the road. The common factor was that these were both situations of high stress for soldiers who were not prepared for it. The soldiers at checkpoints could be left for hours on end in the sun, and were evidently often scared witless. Bryan and Martín were in a van with six other family members—a shadowy group that might be imagined as one of traffickers. In the words of a survivor of another such tragedy that left four dead: "And they suddenly opened fire on us, as if we were enemies."[78]

Human Rights Watch had 16 such cases pending against the Mexican military by mid-2009.[79] The overwhelming content of the complaints was about illegal entries and searches, arbitrary arrests, insulting and threatening behavior, and thefts.[80] Serious enough, these abuses open a window onto the improvised and dangerous conditions in which the army operated. Its rural soldiers would arrive at town after town with some minimum intelligence about their target—but often only a surname. They would break into the houses of, or arrest, anyone they met who shared it. When they had taken losses, like the five in Michoacán in 2007, things could get ugly—70 people were forced to leave their houses, which were then sacked: "in this community there are many people with the surname Mondragón and the soldiers were looking for an assassin of that name."[81] In that community, the army had lost both the support and intelligence-potential of the population.

Militarization made human rights abuses by the army inevitable because the army wasn't trained in intelligence gathering or entrusted with a hearts-and-minds winning strategy. The abuses were inevitable—but the deciding what to do about it was political. Here was the systematic element. High command evidently had a strong interest in providing the armed forces with immunity guarantees. Troop morale wasn't strong enough to do without them. So, 19 soldiers were tried for the killing of the family in June 2007—none sentenced. To public outrage, the same went for the soldiers who executed Jorge Mercado and Javier Arredondo, stole their IDs and reported them as drug traffickers.

The army had an interest in impunity, yet the army was not in the driving seat. The government was; the decisive vote was its. As Anaya Muñoz shows, the vote was against due process; the message that human rights violations by the army were a price worth paying for security. The inevitable was thus guaranteed. In mid-2009 the Supreme Court reviewed the constitutionality of an article of the 1933 Code of Military Justice that allows soldiers accused of crimes against civilians to be tried in exclusively military courts. Here was the stumbling-block to any effective human rights accountability by the armed forces, as the decision on whether to proceed with human rights complaints, such as Human Rights Watch's, in Mexico still rested on the procurator of military justice. From 2007 to mid-2009 his military court had found *one* member of the armed forces guilty of human rights violations, and none for many years prior.

Before the Supreme Court ruling, each of the judges was interviewed by the procurator of military justice in company with Secretary Gómez Mont. The court's ruling was that it was incompetent to rule.[82]

Then, under pressure from both the United States and the Inter-American Court of Human Rights, the executive proposed its own modification of the code of military justice. Military jurisdiction would no longer hold for crimes of rape, forced disappearance and torture. It *would* for extra-judicial executions, illegal arrests and unauthorized entries and searches.[83]

The spectacle continued to be of a democratic government defending the privileges that the military enjoyed under authoritarianism. But the government was gambling with the prestige of the armed forces, traditionally the country's most respected institution. The public accusations of military corruption by the traffickers were already a blow to it, albeit one whose comprehensibility to the public could perhaps be discounted. The shooting of innocents was far more damaging. Sure enough, the army's public rating declined in the Calderón years. Yet it did so in a manner that suggested the government largely won its gamble—declining from 83 percent to 72 percent favorable.[84] Despite the individual tragedies, the public wanted to trust the army.

This in turn allowed the government to pursue its degradation of human rights. It did so by propagating the one assumption that no one seemed to question, not even the NGOs. This was that human rights did not apply to criminals. From December 2006 to February 2010, wrote Gómez Mont in a public letter, the government arrested "almost 72,000 delinquents for crimes against health." Although a lawyer by profession, Gómez Mont didn't think to say *presumed* delinquents.[85] The president went farther: "civilian casualties are the least."[86] The enemy there wasn't even criminal; it was a military combatant. Only the military could destroy it.

No end in sight: 2010

According to one of the standard official lines, Beltrán Leyva's death ought to have fragmented his cartel and reduced violence. Only the first part of that turned out to be true. Beltrán Leyva had been an enforcer who aimed to become a leader. The same had been true of his own enforcer, Edgar Valdez Villarreal, the lieutenant credited with betraying Beltrán Leyva. Valdez Villareal now opened war against brother Héctor Beltrán Leyva, for control of Morelos.[87] A wave of terror hit the state capital of Cuernavaca, even closing it down for one night in April 2010. Corpses were hanged from a prominent bridge; a piled-up heap of six executed "delinquents" contained three teenagers.[88]

The year's major war theater, however, was in the north. Beltrán Leyva's death hadn't ended the conflict there. Vicente Carrillo Fuentes' Juárez cartel remained pitted against the Sinaloans. As the Sinaloans had made inroads into the cartel's territory, so the violence had shot up. The federal police in Ciudad Juárez were accused of working for the Sinaloans by their enemies. In April 2010, six of those police were ambushed and killed. This followed the killing of two US consulate employees and one of their husbands. The acts were a riposte to the government's security operation "We are all Juárez."[89] With 7,000 executions in little over two years, Ciudad Juárez was by 2010 the most violent city on earth.[90] The city's outgoing mayor recorded for those years: "10,000 orphans; 250,000 migrations because of the violence; 10,000 businesses closed; 130,000 jobs lost; and 80,000 addicts."[91] The exodus represented almost 20 percent of the city's population.[92]

Another development was, like others before, unexpected. Despite the extradition of its head, Osiel Cárdenas, the Gulf cartel had remained a united body, led by Cárdenas' brother, with the Zetas as its armed branch. Now it was divided (possibly after Osiel Cárdenas began giving information in the United States against the Zetas).[93] Another fluid coalition was the result: against the Zetas, the Gulf cartel now made common cause with the Sinaloans. Joining the coalition was La Familia. "Cartels United against The Zetas" was the brand name.[94]

Once again then, a super-federation had formed against the cartel singled out as the most violent. It could have been an accident. The Zetas were among those who didn't think it was. In February 2010 they displayed propaganda in 26 cities to denounce the federal government's protection of Joaquín Guzmán.[95] Of the 53,000 criminal cases brought since 2006 by the government, 900 had been against the Sinaloan cartel—90 convictions had resulted.[96] Memoranda came to light that testified to the cartel's levels of infiltration into federal police, intelligence, and naval upper commands.[97] In traditional fashion, the cartel had a winning line for people like the officers of the Third Military Region, based in Mazatlán: their strikes against the cartel's rivals, based on the cartel's intelligence, could be claimed as successes in the war against drugs.[98] As for Joaquín Guzmán himself, back in April 2009 the Archbishop of Durango had told the world where he was living—in the municipality of Guanaceví, just over there towards Sinaloa. Whether or not because it was (in the WikiLeaked diplomatic US words) "parochial and risk-averse," the army took four months to investigate.[99]

One result of the new alignment of forces was that the Zetas' southwards reach was deepened. Their presence in Guatemala had been asserted as of 2008, when they killed 11 members of a trafficking clan there.[100] It was their usual calling card. (The Sinaloans, who had been present for longer in Guatemala, also true to their style had, by contrast, negotiated their way into social orders there.) Within a short time the Zetas' established themselves as a seriously destabilizing force in the country.[101] At the same time, they diversified into human smuggling. This was because of a shift in the main route after 2005 Hurricane Stan's havoc to the railways in the south of Mexico.[102] Central American migrants now had to cross through Zeta territory. In 2009 Mexico's National Human Rights Commission estimated that *18,000* of them were being kidnapped and held to ransom a year.[103] In the summer of 2010, in the municipality of San Fernando in Tamaulipas, the bodies of 72 were discovered, killed by Zetas.

The other result of the new balance of forces, however, was to concentrate the violence within Mexico to the northeast. The Zetas made themselves strong in nine municipalities in Tamaulipas, assassinating a PAN mayoral candidate and his son.[104] Their aim was to control the state's extensive border, with its 15 international bridges to the United States, as well as the coastline, with its access for consignments from the Caribbean and Central America. The entire populations of small towns along the border began to migrate. Within two years, 2008–2010, the population of Ciudad Mier fell from 9,400 to 1,700.[105] The Zetas and the Gulf cartel were fighting there. The PRI's candidate for governor of the state, Rodolfo Torre Cantú, was assassinated.

Neighboring Nuevo León was drawn in. This was not in itself new: it had been a battleground between the Sinaloan and Gulf cartels in the past.

But not its capital, Monterrey. The neighboring state's Reynosa, Nuevo Laredo, Matamoros—these had all suffered, and were still. But *Monterrey?* The proud capital of the north, Latin America's best city to live in, home to multinational companies as well as a formidable business class—for the national psyche, Monterrey's experience of drug violence was the fall of a city. From January to April it was the scene of 159 executions.[106] It became the scene too for a new phenomenon. This was the "drug-blockade," the barriers of hijacked trailers and vehicles that traffickers left blocking major avenues as they made their getaways. It became customary for the very heart of the city to be shut down by dozens of these night-time blockades. Nor did the terror stop there: agricultural production started falling in the state along with Tamaulipas and Chihuahua as control of the roads fell to the traffickers.[107]

While it was true that the violence was quantitatively concentrated in the north, events on other fronts ensured that qualitatively the violence was uncontained. The center of the country—Michoacán, Guerrero, the State of Mexico—was La Familia's sphere of influence. In 2010 as in 2009 it was able to initiate waves of violence against federal police that lasted up to four days. Grenades as well as heavy arms claimed 17 of them in 2009, ten by June of the next year. At the same time, the practice of massacres became set.

- June 2010: 55 bodies discovered in a mineshaft in Guerrero.
- July 2010: 51 bodies discovered in a field outside Monterrey.
- September 2010: 14 young people shot to death in a drug rehabilitation clinic in Ciudad Juárez.
- November 2010: 18 bodies discovered in Guerrero, of men who had been buried alive.
- April 2011: 145 bodies discovered in mass graves around San Fernando, Tamaulipas.

No alternative?

By mid-2010 the president was under pressure. After 85 people were killed in drug violence on one day alone in June, the president publicly confirmed a new line about his government's security policy, one already heralded by his secretary of the interior. "Drug trafficking is only a lesser component" of the threats to Mexico: "this is a battle for the security of Mexicans, it is not a problem of drug trafficking."[108] The president himself introduced the term "National Strategy of Security."[109] Then in July Rodolfo Torre Cantú was assassinated and a car-bomb exploded in Ciudad Juárez. The president responded by convoking a widely publicized series of roundtable discussions called Dialogues for Security.

The moves typified the president's overall dynamic. They were retreats—and advances. The dialogues were broadly attended and lasted 27 hours, but produced no modification of strategy; the government's securitization impetus escalated farther. The 2010 announcement was indeed the complement to the Law of National Security proposed by the executive in April 2009, approved by the legislative in 2010. It gave the president the exclusive authority to declare when the internal security of the country was being disturbed and to order military intervention into any of the 32 states.[110]

If the future was to belong to militarization, the significance of the readjustments of mid-2010 was that they showed how the "war on drugs" could no longer serve as the justification. On every front, the paradigm in Mexico was exhausted. Take its supposed bottom-line—drug seizures. These reached record levels in the time of the administration: 78 tons of cocaine and 4,390 tons of marijuana by mid-2009.[111] "The production and processing of those drugs in Mexico increased," in the words of the 2010 National Evaluation of the Drug Threat.[112] The increase was why Mexico's drug-user population had also risen from 2002's 203,000 to 2008's 361,000.[113] The price paradox of illicit drugs, as discussed in the Introduction, had proved invincible.

Or take the supposed kingpin strategy. The government was still strong enough to "take down" drug leaders. The purely propaganda purpose of this, however, was increasingly plain. After a senior senator from the president's PAN party directly challenged him about the government's protection of the Sinaloa cartel, for example, the army quickly arranged the death of one of its principal associates, Ignacio Coronel Villareal.[114] When the president took to using his tweet to convey his excitement at the closing-in of the hunt for "Tony Storm," a leader of the Gulf cartel killed in November 2010, many questioned his sense of decorum. "The drug cartels have too much power, are undermining and corrupting huge segments of Mexican society," said President Obama, adding: "And so President Calderón has taken them on in the same way that Elliott Ness took on Al Capone back during Prohibition."[115] That was the image. President Calderón himself confessed that it was more complex: "the drug gangs were much stronger than he realized."[116]

"Back during Prohibition": President Obama's careless words explained the most powerful reason for the deterioration to the war on drugs in Mexico. It was anger. During these years the perception gained ground in Mexico that the country was fighting a war on behalf of an ally that remained shockingly ignorant of the role of prohibition in causing the war; that did nothing to reduce its population's illegal drug consumption; that flooded Mexico with firearms; and that gave the Merida Initiative as a paltry tip for carrying on with a failed policy. The perception gained ground because the government suddenly led the way in articulating much of it. The government that had declared there was no alternative to the war on drugs was thus the government that did most to lay the ground for nationalist resentment against the United States. A hitherto unimaginable scenario emerged: campaigning against the war on drugs had the potential to bring votes to the opposition parties.

The Colombia analogy revisited

When he won his exceptionally narrow victory in 2006, President Calderón evidently took as his model Colombia's President Uribe, who reached stratospheric levels of popularity with his so-called democratic security policy. The analogy between Mexico and Colombia was strengthened when the Merida Initiative followed the cue of Plan Colombia. While critics of President Uribe remained, his achievements won over the majority of Colombians and were judged an outstanding success abroad. Why didn't it work out the same for President Calderón?

President Uribe's strategy, first of all, targeted precisely the indicator that President Calderón ignored—violent but common crime. Specific spikes would remain, but overall President Uribe's policy led to real declines in the rates for kidnapping (down by 88 percent since 2002) and homicide (by 50 percent).[117] President Calderón not only ignored ordinary security concerns; his initial approach was to encourage the rise of violence. In this he was a product of the authoritarian tradition in Mexico: due process and human rights were seen as obstacles to the elimination of criminals. President Uribe had the talent to call his security policy democratic, even as his actual stance on human rights was bullishly dismissive.

In Colombia the executive was able to garner the political support necessary to make the state a significant stakeholder in the US-led strategy. Thus, while 80 percent of Plan Colombia's US$5 billion had gone to the military and police forces, in 2006 the Colombian government's own contribution to both was US$4.4 billion—representing 11.6 percent of the national budget and a 30 percent increase from 2001.[118] President Calderón was in no position to convoke Mexico's opposition parties, and assumed a course of action that increased his isolation. His plan for a special forces unit was rebuffed, after which the deployment of the army became hopelessly tangled up in political partisanship.

There were other differences working against the Mexican president, notably that between a rural context of illicit drug production, and an urban one of drug transit in which the presence of the armed forces is infinitely more visible and delicate. On the other hand, the Mexican president didn't face insurgent groups. He chose to act as if he did. His decision would be justified by his discovery—in the autumn of 2006—that over 50 percent of the country's 1,600 police bodies were colluding in organized crime.[119] There was no alternative to the strong hand ... But the decision for militarization was also a decision against police reform. Instead, the federal police corps became footballs in the rivalry between the SSP and the attorney general's office. The status of the attorney general's office was progressively eroded. In Colombia a successful reform of the public prosecutor's office expanded its investigatory capacities.

The Colombian state was strengthened both institutionally, and by its military advances over its enemies. The price was a strong authoritarian bias. Proponents of a political settlement with the FARC were branded terrorist sympathizers, while there was a wave of assassinations of trade unionists—impossible to quantify, and contested by the government, but most likely peaking somewhere between 1,000–2,000 before a decline in 2009.[120] The country's massive flow of internally displaced persons—estimated between 2.5 million and three million by the US General Accounting Office, and at four million by the Colombian Episcopal Conference—continued to grimly testify to the presence of paramilitary land-grabbers in the southern provinces.[121] And in early 2009 the human rights scandal of *los falsos positivos* came to public knowledge—the policy of some members of the armed forces of executing peasants and then claiming their deaths as those of drug traffickers and terrorists. For 2007–2008 alone, more than 900 such murders had been perpetrated, and the Colombian attorney general's office had received another 716 accusations.[122]

The Colombian state had travelled from a partially complete peace process to what many saw as a reconfiguration on the basis of a pact with the power of the paramilitaries—power derived not least from drug trafficking. After demobilization, sectors of them entered into the local political system while striking up a cooperative coexistence with affluent criminal networks.[123] The scandal of this would be called the *parapolítica*. Even as it led to some arrests, it denoted the new power in the state of the paramilitary–political nexus.

In Mexico, a security policy had failed, but had a reconfiguration of the state also been underway? Where was the Mexican state left?

"State failure" revisited

The Weberian image of the strong state that we met in the Introduction could not hold for Mexico in 2011. That image is normative: the state is supposed to ensure security through its possession of the monopoly on the use of force. That is the basis of its supreme and comprehensive claim of authority. When the state does share its authority with other actors and groups, it is expected to do so "on its own terms."[124] It is the convincingly real concentration of power in its hands that has enabled states to successfully claim supremacy for their authority over other competitors.[125] At the end of the day, modern states are more than organized groups of bandits.[126]

Looking at Mexico in this Weberian light will yield the conclusion that it has become a failed state. It no longer exercises the monopoly of violence, and has lost sections of territory—has lost a city as symbolic as Monterrey. The US Joint Forces Command report that we cited in the Introduction saw the risk of "rapid and sudden collapse" of Mexico.

Yet this is a highly unreflective conclusion. It takes a normative map of the state as a description of reality. The historical sociology of the modern state is instead rich in reminders that supremacy has been the result of protracted, often patchy processes. Seldom in history has a state enjoyed an absolute monopoly of coercive power over its territory, and neither is the maintenance of social order reducible to coercive means. Many historic states have fallen short of that aim, and even in the era of the modern state, private security agencies, private military companies and big corporation criminals have long shared in that coercive power. So have other organized groups of bandits.

One reflective advance, then, is to question the uncritical application of the Weberian model. Like this:

> The idea of a State that holds a monopoly on the use of force and that regulates conflict in society is being tested by the existence of criminal groups who are creating parallel powers, backed up by coercion networks willing to use violence, and by clandestine networks that exercise political, economic, and social influence.[127]

That offers a far more valid starting point for thinking about the reality of many states today than the abstractly normative view that condemns them for failing to achieve an ideal. The idea of the monopolistically legitimate state needs to be rethought. Indeed, that is where the state failure tradition itself concluded, when neoliberalism cut into the frame. As we recall from the Introduction, that intervention ended the mainstream political story of state failure. The idea of a state that regulated had gone—no replacement model could match its lost legitimacy.

The mainstream carried state failure in the direction of securitization, but one section branched off. It was represented by scholars like Mark Duffield, Béatrice Hibou, David Keen, Ken Menkhaus and William Reno among others. Indicatively, they worked on Africa, the true origin of the state failure story. And they were able to carry it beyond the impasse between statism and neoliberalism.

Their starting point allows us to advance to the next reflective position, once we have concurred that a government like Mexico's has no superior advantage over the criminal coercion networks willing to use violence to secure protection from the state. What we immediately see is dissolution, chaos. Perhaps we should see more. "Part of the problem is that we tend to regard conflict as, simply, a breakdown in a particular system, rather than as the emergence of another, alternative system of profit and power."[128]

More aphoristically: "one must not be misled by the appearance of anarchy, dissolution of power and a chaotic society."[129]

Then their story was of how privatizations could be successfully transformed by state power to *its* own ends. This was no longer state power with any vestige of legitimacy. Kleptocratic state actors forged partnerships with criminal non-state actors; new orders of power relations emerged—economically illegal and violently predatory upon civilian populations. They emerged from a condition of extreme state collapse. But this, the nightmare scenario of state failure, wasn't the end of state evolution. Privatized forms of conflict and predation might generate an order-in-chaos.[130]

That story is not by any means Mexico's.[131] But we can take much from it. Where the state failure agenda was so focused on insurgencies and terrorism that it clung to the idea that the vast majority of states were bastions against anarchy, here the lens was on a state–crime nexus. The agenda was geared towards collapse because it feared statelessness as an ultimate threat to international order. It defended a particular normative order that had no conceptual space for alternative *factual* orders—including those built on the ubiquity and predictability of violence.[132] Its framework couldn't include state mutation, evolution. And it couldn't see how its own control of the risks of the failed state part of the world was compatible with situations there of "concretely existing anarchy."[133]

The Mexican state, in sum, is both struggling against a particular kind of criminal violence—and adapting in the process. If, after all, the drug cartels had too much power and were undermining and corrupting huge segments of Mexican society, how could that *not* affect the state?

Conclusion

Mexico's security failure broke into view in 2008. It worsened. Not the sole, but the principal reason for this was the government's militarized policy. Premised upon confrontation, it provoked the military branches of the cartels to show and escalate their firepower. Where the army was deployed in Chihuahua, municipality by municipality the effect had been to send the homicide rate soaring.[134] In a January 2011 poll by Mexico's national statistics institute, over 70 percent believed that security had worsened in the country since 2008.[135]

Mexico's security failure, however, had occurred over a far longer time frame. As we argued in Chapter 1, the modern Mexican state developed along with the illicit drug economy. It regulated it, and was affected by it, most saliently by institutionalizing a criminal police. Part of the chaos we see today traces back to how the state never corrected that mutation.

So as we look to the ways the state may be changing now, the first thing we shouldn't be surprised to find are the continuities. These have the power to change the state if they can assert themselves more strongly and openly than in the past. Some of the analysis in Chapter 2 indicates one key area, for the moral of the Zetas is that natural affinities remained between counter-insurgency units of the army and drug traffickers. The paramilitary turn in the conflicts between the traffickers wouldn't have occurred without them. The paramilitary turn also provides an opening for criminals to try to legitimize themselves as social "cleansers" in the context of police absence and judicial impunity. Irregular armed groups have emerged all over the country with just such a purpose; they are behind the half a dozen massacres in drug rehabilitation clinics in Ciudad Juárez.[136]

Other mutations are disguised. President Calderón declared war, but not on the armies of judges, lawyers, bankers, accountants and politicians of organized crime. While the military was deployed, the legal remit of the Treasury's money laundering intelligence unit remained narrow.[137] The interest of the cartels in attaining political influence is denoted by their assassinations of mayors and candidates, but their degree of insertion into the political campaign system is unknown. It has to be deep now. We don't know how deep in part because of a simultaneous combination of factors— the government's selective politicization of drug corruption, the opposition's outrage, and a closing of ranks in the political class that may or may not otherwise have occurred. Julio César Godoy was the only casualty. The moral of Michoacán 2009 was that one scandal sufficed to disguise the new reality of drug money's influence in the legislative branch of the state.

And some mutations are open. Militarization became a prop of government legitimacy. While that happened, the government withdrew from spheres which the Weberian tradition would consider essential for the state to be in. Notably, some generals like Alvarez Icaza noticed: "I ask myself, where are the agencies in charge of providing education, health, where are the programs of prevention against the use of drugs, for developing sport, for giving space to the young?"[138] Under President Calderón the war on drugs proceeded without one alternative crop development program. The country's fiscal ombudsman, Arturo González de Aragón, in 2007 detected the return of thousands of millions of pesos allocated by the government for social policies. There weren't many in place.[139] The larger context of these years was one in which poverty was on the rise in Mexico—for the first time in a decade. Over 25 percent of Mexicans now lived in extreme poverty, unsure of where the next meal was coming from. Over 50 percent—57 million—lived in ordinary poverty, without access to health facilities, regular water, transport.[140]

That other Mexico was the natural constituency of the president's rival in the 2006 election. The PRD's Andrés Manuel López Obrador laid claim to it from a traditional leftist position. In 2006 that claim seemed exclusive because of the weakness of the PRI's candidate. Structurally, though, there was no reason why the PRI couldn't make headway in the world of social programs and mobilizations in which it had so long been undisputed master. Looking to the future, then, there was a clear interest for the incumbent PAN party in finding a trump over both the PRD and PRI. It found it in the coercive idea of security that, as Alejandro Anaya Muñoz argues, meets stoked-up as well as real fears. It also obeys a self-reinforcing logic: it becomes more necessary for the public the more it fails to ensure security for the public. Through the president, the PAN became the party with a monopoly on the only feature of life that could matter more to the population than the economy—security.

So another mutation occurred. The government also withdrew what it could of the state's commitments with the culture of human rights. Those commitments had a pedigree that stretched back to President Salinas, and that had been prominently stamped by the international treaties ratified while Jorge G. Castañeda was foreign secretary. As militarization made human rights abuses by the army inevitable, human rights were denigrated, much as they continued to be in Colombia.

These mutations were open. So was their neo-authoritarian direction. Security would be demanded more by the public; as in 1994 and 2006 security would be the issue that decided the election. The PRD left couldn't be trusted on the issue; the PRI wouldn't win if the election was a referendum on its history with drug trafficking. The country's security crisis would erect a veto against both of the opposition parties. Violent chaos would have generated a newly authoritarian order, with some of the very dark shadows mentioned above.

Is there an alternative? There is, although whether it can be adopted is another question. It would consist in the left—the lefts—overcoming their reflex defensive aversion to the issue of security, and owning it as a principle of democratic right. It would require politicians with the talent to communicate the lesson of Ana Magaloni, that a criminal justice system with a *lower* conviction rate of relatively minor offenders would be more highly effective. Until then, Mexico will remain a bad place to be a petty thief, a paradise for millionaire criminals.

It would need the courage to defend the human rights of criminals; to persuade the public that the strong hand is not the answer to its fears. It would need the reasonable presentation of policies based on a genuine commitment to meeting the country's internal and external security demands. Without that, it would not be possible to challenge the country's subservience to the ever vigilant US security agenda. Without that, the necessary aim of ending the reign of US criminalization of both drug consumption and migration would stand no chance.

Then the public could be reminded that just before President Calderón assumed office in 2006, 18 percent of them had been concerned about insecurity—by which they had meant robbery, assault, kidnapping—1.7 percent had been concerned about drug trafficking.[141] Their democratic right had not been addressed; to the contrary, the country's security failure was the product of many factors, but political choice was high among them.

The president-elect had declared the victory of "the future" over "a past of violence"—a past that "despises the law, abhors institutions."[142] Yet it had been his reckless use of the military arm of the state that had shown the real disrespect for institutions.[143]

Could the Mexican lefts pitch that argument? All past records indicated not. On the other hand, they would be pummeled if they didn't.

Notes

1 On cases of subsidies, Anabel Hernández, *Los Señores Del Narco* (Mexico: Grijalbo, 2010), 357, 373, 375.

2 *Wall Street Journal* 28 January 2011.

3 Sergio Aguayo Quezada, *Vuelta En U: Guía Para Entender Y Reactivar La Democracia Estancada* (Mexico: Taurus, 2010), 167. The rest of this and the following paragraph draws on ibid., 163–213.

4 The other critical factor was the alliance struck up by Calderón with the leader of the one-million-strong teachers union, Elba Ester Gordillo.

5 Cited in ibid., 223.

6 *Reforma* 9 April 2010.

7 *Reforma* 30 October 2010.

8 Carlos Fazio, "Mexico: The Narco General Case," online, available at: www.tni.org/article/mexico-narco-general-case, December 1997.

9 Jorge Carrasco Araizaga, "Al amparo castrense," in Rafael Rodríguez Castañeda, *Los Generales: La militarización del país en el sexenio de Felipe Calderón* (Mexico: temas' de hoy, 2010), 48.

10 Daniel Lizárraga and Francisco Castellanos, "El presidente militarizado," in Rodríguez Castañeda, 23.

11 "Joint Statement on the Merida Initiative," Council on Foreign Relations, 22 October 2007, online, available at: www.cfr.org/publication/14603.

12 Carrasco Araizaga, "Al amparo castrense," 53.

13 Ibid., 37–38.

14 Ibid., 54.

15 Robert A. Donnelly and David A. Shirk, "Introduction," in Donnelly and Shirk, eds., *Police And Public Security In Mexico* (San Diego, CA: University Readers, 2010), 11–12.

16 Carrasco Araizaga, "Al amparo castrense," 38.

17 Miguel Angel Granados Chapa, "Desorganización policiaca," *Reforma* 3 November 2010.

18 Ken Ellingwood, "Mexico Traffickers Bribed Former Anti-Drug Chief, Officials Say," *Los Angeles Times* 22 November 2008; "On the Trail of the Traffickers," *The Economist* 7 March 2009.

19 *La Jornada* 8 November 2008.

20 José Reveles, *El Cártel Incómodo: El Fin De Los Beltrán Leyva Y La Hegemonía Del Chapo Guzmán* (Mexico: Grijalbo, 2009), 173.

21 Hernández, 474.

22 Ibid., 515–516, 524.
23 *La Jornada* 22 November 2008.
24 Reveles, 172.
25 Ricardo Ravelo, "Un Golpe Lleno De Dudas," *Proceso* no. 1729 (December 2009), 16–17; Reveles, 25.
26 Hernández, 509–513.
27 Ibid., 527.
28 Ibid., 529–530.
29 *El Universal* 1 January 2010.
30 The Uppsala Conflict Database, cited in Juan Carlos Garzón, *Mafia and Co. The Criminal Networks in Mexico, Brazil, and Colombia* (Woodrow Wilson International Center for Scholars, 2008), 15.
31 Rafael Segovia, "Se acabó," *Reforma* 1 January 2010.
32 "On the Trail of Traffickers," *The Economist* 7 March 2009.
33 See Martha Crenshaw, "The Logic of Terrorism: Terrorist Behavior as a Product of Strategic Choice," in Walter Reich, ed., *Origins of Terrorism. Psychologies, Ideologies, Theologies, States of Mind* (Washington, DC: Woodrow Wilson Center Press, 1990/1998), 19, 21.
34 *Reforma* 24 August 2009.
35 *Reforma* 16 July 2009.
36 *Reforma* 24 April 2009.
37 *Reforma* 23 October 2010.
38 Miguel Angel Granados Chapa, "Michoacán ocupado," *Reforma* 19 July 2009.
39 Miguel Angel Granados Chapa, "Morelos: sangre y terror," *Reforma* 22 April 2010.
40 *Proceso* special edition no. 29 (July 2010), 20.
41 *Reforma* 24 August 2009.
42 María Amparo Casar, "A legislar," *Reforma* 29 December 2009.
43 (Most of the rest were undecided.) Jorge Alcocer V., "Falta mucho," *Reforma*, 15 December 2009.
44 Cited in Aguayo Quezada, 184.
45 Cited in Carlos Monsiváis, "México en 2009," *Nueva Sociedad*, March–April 2009, 43–44.
46 *Reforma* 11 November 2010.
47 Miguel Angel Granados Chapa, "Michoacán ocupado," *Reforma* 19 July 2009.
48 *Reforma* 6 December 2009.
49 Carrasco Araizaga, "Al amparo castrense," 57.
50 Miguel Angel Granados Chapa, "Desorganización policiaca," *Reforma* 3 November 2010.
51 Carrasco Araizaga, "Al amparo castrense," 54.
52 Lizárraga and Castellanos, 23.
53 *Reforma* 10 October 2010—for the following figures too.
54 Jorge Chabat, "La Policia Federal en México: En Busca de una Policia Profesional," unpublished paper.
55 Carrasco Araizaga, "Al amparo castrense," 57.
56 Miguel Angel Granados Chapa, "¿Escuadrones de la muerte?," *Reforma* 3 November 2009.
57 *El Universal* 21 December 2009.

58 *Reforma* 9 November 2009.
59 Ralph Blumenthal, "What the Mexicans Might Learn from the Italians," *New York Times* 1 June 2008.
60 *Reforma* 2 January 2011.
61 *Reforma* 17 December, 19 December, 24 December 2009.
62 Ravelo, "Un Golpe," 11, 18.
63 Nick Miroff and William Booth, "DEA Intelligence Aids Mexican Marines in Drug War," *Washington Post* 4 December 2010.
64 Juan Gabriel Tokatlian, "La construcción de un 'Estado fallido' en la política mundial: el caso de las relaciones entre Estados Unidos y Colombia," *análisis político* no. 64 (September–December 2008), 79; Stephen D. Krasner and Cralos Pascual, "Addressing State Failure," *Foreign Affairs* 84: 4 (July–August 2005).
65 *Reforma* 6 December 2009; Miguel Angel Granados Chapa, "Marinos en tierra," 16 December 2009.
66 *Reforma* 14 October 2010.
67 Raúl Benítez, cited in Marcela Turati, " 'Ejecuciones' militares," in Rodríguez Castañeda, *Los Generales*, 118.
68 *Reforma* 10 October 2010.
69 *Reforma* 31 October 2010.
70 *Reforma* 31 October 2010.
71 *Reforma* 1 November 2010.
72 *Reforma* 27 December 2009.
73 Jorge Carrasco Araizaga, "Los desertores," in Rodríguez Castañeda, *Los Generales*, 322.
74 Serge Sarmiento, "Innovadora," *Reforma* 11 October 2010.
75 *Reforma* 13 August 2009, 12 May 2010.
76 *Reforma* 8 December 2009.
77 Jorge Carrasco Araizaga, "Ejército represor," in Rodríguez Castañeda, *Los Generales*, 81.
78 Cited in ibid., 83.
79 *Reforma* 11 August 2009.
80 Jorge Carrasco Araizaga, "El Fuero Militar, Oprobiosa Impunidad," in Rodríguez Castañeda, *Los Generales*, 173.
81 Alejandro Gutíerrez, "Pueblos Vejados," in ibid., 93.
82 Miguel Angel Granados Chapa, "Impunidad con Uniforme," *Reforma* 11 August 2009.
83 Jorge Castañeda, "Iniciativa insuficiente," *Reforma* 21 October 2010.
84 Carrasco Araizaga, "El Fuero Militar," 178.
85 Reveles, 117.
86 *Reforma* 17 April 2010.
87 *Reforma* 16 April 2010, 8 May 2010.
88 *Reforma* 10 April 2010.
89 Patricia Dávila, "Golpe a Calderón . . . y a su preferido," *Proceso* (25 April 2010), 7–9.
90 *Proceso* no. 1773 (October 2010), 16.
91 Interview with Patricia Dávila, cited in Miguel Angel Granados Chapa, "Irremediable Ciudad Juárez," *Reforma* 26 October 2010.

92 *New York Times* 9 February 2011.
93 *Milenio* 13 April 2010.
94 *Proceso* special edition no. 29 (July 2010), 13.
95 *Reforma* 15 May 2010.
96 Edgardo Buscaglia, cited in *Reforma* 14 May 2010.
97 Marc Lacey, "Why is Mexican Drug Trafficker Still at Large? Cartel Documents Hint at Answer," *New York Times* 12 May 2010.
98 *Reforma* 21 April 2010.
99 *Proceso* special edition no. 29 (July 2010), 13.
100 International Crisis Group, *Guatemala: Squeezed Between Crime And Impunity* (June 2010), 15.
101 Edgardo Buscaglia cited in Hernández, 571.
102 International Crisis Group, *Guatemala*, 15.
103 *Proceso* no. 1765 (August 2010), 9.
104 *Reforma* 14–15 May 2010.
105 *Reforma*19 December 2010.
106 *Reforma* 1 May 2010.
107 *Reforma* 9 November 2010.
108 *Milenio* 10 April 2010.
109 Jésica Zermeño, "Guerra sin nueva estrategia," *Reforma* 19 December 2010.
110 Carrasco Araizaga, "Al amparo castrense," 59.
111 *Reforma* 20 July 2009.
112 Cited in Hernández, 573.
113 *Reforma* 20 July 2009.
114 Reveles, 116–119; Hernández, 578–582 (in which she casts doubt on the death).
115 On CBS *Face the Nation* March 2009, cited in Froylán Enciso, "Los fracasos del chantaje: Régimen de prohibición de drogas y narcotráfico," in Marco Palacios and Mónica Serrano, "Colombia y Mexico: las violencias del narco-trafico," in Arturo Alvarado and Mónica Serrano, eds., *La Seguridad de Mexico en el Siglo XIX* (Colegio de México, 2010), 88.
116 David Luhnow, "Mexico's 'Eliot Ness' Seeks US Help," *Wall Street Journal* 19 May 2010.
117 John Paul Rathbone, "After the Saviour, what Happens Next?," *Financial Times* 6 April 2010.
118 Anne W. Patterson, "Counternarcotics Strategy in Colombia," Testimony before the House Foreign Affairs Subcommittee on the Western Hemisphere, Washington, DC, 24 April 2007.
119 Ricardo Ravelo, "Oficiales del Ejército vendían armas a bandas rivales," in Rodríguez Castañeda, *Los Generales*, 196.
120 *Semana* 10 October 2009.
121 The figures on IDPs can be found in US Government Accountability Office, "Plan Colombia," October 2008, GAO-09-71, 53. According to other sources, 25–40 percent of IDPs remained unaccounted for. "En 41 percent creció la cifra de desplazados en Colombia, una cifra record en 23 años," *El Tiempo*, 30 September 2008, online, available at: www.eltiempo.com/colombia/justicia/2008–09–30.
122 Las cuentas de los falsos positives," *Semana*, 27 January 2009, online, available at: www.semana.com/noticias-justicia/cuentas-falsos-positivos/120116.aspx.

123 Marco Palacios and Mónica Serrano, "Colombia y Mexico: las violencias del narco-trafico," in Alvarado and Serrano, *La Seguridad de Mexico*, 147.

124 Leslie Green, *The Authority of the State* (Oxford: Oxford University Press, 1988), 1, 75.

125 Michael Mann, *The Sources of Social Power: The Rise of Classes and Nation-States, 1769–1914*, Vol. II (Cambridge: Cambridge University Press, 1993).

126 Charles Tilly, "War Making and State Making as Organized Crime," in Peter B. Evans, Dietrich Rueschemeyer, and Theda Skocpol, eds., *Bringing the State Back In* (Cambridge: Cambridge University Press, 1985).

127 Garzón, 177.

128 David Keen, "Organised Chaos: Not The New World We Ordered," *World Today* (January 1996), 14.

129 Béatrice Hibou, "From Privatising The Economy To Privatising The State: An Analysis Of The Continual Formation Of The State," in B. Hibou, ed., *Privatising The State* (London: Hurst & Company, 2004), 27.

130 Mark Duffield, "Social Reconstruction and the Radicalization of Development: Aid as a Relation of Global Liberal Governance," in Jennifer Milliken, ed., *State Failure, Collapse and Reconstruction* (Oxford: Blackwell, 2003), 291–312.

131 But for an exposition of how part of it was Colombia's, see Eric Hershberg, "Governance in Colombia: A Time for Rethinking Priorities," Social Science Research Council paper (July 2001), online, available at: www.ssrc.org/programs/latinamerica/publications/ColombiaReportWeb.doc.

132 See Denis Wrong, *The Problem of Order: What Unites and Divides Society* (New York: Free Press, 1994), 38, 252.

133 Ulrich Beck, *World Risk Society* (Cambridge: Polity Press, 1999), 56.

134 Fernando Escalante Gonzalbo, "Homicidios 2008–2009: La muerte tiene permiso," *Nexos* no. 397 (January 2011), 43–44.

135 Randal C. Archibald, "In Mexico Drug War, Massacres, but Claims of Progress," *Wall Street Journal* 2 February 2011.

136 Reveles, 190.

137 *Reforma* 3–5 May 2010.

138 *Reforma* 8 December 2009.

139 *Proceso* no. 1764 (August 2010), 10. In similar vein, a program to deliver funds to municipal police forces for their professionalization ran afoul of a requirement that the municipalities contribute 25 percent. Of the country's 2,440 municipalities, only 206 could afford this. They still underspent the 4.14 billion pesos allocated by 790 million pesos. Joint Memo to US Department of State by US and Mexican human rights organizations, 26 May 2010, online, available at: http://wola.org/index.php?option=com_content&task=viewp&id=1106&Itemid=8.

140 *Reforma* 9 December 2009.

141 Ipsos-Bimsa poll, cited in Rubén Aguiliar V. and Jorge G. Castañeda, *El Narco: La Guerra Fallida* (Mexico: punto de lectura, 2009), 40.

142 Cited in Hernández, 525.

143 Under pressure from the Inter-American Court of Human Rights, in July 2011 Mexico's Supreme Court of Justice finally ruled that alleged violations of civilian human rights by military personnel should be tried in civil, not military, courts.

ABOUT THE AUTHORS

Alejandro Anaya Muñoz, Research Professor at the Department of International Studies, Centro de Investigación y Docencia Económicas (CIDE). Alejandro Anaya Muñoz has been Public Policy Scholar at the Woodrow Wilson International Center and has written a book on cultural diversity and human rights in Mexico, as well as articles in *Human Rights Quarterly*, *Journal of Latin American Studies*, *Critical Review of International Social and Political Philosophy* and *International Journal of Human Rights*.

Raúl Benítez, Researcher at the Center on North America, Universidad Nacional Autónoma de México (UNAM); Chairman of the Colectivo de Análisis de la Seguridad con Democracia (Collective Security Analysis with Democracy, CASEDE). A prominent expert on security in Mexico, Raúl Benítez is author of *Atlas de la seguridad y la defensa de México* (2009).

Jorge Chabat, Research Professor at the Department of International Studies, CIDE. Jorge Chabat is one of Mexico's most respected experts on United States–Mexico relations, drug trafficking and organized crime. He is the editor with John Bailey of *Transnational Crime and Public Security: Challenges for Mexico and the US* (2002).

Athanasios Hristoulas, Professor of International Relations at the Instituto Tecnológico Autónomo de México (ITAM), and a founding member of the Colectivo de Analisis de la Seguridad con Democracia. Athanasios Hristoulas is the editor of *Las Relaciones civico–militar en el Nuevo orden internacional* (2002), and has published extensively on Mexican national security policy, Canadian foreign policy and North American security cooperation.

Paul Kenny, former Lecturer in Humanities, King's College, London, and Visiting Professor, Universidad Nacional Autónoma de México (UNAM). Paul Kenny has been editor and translator, and has written on Latin American politics. Over the last years he has been working on a biography of Porfirio Díaz.

Ana Laura Magaloni, Research Professor at the Department of Law, CIDE. Ana Laura Magaloni has established herself as one of Mexico's leading authorities on constitutional and comparative law and the empirical study of the country's criminal justice system. She is the author of *El precedente constitucional en el sistema judicial norteamericano* (2001), and of many influential reports on judicial reform.

Ernesto López-Portillo, founding Director of the Instituto para la Democracia (Insyde), and member of Mexico City's Human Rights Commission. Ernesto López Portillo has been an advisor to the National Institute of Criminal Law, the attorney general's office, the Legislative Assembly of Mexico City, the Chamber of Deputies and Senate of the Republic. His articles have appeared in Mexico's leading newspapers.

Mónica Serrano, Director of Global Center for the Responsibility to Protect, City University of New York; Professor of International Relations, El Colegio de México; Senior Research Associate, Oxford University. Mónica Serrano has been one of the pioneers of security studies within Mexico, and was the permanent co-coordinator of the Ford Foundation project on Mexico's security. Of her many publications, the best known in English are *Transnational Organized Crime and International Security: Business as Usual?* (2002) and *Human Rights Regimes in the Americas* (2010). She has of late been involved in the promotion of the new international norm of the Responsibility to Protect.

Arturo Sotomayor, Assistant Professor, Naval Postgraduate School. Arturo Sotomayor co-coordinated with Mónica Serrano the initial phase of the Ford Foundation project on Mexico's security.

Index